T0323645

Competition

Competition

What It Is and Why It Happens

Edited by

Stefan Arora-Jonsson,
Nils Brunsson,
Raimund Hasse,
and Katarina Lagerström

OXFORD
UNIVERSITY PRESS

OXFORD
UNIVERSITY PRESS

Great Clarendon Street, Oxford, OX2 6DP,
United Kingdom

Oxford University Press is a department of the University of Oxford.
It furthers the University's objective of excellence in research, scholarship,
and education by publishing worldwide. Oxford is a registered trade mark of
Oxford University Press in the UK and in certain other countries

© the several contributors 2021

The moral rights of the authors have been asserted

First Edition published in 2021

Impression: 1

Published in the United States of America by Oxford University Press
198 Madison Avenue, New York, NY 10016, United States of America

British Library Cataloguing in Publication Data

Data available

Library of Congress Control Number: 2020952853

ISBN 978-0-19-289801-2

DOI: 10.1093/oso/9780192898012.001.0001

Printed and bound in the UK by
TJ Books Limited

Preface

This book has a long history. For many years, we have observed a creeping master trend whereby we all become embroiled in various competitions. We have become unwilling or willing extras when schools compete to educate our children; clueless decision-makers who choose the utility providers to supply our electricity or collect our garbage; suspicious academics when the university leadership want us to believe that our university is competing with all other universities of the world; and worried citizens when our politicians suggest that we may be outcompeted by other nations. How did it come to this? Answering or even discussing this seemingly simple question proved far more difficult than we expected, and this difficulty inspired us to write this book.

We believe that competition has snuck up on us not because it is never debated, but because the debate around it is so diffuse and vague. For some people, competition has a positive sheen; various reformers have portrayed the introduction of competition in public administration and in large firms as a promise of efficiency and innovation. For others, competition is treated as a threat: It is imagined that competition will increase in the future, and future competition is used as an argument for radical change in current policies. At the same time, both sides are often vague in telling us what they mean by competition, why one situation and not another is competitive, and to what benefit we should be competing. Competition has felt intrusive, yet ephemeral.

When turning to the academic literature, we found similar vagueness. Many authors rely heavily on the concept of competition, yet leave its definition to the reader. We were also struck by the fact that most discussions about competition presume the context of a market, and that the concepts of competition and market are often confused. Few authors have been interested in the fundamental question of how competition arises, seemingly assuming that it is a natural condition of human existence rather than being actively constructed. Moreover, many authors assume that as observers of social life, they can simply determine the existence of competition without investigating the beliefs of the parties that are allegedly involved. And in some parts of the literature, we found a strange distinction between competition and cooperation that seemed to imply that an individual or organization in a situation of competition could not react with cooperation.

Our conclusion was that much work remains to be done in order to better understand the fundamental and extensive phenomenon of competition in social life. We also realized that such an undertaking would require a clear definition of the concept that could be used for studies in all social areas. The question of how and why competition is constructed is a fundamental one, and in order to answer it, we must be open to the possibility that various processes may be at work: processes of mutual adaptation, institutionalization, and–that which has been the least investigated–processes of organizing.

This book is intended to spark a research program on competition that we believe could stimulate both public and scholarly debate. It provides what we believe is a useful definition of competition that works for any of its forms; it contains analyses of the construction of competition in many social areas; and it includes studies of competition for such goods as money, attention, and status. The book draws from contributions to two conferences: one subtheme at the European Group of Organizational Studies (EGOS) in 2017 and an invitational conference on the organization of competition in Stockholm in 2019. We solicited participation from a wide section of the social sciences and were rewarded with brilliant contributions, ranging from management and sociology to accounting, anthropology, educational studies, and philosophy.

We are grateful for financial support from the Vice Chancellor of Uppsala University. Stefan Arora-Jonsson acknowledges a grant from the Swedish Research Council (Grant 421-2014-1721) and from Handelsbankens forskningsstiftelser (P18-0258). Nils Brunsson was partly financed by a grant from Riksbankens Jubileumsfond (Grant M2007-0244:1-PK).

With the hope of sparking your interest in the question of competition,

Stefan Arora-Jonsson, Nils Brunsson,
Raimund Hasse, and Katarina Lagerström

Luzern and Uppsala
February, 2021

Contents

List of figures and tables

Figures

Tables

List of contributors

Nadine Arnold is a lecturer and postdoctoral researcher at the Department of Sociology, University of Lucerne, Switzerland.

Stefan Arora-Jonsson is Professor of Organization at the Department of Business Studies, Uppsala University, Sweden.

Patrik Aspers is Professor of Sociology at the Seminar of Sociology, University of St Gallen, Switzerland.

Niklas Bomark is a senior lecturer at Örebro University School of Business, Sweden.

Karin Brunsson is an associate professor at the Department of Business Studies, Uppsala University, Sweden.

Nils Brunsson is Professor of Management affiliated with Uppsala University and the Stockholm Centre for Organizational Research (Score), Sweden.

Gino Cattani is Professor of Management and Organizations at the Department of Management and Organizations, New York University Leonard N. Stern School of Business, USA.

Søren Christensen is Associate Professor at the Danish School of Education, Aarhus University, Denmark.

Peter Edlund is a lecturer at the Department of Business and Economics Studies, University of Gävle, and a postdoctoral researcher at the Department of Business Studies, Uppsala University, Sweden.

Fabien Foureault is a postdoctoral researcher at SciencesPO, Centre for Sociology of Organizations, University of Lausanne, Switzerland.

Jason Greenberg is a visiting assistant professor at the Department of Management, Wharton School, University of Pennsylvania, USA.

Raimund Hasse is Professor of Sociology and the head of the Institute for Sociology at the University of Lucerne, Switzerland.

Hanne Knudsen is Associate Professor at the Danish School of Education, Aarhus University, Denmark.

Sebastian Kohl is a senior researcher at the Max Planck Institute for the Study of Societies, Germany.

Katarina Lagerström is Associate Professor in Business Studies at Uppsala University, Sweden.

Emilene Leite is an assistant professor at Örebro University School of Business, Sweden.

Cecilia Pahlberg is Professor of Business Studies at the Department of Business Studies, Uppsala University, Sweden.

Joseph Porac is George Daly Professor in Business Leadership at the Department of Management and Organizations, New York University Leonard N. Stern School of Business, USA.

Katharina Rahnert is a senior lecturer and researcher at the Department of Business Administration, Karlstad University and affiliated with the Stockholm Centre for Organizational Research (Score), Sweden.

Daniel Sands is an assistant professor at the UCL School of Management, University College London, UK.

Abraham Sapién is a postdoctoral researcher at the Institute for Philosophical Research UNAM, Mexico.

Roger Schweizer is an associate professor at the Department of Business Administration, School of Business, Economics and Law, University of Gothenburg. Sweden.

Michael Scroggins is a lecturer at the Institute for Society and Genetics, University of California, Los Angeles, USA.

Daniel Souleles is an associate professor at the Department of Management, Politics and Philosophy, Copenhagen Business School, Denmark.

Linda Wedlin is Professor of Organization at the Department of Business Studies, Uppsala University, Sweden.

1
A new understanding of competition

Stefan Arora-Jonsson, Nils Brunsson, and Raimund Hasse

A central aspect of modern society is the ubiquity of competition in its various forms and shapes. For the past century, competition has been more or less taken for granted as being central to the functioning of economic markets and democracy. More recently, governments have introduced competition in order to govern the provision of almost everything from waste collection to schooling, care of the elderly, and military service. Moreover, competition is an increasingly significant element of popular culture and sports, and has, often triggered by ranking systems, spread into almost every area of society. New areas for competition have thus been added to the common and seemingly mundane competition among individuals for the attention of parents or peers, for love and intimate relationships, or for status.

Despite the importance of competition to social life, social science has been largely silent on its causes and its broader meaning. Although early social scientists saw competition as a fundamental social relationship along with friendship and love, it later became largely confined to a narrow economic meaning with little analytical depth. As a result, the concept of competition has been poorly analysed; it is used primarily as an intermediary concept and is rarely the central subject of investigation. Competition is often used in a loose and undefined way, and when it is defined, the definitions vary across disciplines, leaving social scientists shorthanded in the debate about the rise of competition in new social arenas and about its consequences. Social scientists have even had difficulty addressing the most fundamental questions regarding competition: When does competition (not) exist? Why does it happen? And, how does it emerge? How does a situation change from no competition to one that is experienced as competition? Can competition be exorcised? We believe that competition deserves the full attention of social scientists not only because of its earlier scant theorization, but also because of the normative and ideological connotations that place it at the centre of societal discourse and practice.

To open competition to broader social science investigation, we offer a definition that allows for a grounding of the origins of competition in institutions and organization—one that goes beyond earlier definitions suggested in economics, management, and sociology. *We see competition as a social construction that comprises four core elements: actors, their relationships, desire, and scarcity.* The existence of competition is dependent upon the co-occurrence of all these elements. This definition allows an investigation into the origins of competition

Stefan Arora-Jonsson, Nils Brunsson, & Raimund Hasse, *A new understanding of competition* In: *Competition: What It Is and Why It Happens*. Edited by: Stefan Arora-Jonsson, Nils Brunsson, Raimund Hasse, and Katarina Lagerström, Oxford University Press.

and the role of various actors in rendering a situation competitive. Furthermore, it allows for the analytical separation of competition from its possible behavioural outcomes. Competition can lead to various actions, of which cooperation among competitors is a common one. More fundamentally, our definition does not reify competition as an objectively identifiable situation or a natural state of affairs that arises given the right structural context. Rather, competition needs to be enacted and socially constructed. Some people may see competition in a situation where others see none, because they perceive the existence of its elements differently. There are certain institutional conditions in late modernity that support the emergence of competition. Yet, organizational efforts are often needed for competition to arise. Although efforts at organizing competition are not always successful, a study of the organization of competition is critical to an understanding of why and how competition happens and to the question of who may be responsible for the outcomes of competition.

Most of the earlier literature on competition is based on the presumption that competition already exists and discusses how it is handled by people or organizations. In writing this book, we were more interested in how competition arises and how its origins affect its outcomes. Through a number of empirical studies, we seek to understand the construction of competition by individuals and organizations; for various goods such as money, status, and attention; and in various social settings, such as corporations and schools; and in higher education, sports, auditing, laboratory work, and journalism. We analyse the role of institutions, organizers, and organization in the construction of competition. These studies not only advance our knowledge about competition; they also form the basis for formulating new, intriguing questions for further research. In this chapter, we begin our project by explicating our concept of competition and its consequences.

The popularity of competition

The idea of competition is not new. It has been used for understanding features not only of contemporary society, but of almost any elementary form of life. Even biologists tend to describe the relationships among objects under their investigation as 'competition'. Competition, however defined, seems to be an integral part of life. As a historical perspective informs us, however, competition has also been contentious, and societies have often sought to tame or even abandon it. The strict hierarchy of the Indian caste system and the medieval European guilds may be viewed as expressions of such efforts.

Modern society has placed its trust in the positive effects of competition and, it seems, cannot get enough of it. Strong belief in the usefulness of competition is clearly expressed in our appreciation of democracies, in which parties or candidates compete with each other for votes; and in the institution of competitive markets, which are expected to provide choice opportunities for those who demand a given product or service and to ensure its efficient production. Competition is also thought to motivate athletes and make sports more attractive to mass audiences. It has become constitutive for any type of sport; even new and alternative forms of playful physical activities such as snowboarding or frisbee throwing are sooner rather than later organized as contests in which individuals or teams strive to outperform other individuals or teams. While physical activity is often exercised for its own sake, it is difficult to imagine sports of today to be non-competitive.

In the late 20th century, competition spread into domains that were once organized to temper competition (Castel et al. 2016; Stark 2020; Werron 2015). Since the 1990s, most public administration reforms have been attempts at creating competition among service providers by introducing new incentive systems and by outsourcing some services to private providers (Hood and Dixon 2015). These reforms were backed by the ideological support of such authorities as the Organisation for Economic Co-operation and Development (OECD), which welcomed a transformation of the public into customers as a way of addressing the perceived problems of the traditional welfare states (OECD 1987). In addition, large corporations, spurred on by the idea of returning to its 'core competencies' (Hamel and Prahalad 1990), mixed hierarchical control of its subsidiaries with internal markets in which subsidiaries are expected to compete against each other (Birkinshaw et al. 1998; Tsai 2002).

Likewise, reforms have been introduced in order to strengthen competition in highly professionalized domains, such as culture, science, and health care. In modern science, competition among individuals has always been appreciated and accepted (Ben-David 1991; Mannheim 1982; Merton 1973), but it is a more recent phenomenon that universities and research institutes are viewed (and see themselves) as competitors (Brankovic 2018; Krücken 2019). Consequently, universities that were once viewed as opportunity structures for researchers, described as mere milieux (Luhmann 1992) or even as organized anarchies (March and Olsen 1976), are transforming into strategic actors. This often happens under the assumption that individual scientists should perform as agents who serve their university in its competition with other universities. In the health care system, competition is no longer restricted to pharmaceutical companies competing to sell their drugs; it now includes competition among health insurance companies—a former remit of welfare states. Hospitals are also expected to compete and, like science, thereby re-orient the allegiance of employed professionals from their profession towards the organization in which they are employed.

Competition in the arts is no longer restricted to popular culture that targets mass audiences and celebrates its best-seller charts (Anand and Peterson 2000). Instead, almost all artists are expected to compete for prizes, and even poets are invited to participate in poetry slams, where presentations are evaluated by the audience and a winner is crowned. And states are often seen as competing with each other for the most effective policies or the best climate for business (Pedersen 2011). Such competition among states is fostered by globalization processes and by comparing nation states who, as a response, develop competition strategies in order to be attractive to multinational companies, for example (Kjaer 2015).

As these examples illustrate, the idea of competition is currently found in many, if not most, social domains, such as the economy, politics, sports, higher education, and science. Competition is not endemic to any of these domains, however. Rather, we can observe that competition has been promoted in these areas. Just as the more recent idea of competition among universities or even national research systems has been layered onto—rather than replacing—the earlier individual-level competition among researchers and among research groups, so have Western political systems become characterized by increasingly interwoven layers of competition (Hasse 2003). Not only do parties compete for votes from the municipal level to the national level, often in two chambers, but party members are seen as competing with each other for candidacy in various posts and positions. Furthermore, parties and candidates, particularly in the USA, may compete for donors to finance their campaigns, and they may compete for media attention practically everywhere. Organized interests and various lobby groups are described as competing for political influence (Dahl 1978; Laumann and Knoke 1987), scientific experts and consultants as competing for the opportunity to provide advice to politicians (Jasanoff 1990), and social movements as seeking to push politics towards their agendas against the background of other initiatives. Western political systems may therefore be viewed as a model for illustrating competition as a multidimensional and multi-level phenomenon.

Regardless of its impressive prevalence, competition is also contested, and its legitimacy should not be taken for granted. Although it serves as a core building block of liberal ideological projects (Hirschman 1982; Stiglitz 1992) in which competition is seen as providing many benefits, such as economic efficiency (Hayek 1945; Smith and McCulloch 1838; Stigler 1976), well-balanced and innovative democracies (Schumpeter 1942), or bonding that contributes to social integration (Simmel 1903/2008), sceptics highlight its negative or negligible effects. According to them, competition can erode the innovative capabilities of firms (Rahmandad and Repenning 2016) and result in more segregated schools and health-related deaths (Hsieh and Urquiola 2006; Propper et al. 2004; Rothstein 2007) or simply in a poorer system at higher cost (Hood and Dixon 2015). Reminiscent of the lively European debates of the early 1800s (Dennis 1975), the legitimacy of competition is increasingly questioned, even in its traditional stronghold of economic markets (Rodrik 2011; Stiglitz 1981; Wolff 2006). Likewise, sports fans protest against increased competition that results in the commercialization of sport, people complain about vulgarization of the arts, and there is ambiguity about competition among professionals.

In public debate competition is often connected to, or confused with, discussions about markets, but our examples illustrate that the idea of competition in society is evoked in many other contexts outside economic exchange. In fact, most competition occurs outside markets—organized competition in sports, politics, science, and higher education, for example, and the more generalized competition for status, attention, and power. Rather than seeing competition as being within the purview of economics, we argue that it should be considered along with such other master trends as individualization and rationalization. Therefore, we need a conceptualization of competition that not only derives from or is reliant upon the institution of economic markets. We also need a conceptualization that does not presume that competition arises automatically because economists, reformers or others propagate it.

Conceptualizing competition

Contemporary social scientists play a surprisingly modest role in current debates about competition. In contrast to some of the founders of modern sociology who saw competition as a fundamental form of social interaction that affects most aspects of society (Cooley 1899; Levine et al. 1976), contemporary work has tended to cast the question of competition in narrower terms by evaluating whether it enhances the functioning of markets (Aghion et al. 2005; Besley et al. 2005; Burt 1995; Podolny 1993; Propper et al. 2004). To remedy this situation, social science needs to reclaim a broader perspective on competition and ask more fundamental questions than whether or not and with what effect competition works. Competition, we argue, is one of the intellectual grand challenges of the social sciences, and we aim to provide the theoretical foundations to put forward competition as an object of varied social science research.

The main foil to social science engagement with competition is a piecemeal and disparate theorization across disciplines, a situation that discourages deeper questions and leaves little hope for constructive dialogue. The various definitions of competition have created a major obstacle in overcoming this situation. Some economists see it as a stationary state of optimal resource allocation (Stigler 1957); other economists and human ecologists conceptualize an indirect ongoing process that aligns the actions of myriad individual actors (Hawley 1950; Hayek 1945); political scientists and management scholars often view competition as a direct struggle among few competitors (Downs 1957; Kilduff et al. 2010; Porter 1980); and sociologists often conceptualize competition as indirect vying for the attention of a third party (Burt 1993; Simmel 1903/2008) or as a selection mechanism that shapes populations of organizations (Carroll and Hannan 2000; Hannan and Freeman 1977).

Another problematic aspect of existing theorizations of competition is the theoreticians' agnosticism towards the origins of competition. Particularly common are assumptions about the naturalness of competition, which plays into the myth of the 'hands-free' market economy that is beyond personal interests and politics (Dobbin and Dowd 1997; Lazonick 1993). Earlier work has therefore silenced questions about the origins of competition, thereby downplaying the role of institutions and organization.

In order to address fundamental questions of competition, we conceptualize it as the construction of a relationship among actors that centres on something scarce and desired. Competition exists, therefore, when a focal actor desires something that the actor believes to be scarce, because other actors harbour the same desire. Our emphasis on the constructed nature of competition means that we think of competition as an enactment of a situation, rather than an objectively identifiable situation. Its construction should not be presumed; it requires explanation.

Parsing competition into a combined construction of four elements (actors, relationships, desire, and scarcity) opens the field for a new understanding of the emergence of competition that draws on broader social scientific work on the spread of the social actor (Meyer and Jepperson 1996; Pedersen and Dobbin 1997), the significance of social relationships (Ahrne 2014), and the construction of the sense of scarcity and desire in society (cf. Douglas 2002; Xenos 1987). To view the construction of competition as contingent upon the existence of these elements not only provides an alternative to earlier functionalist explanations based on the assumption that positive effects of competition explain its emergence (cf. Hayek 1945; Hirschman 1982; Schumpeter 1934). Our perspective also offers insights into the question of reversibility of competition. The construction of competition should, for instance, be more difficult to dismantle in contexts in which the constituent elements of competition are taken for granted than it is in contexts in which they are controversial and require ongoing justification.

Conceptualizing competition as a social construction opens the area for new lines of inquiry. Questioning its origins challenges the notion that competition is a natural state of affairs that emerges given the right context (cf. Burt 1993; Hayek 1978). Denaturalizing competition also places into question the idea that its consequences are also natural—most famously expressed in Joseph Schumpeter's (1942) notion of competition as a 'gale of creative destruction'—which allows us to ask how is competition constructed and who is responsible for its outcomes.

To place our perspective on competition in a broader frame, we begin with a brief overview of some of the main prior conceptualizations of competition in theories that touch on competition among organizations and how competition has been thought to happen. Because of the common conceptualization of competition as belonging to the realm of markets, a significant part of the earlier work in this field has been undertaken in economics and management. Yet work in economic sociology and the cognitively oriented management literatures have also provided insights into competition. It is beyond the scope of both this book and our competence to do full justice to the history of ideas and state of the art of all these fields in these few pages. Instead, we focus on the key features and authors that have impacted the discourse on competition. We do not include much of the recent work of experimental and game theory orientation. This research, sophisticated as it is, usually excludes our main focus: the formation of actors and the construction of competition. And, in a sharp contrast to our approach, it conceptualizes competition not as the often-ambiguous social construction of a situation, but in terms of specific actions and behaviour.

The concept of competition in economics, management, and sociology

Economics: The abstraction of competition

Although many people currently associate competition with economics and economists, much of the early work on competition occurred in what would today be recognized as social philosophy by such scholars as Adam Smith and John Stuart Mill (Dennis 1975; McNulty 1967; Stigler 1957). They conceptualized competition as an intricate and dynamic process whereby individuals provoked each other into seeking to outdo one another (Smith and McCulloch 1838). A major conceptual development, which long placed competition primarily within the field of economics was the paradigmatic idea of 'perfect competition' introduced by Cournot and others in the early nineteenth century (Dennis 1975). One of the main drivers in early economic theorizing was the wish for a mathematical conceptualization of an entire competitive economy as a coherent system for resource allocation (McNulty 1968; Stigler 1957). This need for mathematical tractability caused the ambiguities inherent in the earlier individualistic and processual definition to be abstracted away (Stigler 1957; Stiglitz 1992; Vickers 1995). The idea of perfect competition therefore defines competition as a state—the equilibrium point at which prices are stable, characterized by the presence of full information among those involved and the point at which none of the competitors derive sustained profit from their individual actions (Stigler 1957).

Although attractive as an idealized end-state for efficient resource allocation across an entire economy, McNulty (1967) has termed perfect competition behaviourally empty. Economist Friedrich Hayek (1948; 1978) described it as the very antithesis of Adam Smith's notion of competition as a dynamic process. By the early 1900s, this behavioural emptiness began to be redressed in the work of empirically oriented 'field economists' who were interested in the role of individual firms in competition, or, more precisely, the presence of firms that were systematically more profitable than other firms (Bain 1956; Robinson 1969). These economists did not abandon the idea of perfect competition but used it as a conceptual benchmark against which they defined deviations brought about by industrial policy or actions of individual firms that rendered competition 'monopolistic' or 'imperfect'. The number of firms in a market was often taken to be a key indicator of the proximity of a market to its benchmark of perfect competition. Few firms indicated a less perfect market, and more firms were seen as being closer to the ideal type of perfect competition (Caves and Porter 1977; Tirole 1988).

While having re-introduced the firm as an actor, economists have still relied on strong but problematic assumptions about the rationality of the individuals who led these firms in competition (Cyert and March 1992; March and Simon 1958). Moreover, the presence of competition in a market was seen as unproblematic, as it was conceived of as a natural state of affairs generated by the individual's innate drive to 'truck and barter' (Smith and McCulloch 1838). Rather than explaining why firms would perceive a particular situation as competition, economists sought to explain deviations from this situation—imperfections in the competition.

Furthermore, economists have dealt almost exclusively with the case of competition in markets—often to the extent that markets and competition became conflated into market competition (see, for instance, Hirschman 1982). But equating competition with a specific type of market exchange unnecessarily narrows the conceptual scope of competition, thereby undermining efforts at understanding competition as a broadly useful social science concept. It ignores the fact that competition is analytically distinct from markets. Markets are, by definition, a type of voluntary exchange, and a competitive market is one in which there is a choice of possible exchange partners. By contrast, most competition occurs without an exchange process—in the case of competition over status, attention, or a partner, for example.

Management: Competition as a strategic challenge

Mainstream management literature initially adopted the economists' perspective on competition and defined the intensity of competition as the number of competitors (cf. Porter 1980; Rumelt 1991). Although economists (coming from a bird's eye perspective) see many competitors as indicative of and desirable for competition, the typical management scholar (coming from a frog's eye perspective) prefers fewer competitors for the prospects of a focal firm. And, although economists are interested in sharpening the process of competition, management scholars seek to help managers blunt its effects on a specific firm (Porter 1996). As perfect competition negates the possibility of managers to render their firm more profitable than others (cf. Hayek 1978), managers aim to disturb perfect competition to create 'temporary monopolies' in which they can derive sustainable profits (Ghemawat 2002; Peteraf 1993; Porter 1981). A rational market strategy, therefore, is an attempt at escaping competition rather than searching for it (Hasse and Krücken 2013).

The key question for management scholars is not the number of other competitors, in a general sense, but which other specific firms are the main competitors: which organizations are the firm's 'rivals' (Barnett and Carroll 1987; Porter 1980). Rivals are firms that are aware of each other and offer similar things to similar target customers (Kilduff et al. 2010; Porter 1980; 1985); in short, rivals desire money from the same customers. The identification of rivals is not self-evident, however (McGee and Thomas 1986). Some management scholars have solved this problem by defining particular actions as competitive—lowering prices or targeting the core customers of other firms—and define as rivals those firms that respond to each other in this way (Baum and Korn 1996; Chen and Hambrick 1995; Chen and Miller 2012; D'Aveni 1994; Miller and Chen 1996).

Although a definition of competition as the presence of specific actions can help to identify competitors and may be valuable for managers, it is behaviourally deterministic, and therefore problematic. Both earlier and recent work demonstrate that competition can engender a wide variety of actions: a blend of acts of cooperation and antagonistic behaviour (Bengtsson and Kock 2014; Ingram and Roberts 2000; Jarzabkowski and Bednarek 2018; Sonenshein et al. 2017), covert or open cooperation in cartels (Strandqvist 2018), or specific behaviour such as cheating (Kilduff et al. 2016; Schreck 2015). Ingram and Yue (2008) note that the practice of assuming that competition should render antagonistic behaviour is virtually institutionalized within mainstream economic and management literature, but this seems to be an assumption—or wishful thinking—rather than being based in empirical evidence. Antagonistic behaviour may be more likely in market competition, but if we aim to develop a broadly useful understanding of competition for the social sciences, it is important to draw a clear analytical distinction between social structures on the one hand and its possible behavioural responses and intended or unintended outcomes on the other. We need a definition of competition that allows for the fact that it can give rise to many different actions and outcomes—or even none at all.

We find a promising way forward in work that defines competition from a managerial perspective (Reger and Huff 1993). Following a turn towards an interest in managerial cognition in management studies (Kaplan 2011), economic sociologists have taken the perspective of managers in defining who competes with whom over what, and thereby establishing whether or not there is competition (Lant and Baum 1995; Porac et al. 1995). Of interest are not the perceptions of all individual managers, but the perceptions of those whose perceptions are reciprocated, such that there is a cognitively competitive community whereby several managers recognize each other as competitors (Hodgkinson 1997; Porac and Baden-Fuller 1989; Reger and Huff 1993). A cognitively competitive community is created and sustained by both antagonistic and cooperative managerial actions (Porac et al. 1995). It can be maintained by such organizations as industry associations, in which the decision has been made that a number of firms are competitors (Schneiberg and Hollingsworth 1990) and by the classification efforts of significant others (such as industry observers, analysts, and mass media) who inform managers about who their competitors are (Anand and Peterson 2000; Cattani et al. 2017; Kennedy 2008; Rosa and Porac 2002).

A cognitive perspective on competition as developed by these scholars is promising, as it addresses the ambiguity about identifying competitors. It is also useful in that it points to the value of considering competition as a social construction (Cattani et al. 2018). It runs the risk of being a limited perspective, however, if it is based on the assumption that competition is always double-sided, so that the party recognized as a competitor by one party always recognizes the other party as a competitor, because, empirically, this is often not the case. Another limitation is the practice of considering only managerial cognition, which runs the risk of defining competition merely from an inside perspective (Hirshleifer 1978). Such conceptualization excludes other parties that may have a profound impact on those who are seen as competitors. A government that wants to see competition among its railway operators will take action if it does not perceive the railway operators to be competing—no matter how the cognitive community of railway operators perceive competition (cf. Dobbin and Dowd 1997). We therefore need to expand the conceptualization of competition beyond that taken in most management studies and contributions to economic sociology, by looking beyond competitors. Classical sociological contributions offer some promising starting points for that endeavour.

Sociology: Competition as a relationship

According to the seminal work of German sociologist Georg Simmel, there are two types of competition: a 'lower' form, in which at least two actors desire something that is directly available to either of them; and a 'higher' form, in which the desired object is under the control of a third person. It is the higher form of competition that was of greatest interest to Simmel, and he characterized this competition as '*a form of struggle fought by means of objective performances, to the advantage of a third person*' (Simmel 1903/2008: 945, our emphasis). The presence of a third party shifts the attention of the focal competitor from competitors to the third party. Using an example from Adam Smith, when two bakers compete, one will not necessarily win the customer by sabotaging or bad-mouthing the bread of the other, as this may merely shift the consumer away from the consumption of bread. Expanding on Smith's example, Simmel argued, the baker will instead try to win the 'heart and soul' of the third—in this case the consumer. Viewed in this way, competition not only creates the social strain of a struggle; it can also strengthen social cohesion if members of a society strive to 'uncover the innermost wishes of another' (Simmel 1903/2008: 962).

Simmel's conceptualization of competition is a good starting point for a theorization that does not confine competition to the economic sphere of markets, but considers it a fundamental social relationship, along with love and friendship (cf. Coser 1975; Levine et al. 1976). Nevertheless, his work suffers from some shortcomings, which we need to address. Simmel's main limitation is his vagueness and the anecdotal nature of his reasoning, or, as Richard Swedberg (2014: 69) puts it, his writing is more intuitive and artistic than conceptually clear. It is easy to get the impression from his writings that competition exists only if a third party is involved (i.e. higher competition), and Simmel is indeed often read as defining only these third-party forms as competition (cf. Burt 1993; Hannan 1988). On that basis, it is often taken for granted that relations among competitors are always indirect and mediated by third parties.

Yet, there are strong arguments for why direct relationships among competitors should be included even when third parties are involved. For example, in White's (1981) discussion of production markets, such as pharmaceuticals or aircraft construction, third parties in the form of customers are so distant that the competitors have only each other to study for clues about what the customer may want in the future. Similar conditions exist in hotel markets (Lant and Baum 1995). Such direct relationships can be based on mutual observation and information processing (DiMaggio and Powell 1983; Haveman 1993; Lant and Baum 1995; White 1981), or they can be organized and maintained by membership in trade associations and other meta-organizations (Mizruchi 1992; Schneiberg and Hollingsworth 1990). In both cases, direct relations with those who are experienced as competitors compensate the weakness of ties with third parties.

Another question concerns the meaning of 'relation' or 'relationship'. Relations are often viewed as consisting of interaction—communication or the exchange of material goods, for instance. Max Weber (1978: 26–8), by contrast, provided a different understanding with his definition of a relationship. According to Weber, a relationship exists *when actors consider each other and each other's real or assumed behaviours and action.*

Even though relationships can be stimulated by interaction and vice versa, it is possible, given this definition, to have a relationship without interaction (Ahrne 2014; Ahrne and Brunsson 2019). The relationship between a fan and a star or the relationship of a believer and God are illustrative. Competitive relationships in this understanding are a type of sensemaking (Cattani et al. 2018; also Chapter 2, this volume), involving actors that consider others as frames of reference for their decision-making, but it does not require that competitors interact with each other. In fact, competition may be the prime example of relationships that need not and tend not be based on interaction, because competition requires only that a focal actor envisions competitors and utilizes a personal understanding of these competitors as a frame of reference when making choices about social action.

Whereas Weber seemed to assume that relationships are mutual, we are open to the possibility that they can be one-sided: one actor has a relationship with another, but the reverse is not necessarily true. Competition can thus be asymmetrical. Research on managers suggests that it is no trivial issue to determine if a relationship exists between two firms—and the extent to which any such relationship is viewed as competitive. In their case study of Polaroid Corporation, Tripsas and Gavetti (2000) showed how its management did not identify the new electronics firms producing digital images as firms requiring consideration. Competition, in their view, was with the older firms that manufactured physical film. Consequently, Polaroid tailored its market strategies and actions towards the old firms, and when it lost market shares, managers interpreted their loss as having been caused by exogenous demand shifts rather than Polaroid's poor performance in relation to the digital producers. Similar stories of dominant industry incumbents being blindsided and failing to consider new entrants to the industry as competitors are well documented in technology and innovation studies (cf. Anderson and Tushman 1990; Henderson and Clark 1990), but such forms of asymmetric competitive relationships can also be found in politics, science, and sports.

In summary, a common shortcoming of the literatures we have surveyed is an almost exclusive interest in markets as the setting for competition and a lack of interest in the origins of competition. Another, but related problem is that economics, management studies, and sociology tend to stay with a narrow and often unclear conceptualization of competition. Furthermore, instead of problematizing the existence of competition, its existence is taken for granted; the discussion is instead concentrated on how competitors act, how they should act, or how competition allocates resources.

Defining competition

Based on our review of various approaches to competition, we can now provide a more precise definition. Competition is the construction of *a particular relationship* (in the Weberian sense and as previously outlined). It covers relationships in which *a focal actor desires something that this actor perceives as scarce, because of a belief that other actors have the same desire.* Products, money, attention, status, and many other things can become objects of competition. Before we dig into the research implications of this definition, we must have a closer look at its components.

We begin with the question of *desire*—a term we use for anything an actor is longing for. 'Desire' has a psychological connotation, but as a concept it has attracted much broader attention in the social sciences and in humanities since the writings of Jacques Lacan (see Chapter 10, this volume) For our definition of competition, 'desire' is a more appropriate term than 'needs'—a term that refers to functional lines of thinking in anthropology and sociology; or 'demands', which are often reduced to markets and understood as the expressed willingness and capacity to pay for a given product or service. 'Desire' in our understanding is closer to 'goals' in organization theory (Cyert and March 1992): organizations often have goals as a frame of reference for their decision-making. Various things may be desired, but for a desire to be an element in a competitive relationship, we argue that an actor must *realize or imagine that another actor shares the same desire.* The baker or the managers of Polaroid Corporation must recognize or believe that there is another baker or another firm with the same desire. Without that recognition, the situation is not one of competition.

It is noteworthy that we are discussing how actors *understand* or *construct* a situation with respect to the desires of others. One suitor can believe that another person shares the desire for a third person, regardless of what that other person actually thinks or feels. A government can convince some schools that they are competing with other schools for students; yet those other schools may be of a different opinion. In either case, the first necessary element of competition is for a focal actor to believe that someone else shares a desire.

To this point we have been using the term 'actor' quite freely, but our theorization requires an understanding of actors as considered by others as capable of desire; as capable of recognizing the desires of others; and as having the capability to act on desires. In other words, competition requires entities that are inscribed with 'actorhood' (Meyer and Jepperson 2000), because actorhood implies the capability of making decisions in line with one's desire and the willingness and ability to implement those decisions.

Earlier work on competition has typically been based on the assumption that actors are present, but this is a precarious assumption that obscures our understanding of how competition occurs. Importantly, it is an assumption that divorces the study of competition from the richness of work on actors and actorhood in the broader social science. No entity is a social actor by nature or in isolation. Actorhood is the result of institutions or organization (Hasse 2017; Meyer and Jepperson 2000; Sewell Jr 1992), which means that it is contingent upon history and geography (King et al. 2010; Meyer 2010; Pedersen and Dobbin 1997). In current society, it is mainly individuals, organizations, and states that gain actor status; other entities such as classes or clans, once considered actors, are no longer seen in that way (Hasse 2017). Furthermore, it seems that any state, organization, or individual is now expected to develop an identity as actor (Brunsson and Sahlin-Andersson 2000; Hasse 2017).

Although actors are generally recognized as having the ability to desire and to consider the desire of other actors, actorhood is dependent on the situation. A common, situational limitation on the capacity to act is a lack of resources. Many people may desire to have a Picasso painting over their fireplace, but because they are not wealthy, they are not competitors to affluent art collectors or museums. Studies of what other firms that a focal firm recognizes as a competitor suggest an asymmetry: smaller firms identify larger firms, but larger firms do not recognize the smaller (Baum and Haveman 1997; Lant and Baum 1995).

At times, decisions or institutions limit what is seen as legitimate actorhood. Social standing, supported by such institutions as aristocracy, can delineate who is and is not a competitor to become the next sovereign. The complications of becoming a legitimate competitor for affection when violating such institutions is a common theme of popular literature. In sports, being considered a competitor is usually contingent upon conforming with categories like gender and age (Obel 1996). The capacity of an actor to be a competitor can also have moral dimensions (Wolff 2006). Norms about the appropriateness of same-sex attraction have been key constraining factors for who is considered a legitimate competitor for affection (cf. Adut 2005). Becoming a competitor is thus institutionally enabled and often circumscribed through social classification (cf. Zelizer 2005; Zerubavel 1996).

Actors who recognize each other's desire for something is a necessary, but not sufficient, element of competition. There are many situations of shared desire that do not constitute competition. One can think of regions with winter tourism which may share a desire for snow, for example. Competition requires a sense of *scarcity* and that, at least to some extent, this scarcity is viewed as caused or strengthened by the desire of others.

In earlier treatments of scarcity in competition, it has often been unclear who controls the scarce good. There is widespread confusion regarding this issue, and it is often said that firms compete for each other's market shares, or that two states compete for the territory of one. We prefer to reserve the term 'competition' for instances in which the desires concern something that *none of the competitors already* has. This is obviously the case when the object of competition is under the control of a third party and none of the competitors already has that object. Accordingly, firms do not compete for the money that the customer has already given to one of them, but for the money still in the pockets of the customer. The market shares that are of interest to a firm are those that can be won tomorrow—not those of yesterday. Lovers do not compete for the time already spent with another, but for the time yet to share with the loved one. In an election, it is not the votes of the last election but those who are yet to be cast that the parties desire. Thus, competition is about the future, an important aspect that is seldom made explicit in the competition literature (cf. Emirbayer and Mische 1998).

Implications: asymmetries, fourth parties, and behavioural effects

Conceptualizing competition as a construction accentuates the question of who constructs a situation as competition, and it also implies that there can be several constructions at the same time. Social constructions do not need to be symmetric; one actor may construct a situation as competition with respect to another actor who does not share this construction. The potential for asymmetric constructions increases by expanding the scope of those who can construct competition to include observers. Not only can people see themselves as competing with others, they can also act as observers of others and judge their relationships as competitive or not. A biologist studying minnows may see the pike as competing with each other because they desire the same scarce minnows. And an economist observing many firms selling similar products may view them as competing, even assuming that the more firms there are, the more competition. The observers' view may, however, not coincide with the view of the allegedly competing actors—they may have no idea that they are competing. Therefore, scholars who act as observers need to clarify their analytical viewpoint and recognize that they define competition from their omniscient perspective—which also means that they should not infer competitive awareness among those they consider competitors.

Other observers are those who often, but not under all circumstances, adjudicate the outcome of competition—voters in politics and customers in markets, for example. Such 'third parties' (Simmel 1903/2008) may think that several actors compete for their votes or their money; yet one or more of those actors may not see themselves as competitors. Conversely, third parties may believe that they cannot choose among offers from several competitors, whereas one or several of the alleged competitors do believe that there is competition.

Further asymmetries need to be considered if we consider actors that are not competing or adjudicating, but whose decisions have an impact on the competition on others. Extending Simmel's conceptualization which has emphasized the role of third parties, we label these actors *fourth parties*. Fourth parties contribute to the establishment and maintenance of the construction of a situation as competition. Many individuals and organizations can act as fourth parties. Among these are regulators, prize givers, contest organizers, and experts who make comparisons, evaluations, or rankings. In many cases, these fourth parties are crucial for the construction of competition, but sometimes they are the only ones who believe that they have launched a competition; what they see as competition may not be seen as competition by those they consider as competitors or as third parties.

Our definition also allows the analytical distinction between competition and the specific actions that it may give rise to. This distinction is significant for two reasons. First, it clarifies our position that competition is not, as many think, specific actions—innovating more or lowering prices, for instance (cf. Miller and Chen 1996)—actions that can be caused by many circumstances and ideas other than competition. Competition is a relationship that can give rise to actions; it is not the action in itself. Second, competition can lead to many types of action, and we cannot merely presume that any one type will materialize. Seeing a situation as competitive may even discourage action. Even if a situation is understood to be competitive, one common reaction is that it will not matter much one way or the other what one chooses to do. Experimental studies at the individual level have demonstrated that having won earlier competitions can motivate further action, but having lost tends to induce passivity (Murayama and Elliot 2012; Reeve and Deci 1996).

Competition may or may not induce interaction among competitors. Most of the hopes pinned on competition rely on the idea that competition induces action—but not interaction—that it motivates a competitor to 'shape up' and improve performance (Hirschman 1970), or in the words of Simmel, that the competitor strives to divine the 'innermost wishes' of the third party (1903/2008). But competition may also lead to interaction with competitors, an outcome that is often seen as negative. It can motivate attempts to undermine the capacity of a competitor to compete or even to destroy them—through a hostile take-over of a firm, for instance. Or competition leads to cooperation among competitors, which is a common outcome.

By distinguishing between competition and its behavioural effects, we see that competition is *not* the opposite of collaboration or cooperation as is commonly assumed in some of the literature (see, for instance, Brandenburger and

Nalebuff 1997; Chen and Miller 2012; Fehr and Schmidt 1999). Collaboration or cooperation are examples of interactive responses to competition; they do not define away a situation as competitive. Cooperation as a response to competition does not eliminate the competitive relationship; it simply means that those involved in the relationship have decided on a particular response. Take the example of a cartel. Firms in a cartel are still in a competitive relationship with each other over the customer's money, but they have agreed to act in a certain manner in order to handle their competitive relationship—by determining maximum production volumes or minimum prices, for instance. As with all forms of cooperation, rather than reducing competition, cartels may focus, increase, and stabilize competition, because they make it clear that there are competitors and identify who those competitors are—something that may not be as clear without cooperation.

Investigating competition

We miss the lively debate that should be taking place among social scientists about the implications of competition in societies—not only in terms of market competition but also in other domains. We believe that a social science contribution to the public debate about competition has been hindered by a lack of an inclusive and coherent way to define competition. As a consequence, we are overwhelmed by disparate definitions of competition, most of which do not lend themselves to a deeper social science analysis of competition, its origins, or its consequences.

In this book, we begin the task of addressing questions of competition from a broader social science perspective through chapters that variously discuss and investigate how competition is introduced, managed, and removed in different social settings. Compared to earlier work, we provide a highly encompassing, yet precise, definition of competition. The following chapters reflect this inclusiveness in their different analytical stands, breadth of empirical settings, and variation in type of good the competitors desire.

Conceptualizing competition as the social construction of four constitutive elements opens up for new questions and new lines of research. Although the significance of relationships and the existence and institutionalization of scarcity, desire, and actorhood have been extensively and separately dealt with in the social science literature, little effort has been made to relate these developments to the rise of competition.

It is important to consider the elements of competition not only in the analysis of existing competition, but more crucially when seeking to understand the introduction of competition. In that case, all elements of competition are required. Analogously, the removal of competition requires the deconstruction of any one of these elements. There is no competition without actors, or where the actors lack desire, or if they desire only what is not scarce, or where actors are not aware that there are other actors with the same desire to which they relate themselves. There are three types of actor relevant for the construction of competition and these parties may neither share each other's ideas whether there is competition nor the ideas of external observers. Competition, one may conclude, then, is a fragile social arrangement whose emergence and maintenance cannot be taken for granted.

Another topic regards the direct and indirect impact of competition on society. Durkheim began this line of questioning at the turn of the nineteenth century. He argued that competition resulted in a division of labour that eroded established forms of solidarity. His perspective is as relevant today as it was over a century ago, but now competition exists on a global scale with off-shoring and global value chains. Furthermore, more and more status orders have become global. What are the effects of an increasing part of the relationships in a (world) society being seen as competitive? Georg Simmel suggested that we should see competition in the positive light of increasingly orienting persons towards each other, thus contributing to social inclusion (Simmel 1903/2008). Others have argued that the consideration of other social norms of behaviour are pushed to the side when a situation is constructed as competition (Kilduff et al. 2016; Schreck 2015), suggesting that a more competitive society is colder and more antagonistic.

Chapter 2 presents a theorization of competition from the perspective of managers, using the case of restaurants in New York. It shows the often-underestimated complexities of analysing competition even in a relatively simple market setting—illustrating the differences in perceptions of competition by competitors and by the scholars who work with different theoretical, omniscient, research perspectives. That chapter follows the tradition of economic science by beginning with a setting that is already assumed to be competitive, but Chapter 3 investigates how competition can emerge, specifically by processes of mutual adjustment. Christmas decorators and producers and consumers of fashion can all create competition without necessarily wanting or meaning to. Thus, competition can originate beyond the intention of individual actors. Chapter 4 brings together and systematizes our theorizing, arguing that the origins of most competition lie in institutions and organization. Several aspects of modern institutions facilitate the construction of competition, but competition is usually the intentional or unintentional result of various forms of organization. These initial four chapters lay the foundation for the empirical studies in the rest of the book.

Chapters 5–9 examine the construction of the different elements of competition in a number of settings and with a broad selection of 'fourth parties'. Competition is not merely a matter of the promulgation of a reform; it is also hard work, fraught with uncertainty. Chapter 5 details the intensive and varied organizational efforts of a Swedish municipality that worked with different levels of success over two decades, in order to introduce competition among its upper secondary schools. One key challenge was to construct the schools into actors that viewed themselves and each other as legitimate competitors for students. Whereas the object of competition in Chapter 5 was, indirectly, money, Chapter 6 discusses competition for status, using public sports and higher education as the main examples. The allocation of status may be organized through the use of meta-organizations, ratings, rankings, or prizes, but it is far from certain that these forms of organization oblige individuals or organizations to construct competition. Chapter 6 details the complexities of the relationship between organization and competition.

One specific challenge is to ensure the desirability of the object of competition—a place in a ranking table, for instance. Chapter 7 demonstrates that the attempts of rankers of waste-management organizations at creating desire are not always successful— particularly when there are alternative rankings towards which desires can be directed. It is not only what is to be desired that can be constructed differently; Chapter 8 details the history of how Swedish auditors began to compete with each other. In this process, they constructed the firms to be audited as the relevant third party rather than the investors and others who required the audit information. One key implication is that studies that take the prevailing construction of competition as a given miss the other ways in which competition could have been constructed, thereby tending to accept the negative but avoidable effects of the prevailing constructions. Moreover, this perspective ignores the efforts and costs required to introduce competition in the first place.

A central challenge across these studies has been to motivate those who are sup- posed to compete to see themselves and their peers as competitors. In some cases, however, other actors and institutional conditions help to construct competition. Chapter 9 conceptualizes competition as a social drama and demonstrates how researchers and financial actors can be funnelled and lured into competition through contests and prizes and journalists are fond of describing what they see as contests at the expense of other, perhaps more important processes.

Once competition is introduced into a setting, it may need to be maintained, and its effects may need to be managed. The effects of competition are often not those imagined by the fourth parties that introduced it. The management of competition is analysed in Chapters 10–12. The goal of competition can be ambiguous, as in the case of schools, where it is seen as a promise and incentive on the one hand and a possible threat to the ideals of equality on the other hand. Balancing the different expectations of competition in a classroom of children is a delicate managerial task, as illustrated in Chapter 10. A similar ambiguity is common within complex organ- izations that act in an economic setting. Multinational corporations often stimulate competition among its subsidiary units as a way of allocating resources and encour- aging initiatives, but they do not want the competition that is constructed to quell cooperation among its units. Chapter 11 shows how headquarters, in the role of a third and fourth party, can circumvent competition and use a variety of managerial tools in order to guide subsidiaries to react to the competition by cooperating. Sometimes managers want to revoke competition. Chapter 12 addresses the post- merger organizational efforts of a private equity firm that sought to encourage for- mer competing firms to construct their situation as less competitive. That chapter provides a good illustration of the forward-looking aspect of competition: although the personnel in the merged units could see that they were not competing today, they did not trust that they would not compete tomorrow, and they were reluctant to cooperate with each other in a way that could weaken their future positions.

Chapter 13 takes a step back from the empirical work to argue, from a more philosophical standpoint, that the consequences of competition need to be radically rethought. The holy trinity of competition, individualism, and meritocracy needs to be reconsidered, as neither the sense of deserving associated with winning or the blame associated with losing a competition can and should be attributed to individuals. Competition is far too relational for that. Chapter 14 closes the book with conclusions, reflections, and pointers for future research concerning how, when, and why competition is constructed; the many possible consequences of competition; and how competition can be removed.

References

Adut, A. 2005. 'A theory of scandal: Victorians, homosexuality, and the fall of Oscar Wilde'. *American Journal of Sociology* 111 (1): 213–48.

Aghion, P., Bloom, N., Blundell, R., Griffith, R., and Howitt, P. 2005. 'Competition and innovation: an inverted-U relationship'. *Quarterly Journal of Economics* 120 (2): 701–28.

Ahrne, G. 2014. *Samhället mellan oss: om vänskap, kärlek, relationer och organisationer*. Stockholm. Sweden: Liber.

Ahrne, G. and Brunsson, N. 2019. Organization Unbound. In *Organization outside Organizations. The Abundance of Partial Organization in Social Life*, edited by G. Ahrne and N. Brunsson. Cambridge: Cambridge University Press: 3–36.

Anand, N. and Peterson, R. A. 2000. 'When market information constitutes fields: sensemaking of markets in the commercial music industry'. *Organization Science* 11 (3): 270–84.

Anderson, P. and Tushman, M. 1990. 'Technological discontinuities and dominant designs: a cyclical model of technological change'. *Administrative Science Quarterly* 35 (4): 604–34.

Bain, J. S. 1956. *Barriers to New Competition*. Cambridge, MA: Harvard University Press.

Barnett, W. P. and Carroll, G. R. 1987. 'Competition and mutualism among early telephone companies'. *Administrative Science Quarterly* 32 (3): 400–21.

Baum, J. A. C. and Korn, H. 1996. 'Competitive dynamics of interfirm rivalry'. *Academy of Management Journal* 39 (2): 255–91.

Baum, J. A. C. and Haveman, H. A. 1997. 'Love thy neighbor? Differentiation and agglomeration in the Manhattan hotel industry, 1898–1990'. *Administrative Science Quarterly* 42: 304–38.

Ben-Dayid, Y. 1991. *Scientific Growth: Essays on the Social Organization and Ethos of Science*. Berkeley: University of California Press.

Bengtsson, M. and Kock, S. 2014. 'Coopetition—Quo vadis? Past accomplishments and future challenges'. *Industrial Marketing Management* 43 (2): 180–8.

Besley, T., Persson, T., and Sturm, D. 2005. *Political Competition and Economic Performance: Theory and Evidence from the United States*. Cambridge, MA: National Bureau of Economic Research.

Birkinshaw, J., Hood, N., and Jonsson, S. 1998. 'Building firm-specific advantages in multinational corporations: the role of subsidiary initiative'. *Strategic Management Journal* 19 (3): 221–41.

Brandenburger, A. M. and Nalebuff, B. J. 1997. *Co-opetition: A Revolution Mindset that Combines Competition and Cooperation: The Game Theory Strategy that's Changing the Game of Business.* Currency paperback edition. New York: Doubleday.

Brankovic, J. 2018. 'The status games they play: unpacking the dynamics of organisational status competition in higher education'. *Higher Education* 75 (4): 695–709.

Brunsson, N. and Sahlin-Andersson, K. 2000. 'Constructing organizations: the example of public sector reform'. *Organization Studies* 21 (4): 721–46.

Burt, R. S. 1993. 'The social structure of competition'. *Explorations in Economic Sociology* 65: 103.

Burt, R. S. 1995. *Structural Holes.* Cambridge, MA: Harvard University Press.

Carroll, G. R. and Hannan, M. T. 2000. *The Demography of Corporations and Industries.* Princeton: Princeton University Press.

Castel, P., Hénaut, L., and Marchal, E. 2016. *Faire la concurrence. Retour sur un phénomène social et économique.* Paris: Presses des Mines.

Cattani, G., Porac, J. F., and Thomas, H. 2017. 'Categories and competition'. *Strategic Management Journal* 38 (1): 64–92.

Cattani, G., Sands, D., Porac, J., and Greenberg, J. 2018. 'Competitive sensemaking in value creation and capture'. *Strategy Science* 3 (4): 632–57.

Caves, R. and Porter, M. 1977. 'From entry barriers to mobility barriers: conjectural decisions and contrived deterrence to new competition'. *Quarterly Journal of Economics* 91 (2): 241–61.

Chen, M.-J. and Hambrick, D. C. 1995. 'Speed, stealth, and selective attack: how small firms differ from large firms in competitive behavior'. *Academy of Management Journal* 38: 453–82.

Chen, M.-J. and Miller, D. 2012. 'Competitive dynamics: themes, trends, and a prospective research platform'. *The Academy of Management Annals* 6 (1): 135–210.

Cooley, C. H. 1899. *Personal Competition: Its Place in the Social Order and Effect upon Individuals: With Some Considerations on Success.* In *Sociological Theory and Social Research: Being Selected Papers of Charles Horton Cooley*: 163–226. Originally published in *Economic Studies* 4 (2). The Mead project. (https://brocku.ca/MeadProject/Cooley/Cooley_1899.html)

Coser, R. L. (ed.). 1975. 'The complexity of roles as a seedbed of individual autonomy'. *The Idea of Social Structure: Papers in Honor of Robert K. Merton.* Piscataway, NJ: Transaction: 237–63.

Cyert, R. M. and March, J. G. 1992. *A Behavioral Theory of the Firm.* Cambridge, MA: Blackwell Business.

D'Aveni, R. 1994. *Hypercompetition.* New York: Free Press.

Dahl, R. A. 1978. 'Pluralism revisited'. *Comparative Politics* 10 (2): 191–203.

Dennis, K. G. 1975. *Competition in the History of Economic Thought.* Thesis (Ph.D). Oxford: University of Oxford.

DiMaggio, P. J. and Powell, W. W. 1983. 'The iron cage revisited: institutional isomorphism and collective rationality in organizational fields'. *American Sociological Review* 48: 147–60.

Dobbin, F. R. and Dowd, T. J. 1997. 'How policy shapes competition: early railroad foundings in Massachusetts'. *Administrative Science Quarterly* 42 (3): 501–29.

Douglas, M. 2002. *The World of Goods: Towards an Anthropology of Consumption*, volume 6. New York: Psychology Press.

Downs, A. 1957. 'An economic theory of political action in a democracy'. *Journal of Political Economy* 65 (2): 135–50.

Emirbayer, M. and Mische, A. 1998. 'What is agency?'. *American Journal of Sociology* 103 (4): 962–1023.

Fehr, E. and Schmidt, K. M. 1999. 'A theory of fairness, competition, and cooperation'. *Quarterly Journal of Economics* 114 (3): 817–68.

Ghemawat, P. 2002. 'Competition and business strategy in historical perspective'. *Business History Review* 76 (1): 37–74.

Hamel, G. and Prahalad, C. K. 1990. 'The core competence of the corporation'. *Harvard Business Review* 68 (3): 79–91.

Hannan, M. T. and Freeman, J. 1977. 'The population ecology of organizations'. *American Journal of Sociology* 82 (March): 929–64.

Hannan, M. T. 1988. 'Social change, organizational diversity, and individual careers'. *Social Structures and Human Lives* 1: 161–74.

Hasse, R. 2003. *Wohlfahrtspolitik und Globalisierung*. Wiesbaden: Springer.

Hasse, R. and Krücken, G. 2013. 'Competition and actorhood: a further expansion of the neo-institutional agenda'. *Sociologia Internationalis* 51 (2): 181–205.

Hasse, R. 2017. 'About actors: an institutional perspective'. In *Theory in Action: Theoretical Constructionism*, edited by P. Sohlberg and H. Leiulfsrud. Leiden: Brill: 189–205.

Haveman, H. A. 1993. 'Follow the leader: mimetic isomorphism and entry into new markets'. *Administrative Science Quarterly* 38: 593–627.

Hawley, A. 1950. *Human Ecology: A Theory of Urban Structure*. New York: Ronald Press.

Hayek, F. A. 1945. 'The use of knowledge in society'. *American Economic Review* 35 (4): 519–30.

Hayek, F. A. 1948. 'The meaning of competition'. *Individualism and Economic Order* 92: 98.

Hayek, F. A. 1978. 'Competition as a discovery procedure'. In *New Studies in Philosophy, Politics, Economics, and the History of Ideas*, edited by F. A. Hayek. London: Routledge: 179–90.

Henderson, R. M. and Clark, K. B. 1990. 'Architectural innovation: the reconfiguration of existing product technologies and the failure of established firms'. *Administrative Science Quarterly* 35: 9–30.

Hirschman, A. O. 1970. *Exit, Voice, and Loyalty: Responses to Decline in Firms, Organizations, and States*. Cambridge, MA: Harvard University Press.

Hirschman, A. O. 1982. 'Rival interpretations of market society: civilizing, destructive, or feeble?'. *Journal of Economic Literature* 20 (4): 1463–84.

Hirshleifer, J. 1978. 'Competition, cooperation, and conflict in economics and biology'. *American Economic Review* 68 (2): 238–43.

Hodgkinson, G. P. 1997. 'The cognitive analysis of competitive structures: a review and critique'. *Human Relations* 50 (6): 625–54.

Hood, C. and Dixon, R. 2015. *A Government that Worked Better and Cost Less? Evaluating Three Decades of Reform and Change in UK Central Government*. Oxford: Oxford University Press.

Hsieh, C.-T. and Urquiola, M. 2006. 'The effects of generalized school choice on achievement and stratification: evidence from Chile's voucher program'. *Journal of Public Economics* 90 (8): 1477–503.

Ingram, P. and Roberts, P. W. 2000. 'Friendships among competitors in the Sydney hotel industry'. *American Journal of Sociology* 106 (2): 387–423.

Ingram, P. and Yue, L. Q. 2008. 'Structure, affect and identity as bases of organizational competition and cooperation'. *Academy of Management Annals* 2 (1): 275–303.

Jarzabkowski, P. and Bednarek, R. 2018. 'Toward a social practice theory of relational competing'. *Strategic Management Journal* 39 (3): 794–829.

Jasanoff, S. 1990. *The Fifth Branch: Science Advisers as Policymakers*. Cambridge, MA: Harvard University Press.

Kaplan, S. 2011. 'Research in cognition and strategy: reflections on two decades of progress and a look to the future'. *Journal of Management Studies* 48 (3): 665–95.

Kennedy, M. T. 2008. 'Getting counted: markets, media, and reality'. *American Sociological Review* 73 (2): 270–95.

Kilduff, G., Galinksy, A., Gallo, E., and Reade, J. 2016. 'Whatever it takes to win: rivalry increases unethical behavior'. *Academy of Management Journal* 59 (5): 1508–34.

Kilduff, G. J., Elfenbein, H. A., and Staw, B. M. 2010. 'The psychology of rivalry: a relationally dependent analysis of competition'. *Academy of Management Journal* 53 (5): 943–69.

King, B. G., Felin, T., and Whetten, D. A. 2010. 'Perspective—finding the organization in organizational theory: a meta-theory of the organization as a social actor'. *Organization Science* 21 (1): 290–305.

Kjaer, P. F. 2015. 'Context construction through competition: the prerogative of public power, intermediary institutions, and the expansion of statehood through competition'. *Distinktion: Journal of Social Theory* 16 (2): 146–66.

Krücken, G. 2019. 'Multiple competitions in higher education: a conceptual approach'. *Innovation: Organization and Management*. https://doi.org/10.1080/14479338.201 9.1684652 (Accessed 1 February 2021).

Lant, T. K. and Baum, J. A. 1995. 'Cognitive sources of socially constructed competitive groups: examples from the Manhattan hotel industry'. In *The Institutional Construction of Organizations—International and Longitudinal Studies*, edited by R. W. Scott and S. Christensen. California: SAGE: 15–39.

Laumann, E. O. and Knoke, D. 1987. *The Organizational State: Social Choice in National Policy Domains*. Madison: University of Wisconsin Press.

Lazonick, W. 1993. *Business Organization and the Myth of the Market Economy*. Paperback. New York, USA: Press Syndicate of the University of Cambridge.

Levine, D. N., Carter, E. B., and Gorman, E. M. 1976. 'Simmel's influence on American sociology. I'. *American Journal of Sociology* 81 (4): 813–45.

Luhmann, N. 1992. *Universität als Milieu: Kleine Schriften*: Bielefeld, Germany: Haux.

Mannheim, K. 1982. 'Die Bedeutung der Konkurrenz im Gebiete des Geistigen'. In *Der Streit um die Wissenssoziologie*, edited by V. Meja and N. Stehr. Vol. 1. Frankfurt a M: Suhrkamp: 325–70.

March, J. G. and Simon, H. A. 1958. *Organizations*. New York: Wiley.

March, J. G. and Olsen, J. P. 1976. *Ambiguity and Choice in Organizations*. Bergen: Universitetsforlaget.

McGee, J. and Thomas, H. 1986. 'Strategic groups: theory, research and taxonomy'. *Strategic Management Journal* 7: 141–60.

McNulty, P. J. 1967. 'A note on the history of perfect competition'. *Journal of Political Economy*, 75 (4): 395–9.

McNulty, P. J. 1968. 'Economic theory and the meaning of competition'. *Quarterly Journal of Economics* 82 (4): 639–56.

Merton, R. K. 1973. *The Sociology of Science: Theoretical and Empirical Investigations*. Chicago, USA: University of Chicago Press.

Meyer, J. W. and Jepperson, R. 1996. 'The actor and the other: cultural rationalization and the ongoing evolution of modern agency'. Paper presented at the Institutional Analysis Conference, Tucson, Arizona, April.

Meyer, J. W. and Jepperson, R. L. 2000. 'The "actors" of modern society: the cultural construction of social agency'. *Sociological Theory* 18 (1): 100–20.

Meyer, J. W. 2010. 'World society, institutional theories, and the actor'. *Annual Review of Sociology* 36: 1–20.

Miller, D. and Chen, M. J. 1996. 'Nonconformity in competitive repertoires: a sociological view of markets'. *Social Forces* 74: 1209–34.

Mizruchi, M. S. 1992. *The Structure of Corporate Political Action: Interfirm Relations and their Consequences*. Cambridge, MA: Harvard University Press.

Murayama, K. and Elliot, A. J. 2012. 'The competition–performance relation: a meta-analytic review and test of the opposing processes model of competition and performance'. *Psychological Bulletin* 138 (6): 1035.

Obel, C. 1996. 'Collapsing gender in competitive bodybuilding: researching contradictions and ambiguity in sport'. *International Review for the Sociology of Sport* 31 (2): 185–202.

OECD. 1987. *Administration as Service: The Public as Client*. Paris: OECD.

Pedersen, J. S. and Dobbin, F. 1997. 'The social invention of collective actors: on the rise of the organization'. *American Behavioral Scientist* 40 (4): 431–43.

Pedersen, O. K. 2011. *Konkurrencestaten*. Copenhagen: Hans Reitzels Forlag.

Peteraf, M. A. 1993. 'The cornerstones of competitive advantage: a resource-based view'. *Strategic Management Journal* 14: 179–91.

Podolny, J. M. 1993. 'A status-based model of market competition'. *American Journal of Sociology* 98 (4): 829–72.

Porac, J. F. and Baden-Fuller, C. 1989. 'Competitive groups as cognitive communities: the case of Scottish knitwear manufacturers'. *Journal of Management Studies* 26: 397–416.

Porac, J. F., Thomas, H., Wilson, F., Patson, D., and Kanfer, A. 1995. 'Rivalry and the industry model of Scottish knitwear producers'. *Administrative Science Quarterly* 40 (2): 203–27.

Porter, M. 1980. *Competitive Strategy: Techniques for Analyzing Industries and Competitors*. New York: Free Press.

Porter, M. 1981. 'The contributions of industrial organization to strategic management'. *Academy of Management Review* 6 (4): 609–20.

Porter, M. 1985. *Competitive Advantage, Creating and Sustaining Superior Performance*. New York: Free Press.

Porter, M. 1996. 'What is strategy'. *Harvard Business Review* (November–December): 61–78.

Propper, C., Burgess, S., and Green, K. 2004. 'Does competition between hospitals improve the quality of care? Hospital death rates and the NHS internal market'. *Journal of Public Economics* 88 (7): 1247–72.

Rahmandad, H. and Repenning, N. 2016. 'Capability erosion dynamics'. *Strategic Management Journal* 37 (4): 649–72.

Reeve, J. and Deci, E. L. 1996. 'Elements of the competitive situation that affect intrinsic motivation'. *Personality and Social Psychology Bulletin* 22 (1): 24–33.

Reger, R. K. and Huff, A. S. 1993. 'Strategic groups: a cognitive perspective'. *Strategic Management Journal* 14 (2): 103–23.

Robinson, J. 1969. *The Economics of Imperfect Competition*. Springer. New York.

Rodrik, D. 2011. *The Globalization Paradox: Why Global Markets, States, and Democracy Can't Coexist*. Oxford, UK: Oxford University Press.

Rosa, J. A. and Porac, J. F. 2002. 'Categorization bases and their influence on product category knowledge structures'. *Psychology and Marketing* 19 (6): 503–31.

Rothstein, J. 2007. 'Does competition among public schools benefit students and tax-payers? Comment'. *American Economic Review* 97 (5): 2026–37.

Rumelt, R. P. 1991. 'How much does industry matter?'. *Strategic Management Journal* 12 (3): 167–85.

Schneiberg, M. and Hollingsworth, J. R. 1990. 'Can transaction cost economics explain trade associations?' In *The Firm as a Nexus of Treaties*, edited by M. Aoki, B. Gustafsson, and O. Williamson. London: SAGE: 233–46.

Schreck, P. 2015. 'Honesty in managerial reporting: how competition affects the benefits and costs of lying'. *Critical Perspectives on Accounting* 27: 177–88.

Schumpeter, J. A. 1934. *The Theory of Economic Development*. Cambridge, MA: Harvard University Press.

Schumpeter, J. A. 1942. *Capitalism, Socialism and Democracy*. New York: Harper and Brothers.

Sewell Jr, W. H. 1992. 'A theory of structure: duality, agency, and transformation'. *American Journal of Sociology* 98: 1–29.

Simmel, G. 1903/2008. 'Sociology of competition'. *Canadian Journal of Sociology/Cahiers Canadiens de Sociologie* 33 (4): 957–78.

Smith, A. and McCulloch, J. R. 1838. *An Inquiry into the Nature and Causes of the Wealth of Nations*. A. and C. Black and W. Tait.

Sonenshein, S., Nault, K., and Obodaru, O. 2017. 'Competition of a different flavor: how a strategic group identity shapes competition and cooperation'. *Administrative Science Quarterly* 62 (4): 626–56.

Stark, D. 2020. *The Performance Complex: Competition and Competitions in Social Life*. Oxford: Oxford University Press.

Stigler, G. J. 1957. 'Perfect competition, historically contemplated'. *Journal of Political Economy* 65 (1): 1–17.

Stigler, G. J. 1976. 'The existence of x-efficiency'. *American Economic Review* 66 (1): 213–16.

Stiglitz, J. E. 1981. 'Potential competition may reduce welfare'. *American Economic Review* 71 (2): 184–9.

Stiglitz, J. E. 1992. 'The meanings of competition in economic analysis'. *Rivista Internazionale di Scienze Sociali* 100 (2): 191–212.

Strandqvist, K. 2018. 'From a free market to a pure market' in *Organizing and Reorganizing Markets*, edited by N. Brunsson and M. Jutterström. Oxford, UK: Oxford University Press: 232–48.

Swedberg, R. 2014. *The Art of Social Theory*. Princeton: Princeton University Press.

Tirole, J. 1988. *The Theory of Industrial Organization*. Cambridge, MA: MIT press.

Tripsas, M. and Gavetti, G. 2000. 'Capabilities, cognition and inertia: evidence from digital imaging'. *Strategic Management Journal* 21 (10/11): 1147–61.

Tsai, W. 2002. 'Social structure of "coopetition" within a multiunit organization: coordination, competition, and intraorganizational knowledge sharing'. *Organization Science* 13 (2): 179–90.

Vickers, J. 1995. 'Concepts of competition'. *Oxford Economic Papers* 47 (1): 1–23.

Weber, M. 1978. *Economy and Society: An Outline of Interpretive Sociology*. Berkeley: University of California Press.

Werron, T. 2015. 'Why do we believe in competition? A historical-sociological view of competition as an institutionalized modern imaginary'. *Distinktion: Journal of Social Theory* 16 (2): 186–210.

White, H. C. 1981. 'Where do markets come from?' *American Journal of Sociology* 87 (3): 517–47.

Wolff, J. 2006. 'Libertarianism, utility, and economic competition'. *Virginia Law Review* 92 (7): 1605–23.

Xenos, N. 1987. 'Liberalism and the postulate of scarcity'. *Political Theory* 15 (2): 225–43.

Zelizer, V. 2005. 'Culture and consumption'. In *The Handbook of Economic Sociology*, edited by N. J. Smelser and R. Swedberg. Princeton: Princeton University Press and New York: Russell Sage Foundation: 331–55.

Zerubavel, E. 1996. 'Lumping and splitting: notes on Social Classification'. Sociological Forum. Vol. 11. No. 3. Kluwer Academic Publishers-Plenum Publishers.

2

Competition as sensemaking

Daniel Sands, Gino Cattani, Joseph Porac, and Jason Greenberg

The concept of competition has long been a central theme in different literatures concerned with markets. Depictions of competition, however, have varied considerably, both across disciplines and over time. While research in industrial organization can often treat competitive forces as uniform and exogenous constraints on strategic choices (e.g. Bain 1952; Porter 1980), socio-cognitive accounts of competition have emphasized how competitive forces are at least partially endogenous. These developments have drawn the attention to the social and cognitive processes that underlie how firms detect, define, and conceptualize their competitive relationships with other firms (see Cattani et al. 2017; 2018). The purpose here is to elucidate further why such an account is not only useful but also necessary for studying how firms make sense of their competitive environment and, accordingly, make choices. We expect that this chapter can help problematize competition by focusing on the often taken-for-granted assumptions underpinning definitions of competition across different literatures. We hope that our analysis will underscore the inherent challenges in studying competition empirically and that our sensemaking perspective will contribute to the interdisciplinary dialogue on the topic. In this way, our chapter also speaks to some of the issues contemplated in other chapters—particularly the definition and institutionalization of competition (see Chapters 1 and 4, this volume), as well as the notion of competition playing out at multiple levels. (See also Chapter 3, this volume.)

Consistent with other recent work (e.g. Arora-Jonsson et al. 2020), we move away from the notion that competition is simply out there, passively waiting to be observed and then recognized as such. Instead, we argue that competition is the ongoing sensemaking process where different actors (e.g. transaction partners, managers, other firms, and even non-contractually involved external audiences) interact and where market boundaries are continuously defined, contested, and redefined. Competition, thus, is socially constructed, and accounts of competition extend from the collective mental models of different actors that weave in and out of the marketplace. Reconsidering fundamental assumptions about competition offers an opportunity to better understand its institutional and organizational foundations (cf. Chapter 4, this volume), while also recognizing its agentic—and, by extension, strategic—nature. The sensemaking approach, for which we advocate, provides such an orientation.

Daniel Sands, Gino Cattani, Joseph Porac, & Jason Greenberg, *Competition as sensemaking* In: *Competition: What It Is and Why It Happens*. Edited by: Stefan Arora-Jonsson, Nils Brunsson, Raimund Hasse, and Katarina Lagerström, Oxford University Press.

We begin this chapter by first exploring conventional conceptualizations of competition used in different literatures. We then investigate the multi-level cognitive embeddedness of competition among restaurants in New York City through three case studies. These case studies allow us to concurrently portray how prior definitions of competition map onto managerial perceptions of competition. Notably, the New York City restaurant industry is ideal for our research purposes as it allows us to address core questions concerning competitive boundaries that cut across transactional, organizational, and categorical analytical perspectives. Hence, our question-driven empirical approach allows us to exploit the richness of our research setting for the purpose of addressing fundamental issues about competition that go beyond the scope of existing theories and perspectives. Ultimately, we posit that different perspectives of competition (transactional, organizational, and categorical) are only loosely coupled, and we contend that competition is, in fact, construed through a sensemaking process that deploys heterogeneous representations of markets. Finally, we wrap up our chapter by briefly discussing how a cognitively embedded conceptualization of market competition is needed to help overcome the inconsistencies that emerge from more reductionist perspectives of competition, highlighting the inherent strength of the sensemaking approach.

Definitions of market competition

Defining competition in markets is an old problem in the social sciences (see Chamberlin 1933; Robinson 1933), and various disciplines have grappled with the complexities of recognizing and defining competitive relationships in different ways. In particular, three approaches have dominated the economics, strategy, and organizations literatures: (1) cross-elasticities of demand, (2) strategic groups, and (3) the categorical structure of markets. In briefly reviewing these three literatures, our goal here is to explore their strengths and weaknesses and identify how each literature defines competitive relationships in markets.[1]

Cross-elasticities of demand

Since Robinson (1933), economists have viewed imperfect competition as a matter of substitution among products. As Bain once put it, 'The general criterion for inclusion of products in an industry becomes close substitutability, of which perfect substitutability is a special and extreme case' (1952: 24–5). Triffin (1940) formalized the notion of substitutability in promoting the 'cross-elasticity' of demand and supply as a metric for determining the degree of competition among products and firms.

---

[1] For a more comprehensive review of these three approaches, refer to Cattani et al. 2017; see also Arora-Jonsson et al. 2020 for other conceptualizations related to the origins of competition.

Cross-elasticities depict competition as a relative measure of how sensitive one economic actor is to the behaviour of another. As such, cross-elasticity measurements have become the central metric for defining competitive relationships within industrial organization economics, spawning a large and deep literature on market structure and market power over the years (e.g. Baker and Bresnahan 1985; Bresnahan 1987; Elzinga and Hogarty 1973; Froeb and Werden 1991; Horowitz 1981; Petrin 2002; Scheffman and Spiller 1996; Slade 1986).

Since the 1950s, cross-elasticity metrics have also been at the centre of questions about market power within antitrust deliberations (e.g. Baker and Bresnahan 2008; Werden 1992; 1997); indeed, defining which firms are in a competitive relationship with which other firms (if any) _is_ the central question. Recent advances in cross-elasticity measurement combine advanced econometrics with simulations as a way of constructing counterfactual definitions of competitive space within structural estimations of supply and demand (e.g. Berry et al. 1995; 2004). This helps mitigate the complex dimensionality problem by comparing different sets of product and buyer attributes and their best fit with empirical estimations of supply and demand. Such counterfactual analysis has become a widely accepted technique in antitrust regulation as well (e.g. Werden 1997).

Notably, however, cross-elasticity estimation is inherently a backward-looking measure. Hence, much depends on stable competitive relationships and product attributes to estimate future competitive positions (Pleatsikas and Teece 2001). These requirements and deficiencies are sometimes overlooked in academic scholarship, but they are confronted regularly in antitrust courts (e.g. Baker and Bresnahan 2008; Werden 1997). Echoing this broader point, Baker and Bresnahan (2008: 15) concluded their review of the antitrust econometrics literature by suggesting that the inherent complexity of markets and market power 'makes the use of multiple sources of evidence particularly valuable'. Cross-elasticity of demand, therefore, cannot be the only empirical criterion for the demarcation of competitive boundaries.

Strategic groups

A long-standing criticism of cross-elasticity measurements, given their backward-looking nature, has been that they do not directly assess the active and strategic aspect of what constitutes a competitive relationship. Indeed, cross-elasticity measures do not account for the managerial intent that leads firms to pursue similar strategies and respond cooperatively or competitively to one another. As Weintraub (1942) noted long ago, such inter-firm action and reaction complicates cross-elasticity estimation and also opens up competition to a variety of second-order managerial influences. A firm's decision to compete directly with another firm on particular dimensions and at a given price is driven by managerial strategic intent. This intent is partially rooted in managerial mental models about the competitive space (e.g. Daniels et al. 2002; Porac et al. 1995), and it is an open question how these models shape, and are shaped by, cross-elasticity metrics.

Relational sociology offers particularly useful insights here as it provides a distinction between market *transactions* and competitive *relationships* (e.g. Tilly 2005; White 1992; 2004). Conceptually, this corresponds to the importance of strategic intent and strategic interaction among competing firms, which was a key motivation for the development of the concept of 'strategic groups' in the strategic management literature. Hunt's (1972) observation of group-level heterogeneity in the home appliance industry was extended by Caves and Porter (1977) and Porter (1976; 1979; 1980), and these works suggest that competition exists because there are 'group of firms in an industry following a same or similar strategy along strategic dimensions' (Porter 1980: 129). In considering the inherent endogeneity of competition within strategic groups, Caves and Porter (1977: 251) argue that 'Because of their structural similarity, group members are likely to respond in the same way to disturbances from inside or outside the group, recognising their interdependence closely and anticipating their reactions to one another's moves quite accurately'.

The strategic groups literature, thus, suggests that activities in markets are not only a function of underlying economic fundamentals such as supply and demand, but they are also derived from socially constructed representations of market-membership. However, this literature can also be portrayed as overly inward-looking since it often overlooks how external audiences can impose categorical structures that frame competitive boundaries. And while the socio-cognitive bases of strategic groups have been explored in several empirical studies to good effect (e.g. McNamara et al. 2003; Ng et al. 2009; Osborne et al. 2001; Porac et al. 1995; Reger and Huff 1993; Wry et al. 2006), there has been almost no research outside the discussions in prior conceptual work devoted to investigating relationships between mental models of strategists and the nature of cross-elasticities among firms.

The categorical structure of markets

Over the past two decades or so, economic sociologists and organizational theorists have explored the structure of competitive markets from a social constructionist perspective. A general approach to market boundaries has begun to take hold, emphasizing the critical role of semantic categories in structuring market relationships (Vergne and Wry 2014). Drawing from research in cognitive psychology, categories are considered key elements in classification systems that impose coherence and create shared understandings of the organizational world that facilitate exchange in markets (Hannan et al. 2007; 2019; Koçak et al. 2014; Porac and Thomas 1994). They do so by establishing semantic boundaries around similar kinds of entities such as products, technologies, genres, people, or organizational forms (DiMaggio 1987; Goldberg, Hannan, and Kovács 2016; Lamont and Molnár 2002; Lounsbury and Rao 2004; Rosa et al. 1999).

In Hannan et al.'s (2007: 33) words, 'members of audiences observe producers and products, notice similarities, try to make sense of them by clustering similar producers/products, and possibly assign labels to clusters'. Hence, research from this perspective would suggest that the two actors are competitors in the same market if there is a semantic category that is consensually understood by buyers and sellers and that binds their transactions together via common category membership. Research has, indeed, established relationships between the socio-cognitive categorical structure of organizational fields and outcomes such as firm revenues (e.g. Hsu 2006; Zhao et al. 2013), costs (e.g. Ody-Brasier and Vermeulen 2014), perceptions of quality (e.g. Bowers and Prato 2018; Sands 2021), capital inflows (e.g. Pontikes 2012; Smith 2011), and stock prices (e.g. Zuckerman 1999).

Market category research in sociology has contributed to the study of markets in several ways. It calls attention to how collective and culturally produced semantic categories organize and institutionalize markets and industries. Moreover, given that much of this research has measured categories by coding linguistic output from external audience market mediators, such as analysts, critics, and journalists, it has also demonstrated how these external audiences contribute to labelling, codifying, and evaluating individual firms and products in accepted categories. In this way, category research has called attention to the 'category producing infrastructure' of markets and industries, and the set of external audience actors who are involved in making sense of the structure of market transactions and developing category systems for describing them (Cattani et al. 2017). An implication of this latter contribution is that such research *endogenizes* category systems by making them a mutually constitutive part of the market-making process, rather than viewing them as exogenous and unexplained market classification systems. Also, a single omnibus category system for describing intra-industry variation may not be viable as different external audiences may have different categorical perspectives on the same firm. Yet, missing from much of the category research is an explicit focus on firms and their managers as loci for competitive sensemaking and decision-making or the relationship between categorical membership and cross-elasticity measures. Likewise, how the strategic choices of firms are influenced by managerial interpretation and use of collective categories has only recently been investigated (e.g. Pontikes 2018; Pontikes and Kim 2017; Rhee 2015).

Case studies

Our review of the literature, following the heuristic framework provided by Cattani et al. (2017: 79), suggests that there are three analytical perspectives of identifying competitive relationships, each of which corresponds to alternative definitions of competitive relationships as defined by different orientations to markets: transactional (the cross-elasticities of demand perspective), organizational (the strategic groups perspective), and categorical (the categorical structure of markets perspective).

Comparing the coherence and correspondence of competitive relationships (and their metrics) across these three perspectives is a crucial step in refining our understanding of competition in markets. We have described how different literatures have conceptualized and attempted to identify competitive relationships among firms at one of the three analytical perspectives, thus providing a reductionist view of what, in fact, is a more complex phenomenon. Integrating these different literatures into a heuristic framework of competition and introducing measures of competitive relationships across all three of them will afford a window to view where possible (in)consistencies in market definitions occur. This comparative examination, thus, raises the key research question that forms the basis for our study: *what is the correspondence between the identified competitive relationships across transactional, organizational, and categorical analytical perspectives?*

Case construction

In this chapter, we develop three case studies of restaurants to explore the nuances of transactional, organizational, and categorical representations of competitive space. The three restaurant cases were chosen to represent three different cuisine types that exist amongst many within a single zip code in New York City but were randomly selected from within their cuisine category. They allow us to present a detailed comparison of competitive representations given that we can compare specific data from all three analytical perspectives.

For purposes of this study, we use menu items and price data to serve as a proxy for transactional interdependencies. We developed measures for menu overlap between restaurants and the median price for a main course for the restaurants in our sample. That is to say, for each restaurant, we used menu data in order to construct a list of items and prices. For each restaurant, we then calculated the median price of a main course, and for any given pair of restaurants, we calculated how many individual items appeared on both menus (i.e. the overlap in menu offerings between a pair of restaurants).

From the organizational perspective, we develop an understanding of how restaurant owners defined and comprehended the dimensions along which they compete and differentiate among other restaurants through semi-structured interviews of restaurateurs in New York City with a focus on a particular neighbourhood in Manhattan. All respondents were either the owner of the restaurant, the head manager, or both. Interviews began with background questions concerning the history and founding of the restaurant, as well as the training and prior entrepreneurial, business, professional, and networking experiences of the founders. Background questions were followed with those concerning the identity of the restaurant, how the restaurant competes and differentiates, as well as with whom, to what extent, and why. We depict any competitors as 'Competitor 1', 'Competitor 2', and so on, for confidentiality reasons.

In order to assess the categorical structures imposed on restaurants by external audiences, we track the cuisine categories into which New York City restaurants have been classified by three prominent external audience evaluation aggregator websites, *Yelp*, *OpenTable*, and *TripAdvisor*. While each of these review websites has different primary audiences (e.g. general diners, diners making reservations, and travelling diners, respectively), together they provide ample evidence for how restaurants are depicted across the broader external audience category producing infrastructure. To maintain the confidentiality of those restaurants included within our sample, we do not disclose which external audience websites categorized which restaurants; therefore, we list these external audience evaluation aggregators as simply 'Review Website 1', 'Review Website 2', and 'Review Website 3' in our data tables.

Counterfactual competition

As noted in the previous section, we asked each interviewee to list other local restaurants that were competitors, why they listed a particular restaurant, and how their restaurant compared to a competitor on certain key attributes. From this, we constructed a competitor matrix to summarize a restaurateur's representation of their principal competition. For each of the cases, we compare this competitor matrix with external audience cuisine categorizations and review information, along with data on geographic location, menu overlap, and prices. These comparisons represent the core of our data analysis. In addition, following the logic of counterfactual analysis in identifying market structures (e.g. Berry et al. 1995; 2004; Petrin 2002), we constructed 'counterfactual' representations of the competitive landscape for each restaurant and compared these counterfactuals with each restaurateur's representation. Notably, our qualitative counterfactual analysis draws inspiration from related techniques that have long been used in a wide range of disciplines such as political science (e.g. Allison 1971; Levy 2008; Tetlock and Belkin 1996), philosophy (e.g. Goodman 1947), history (e.g. Black 2015), sociology (Mahoney and Barrenechea 2019), and law (Grossman and Shapiro 1986; Stoljar 2001).

In our case, we construct counterfactuals that represent restaurants that maximized the similarity between one of our sample restaurants on the dimensions of geographic distance, menu overlap, prices, and external audience-defined cuisine categorization. That is, our counterfactual set of competitors is our best estimate of the most plausible definition of competitive relationships for the focal restaurant (of each of our three restaurant cases), considering distance, menu overlap, prices, and external audience-defined cuisine categorization. We selected these dimensions based on their theoretical relevance and pragmatic availability and because these dimensions were most commonly referenced within our exploratory interviews of restaurateurs. Figure 2.1 depicts our empirical strategy showing how we combine data from different sources to map onto the managerial set of competitors, as well as our counterfactual set of competitors.

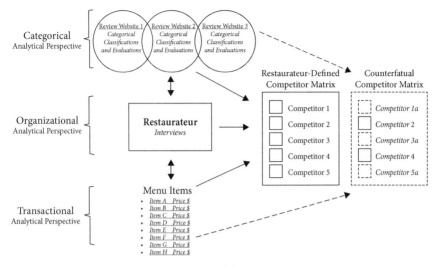

Figure 2.1 Analytical perspectives, data, and the construction of competitor matrices

Notes: Figure depicts how data from multiple sources are integrated to construct the restaurateur-defined and counterfactual competitor matrices.

Case analyses

Case study one: Blue Poppy

The focal restaurant in the first case study will be referred to as 'Blue Poppy'.[2] Blue Poppy had been in business for fourteen years at the time of our first interview. At the time of our interviews, it was run by an owner-manager, but it had been founded by the manager's father and brother. Blue Poppy is a vegetarian restaurant, with vegan options, serving food items that resemble non-vegetarian items but are solely plant based. The restaurant identifies as being a purveyor of 'vegan comfort food', serving common dishes such as chicken parmesan (but without actual chicken). More precisely, the manager defined Blue Poppy's competitive positioning by stating: 'I [Blue Poppy] have a unique brand of food, I am not serving raw or organic vegetables. I am serving things that look like meat and seafood. That is my niche.' Therefore, this restaurant is categorized by some review websites based on dietary restriction (e.g. 'Vegetarian', 'Vegan'), and in others based on cuisine genre (e.g. 'Soul Food', 'American'), albeit inconsistently. Two of the three review websites listed the restaurant as 'Vegetarian'. A different pair of review websites listed it as 'Asian', and yet a different pair of review websites as either 'American' or 'Soul Food'. Thus, no two review websites categorize the restaurant in precisely the same categories. In perusing the menu—as well as all online reviews (several thousand from one external audience evaluation aggregator website)—it is clear that the restaurant serves both American soul food (e.g. southern and BBQ-style) dishes and Asian dishes (Table 2.1).

---

[2] Cattani et al. 2018, 647–8, make use of this particular case in developing a depiction of the 'comparability' component of competitive sensemaking.

Table 2.1 Competitor matrix: Blue Poppy

	Categorization by Review Website 1	Categorization by Review Website 2	Categorization by Review Website 3	Median Cost Main Menu Item	Mean Consumer Evaluation	Number of Menu Overlaps	Distance to Focal Restaurant (Miles)
FOCAL RESTAURANT: Blue Poppy	Vegetarian, Soul Food, Vegan	American, Asian, Vegetarian Friendly	Asian	$13	4.25		
RESTAURATEUR-DEFINED COMPETITOR MATRIX							
Competitor 1	American, Asian, Fusion	Vegan, Asian Fusion, Kosher	N/A	$16	4.25	2	0.1
Competitor 2	Vegetarian, Vegan	Vegetarian/Vegan	America, Vegetarian Friendly, Vegan Options	$22	4.3	4	12
Competitor 3	Vegan, Gluten-Free, Sandwiches	American, Café, Vegetarian Friendly	N/A	$21	4.25	3	3.9
Competitor 4	Vegetarian, Vegan, Kosher	Vegetarian Friendly, Vegan Options, Gluten Free Options	Gastro Pub	$16	3.75	2	0.2
Competitor 5	Continental	Cocktail Bars, American (New)	American, Vegetarian Friendly	$24	4	0	1.7
Mean (Competitors)				19.80	4.11	2.20	1.42
Standard Deviation (Competitors)				3.63	0.23	1.48	1.54

COUNTERFACTUAL COMPETITOR MATRIX

Competitor 1	American, Asian, Fusion	Vegan, Asian Fusion, Kosher	N/A	$16	4.25	2	0.1
Competitor 2	Coffee & Tea, Vegan, Gluten-Free	Café, American, Vegetarian Friendly	N/A	$13	4.25	7	0.5
Competitor 3	Vegetarian, Vegan	American, Vegetarian Friendly, Vegan Options	N/A	$12	4.25	7	0.2
Competitor 4	Vegetarian, Vegan, Kosher	Vegetarian Friendly, Vegan Options, Gluten Free Options	Gastro Pub	$16	3.75	2	0.2
Competitor 5	Vegan, Burgers, Ice Cream & Frozen Yogurt	American, Vegetarian Friendly, Vegan Options	Vegetarian	$10	4.25	4	0.2
Mean (Competitors)				13.40	4.15	4.40	0.024
Standard Deviation (Competitors)				2.61	0.22	2.51	0.15

Note: This table contains the restaurateur-defined (top) and counterfactual (bottom) competitor matrices. For each matrix, five competitors are listed along with information about these restaurants and their relationship to the focal restaurant (*Blue Poppy*).

When asked to name the competition, the manager provided the name of five competitors. However, in discussing why these are the competitors she selected, the manager ultimately dismisses them (and, by implication, cross-firm interdependencies) because she does not believe that Blue Poppy's consumers consider other restaurants to be reasonable alternatives. An example of this appears within the following quote:

> When my restaurant is packed they have the option but they don't go [to Competitor 1]. So they are definitely not a competition. You could get a pizza and people actually do. What I do is tell the customer: "Hey guys, this is our routine. Let me take your name and number. You can walk around the park and I will give you a call in 45 minutes." People are so happy with that. If they don't want to wait I tell them they can do a takeout. Give me ten minutes and you can eat in the park. Give these people options [of going to an alternative restaurant] and they will still buy your food.

The restaurateur does not believe that her selected competitors are viable substitutes for her restaurant. This sentiment was reinforced when discussing Competitor 4: 'They [Competitor 4] are vegetarian but they offer different products than us. I don't see them as competition. Even though they are three blocks down, they are just different.' The restaurateur even includes restaurants that are not geographically near or at the same price point. Competitor 5 is not a vegetarian restaurant but offers things that the restaurateur finds appealing: 'I actually went there [Competitor 5] two months ago. I do like the atmosphere. They do serve meat but it is more like health-conscious.'

The set of restaurants that we observe in the restaurateur-defined competitor matrix is not indicative of a lack of more similar restaurants in the area, which could be substitutes. When we compare her matrix to our counterfactual competitor matrix generated by using external audience review websites whose businesses are predicated on defining, ranking, and rating substitutes, we only observe two restaurants (Competitors 1 and 4) appearing in both lists. The counterfactual competitor matrix contains restaurants that are more similar to the focal restaurant on observable characteristics. Notably, the competitors listed by the manager show a median main menu item cost that is 50 per cent higher than Blue Poppy. Likewise, the counterfactual competitor matrix has a 100 per cent increase in menu overlaps compared to the set of competitors listed by the manager. Just like our focal restaurant seeks to offer a menu full of items that appear to be traditional dishes but are actually meat-free alternatives, counterfactual Competitors 3 and 5 offer similar menu items. This case study highlights how a restaurateur does not necessarily define competition as a substitute, as an elasticity-based orientation would presume. Additionally, this restaurateur omitted potential competitors that were geographically near and categorically similar to them. In fact, the mean walking distance between Blue Poppy and the restaurateur-defined competitors was 1.42 miles (and our counterfactual competitors were only 0.24 miles away).

Case study two: Clifford's

The focal restaurant used in the second case study we call 'Clifford's'. Clifford's was founded in the early 2010s by a first-time restaurateur who had originally been a banker but finally decided to open a restaurant after years of deliberation. In the interview, she describes that their intent with founding Clifford's was to establish a restaurant that placed 'a big emphasis on taking care of people'. With only sixteen items on their menu, Clifford's serves dishes such as salads, sandwiches, and pizzas. This restaurant is categorized rather differently across the various review websites (e.g. 'American Traditional', 'Italian', 'Café', 'Pizza', 'Sandwiches'). We speculate that this is, in part, because its identity is based on a regional cuisine. The main menu item is pizza, and the other menu items are very diverse (Table 2.2).

The restaurateur-defined competition matrix is particularly striking when considering that the first listed competitor is only a takeout pizza shop; they do not even carry a full range of menu offerings, nor waiter service, and they are priced significantly lower than Clifford's. Competitor 3 and Competitor 4, while also geographically near,[3] do not even have pizza on their menus. Competitor 3's median main menu item is more than double that of the focal restaurant. Competitor 2 and Competitor 5 are so geographically distant that a patron could not travel between the locations without a more-than-thirty-minute taxi or subway ride; accordingly, it is unlikely that consumers would alternate between these options provided a price change or supply constraint. While these distances may be reasonable for defining competitive relationships in some cases (e.g. niche genres or venues focused on special events), the identity of Clifford's (and even the restaurateur-defined competition) does not seem to warrant such expansive competitive boundaries. Moreover, the median menu item ($12) would be less expensive than a taxi ride from Clifford's to Competitors 2 or 5. Accordingly, there are seemingly no conditions under which a standard consumer would consider these particular restaurants as viable alternatives.

Our counterfactual list is mostly made up of restaurants that are defined by pizza. Only one of the restaurants, Competitor 4, appears in the restaurateur-defined competitor matrix. All of these restaurants are within a few dollars of the interviewed restaurant, and four of five are within a 0.2-mile walk. Notably, the most distant restaurant of the counterfactual competitor matrix (but not as distant as restaurants appearing on the restaurateur-defined competitor matrix), Competitor 5, classifies its cuisine type (regional American cuisine with an emphasis on pizza) in nearly the same way as the focal restaurant, but it does not appear on the restaurateur-defined competition list. Moreover, the restaurateur-defined competitors have a median menu item cost that is 40 per cent more expensive than Clifford's, and the counterfactual set of competition has twice as much menu item overlap compared to the restaurateur-defined set.

---

[3] 'Near' within New York City can be conceptualized as within a neighbourhood boundary or in an adjacent and accessible neighbourhood. Practically, crossing from one adjacent neighbourhood to another takes no more than fifteen minutes via walking or public transportation. In much of New York City, traveling fifteen minutes would lead an individual to pass by hundreds of restaurants.

Table 2.2 Competitor matrix: Clifford's

	Categorization by Review Website 1	Categorization by Review Website 2	Categorization by Review Website 3	Median Cost Main Menu Item	Mean Consumer Evaluation	Number of Menu Overlaps	Distance to Focal Restaurant (Miles)
FOCAL RESTAURANT: Clifford's	American Traditional, Pizza, Sandwiches	Italian, Pizza, American	Café	$12	4.25		
		RESTAURATEUR-DEFINED COMPETITOR MATRIX					
Competitor 1	Pizza	Italian, Pizza, Fast Food, Vegetarian Friendly	N/A	$6	4.3	1	0.3
Competitor 2	Pizza	Italian	Italian, Pizza	$15	4.6	2	4
Competitor 3	Breakfast and Brunch, Salads and Sandwiches	American	Seafood, American, Contemporary, Vegetarian Friendly, Gluten Free Options, Vegan Options	$34	4.3	1	0.1
Competitor 4	Italian	Italian Vegetarian Friendly	Italian	$14	3.9	1	0.2
Competitor 5	Pizza, Italian	Italian, Pizza, Vegetarian Friendly, Vegan Options	Italian	$17	4.25	1	4.4
Mean (Competitors)				17.20	4.27	1.20	1.80
Standard Deviation (Competitors)				10.28	0.25	0.45	2.20

COUNTERFACTUAL COMPETITOR MATRIX

Competitor 1	Pizza, Italian	Italian, Pizza, Mediterranean, Vegetarian Friendly, Vegan Options	Italian	$16	4.4	2	0.1
Competitor 2	Pizza, Italian	Italian, Pizza, Vegetarian Friendly	Italian	$15	4.1	3	0.1
Competitor 3	Italian, Pizza	American	Italian, Pizza, Vegetarian Friendly	$12	4	2	0.1
Competitor 4	Italian	Italian Vegetarian Friendly	Italian	$14	3.9	1	0.2
Competitor 5	Pizza	Italian, Pizza	N/A	$12	4	4	2.1
Mean (Competitors)				13.80	4.08	2.40	0.52
Standard Deviation (Competitors)				1.79	0.19	1.14	0.88

Note: This table contains the restaurateur-defined (top) and counterfactual (bottom) competitor matrices. For each matrix, five competitors are listed along with information about these restaurants and their relationship to the focal restaurant (*Clifford's*).

The previous evidence suggests how categories do not reconcile the restaurateur-competitor list, nor does the elasticity-substitution logic seem to explain how restaurateurs perceive a competitor. It is also not the case that the restaurateur lacks a sophisticated view of the market; in fact, she notes how much effort (and expense) is put into making sound strategic decisions: 'It takes a lot of money to open a restaurant. Now it is such a good calculated move with investors and consultants.' Likewise, the restaurateur is well aware of the other key actors in the market and is highly embedded in the New York City restaurant industry; she describes socializing with other owners 'all the time. More since I opened, since we get along better. [We're] like-minded individuals. You share the same struggles.' Provided the restaurateur's sophistication and embedded position in the market, it is perhaps surprising that our counterfactual competitor matrix provides greater overlap with categorical, distance, and price measures. By all quantitative and qualitative measures, the counterfactual competitors are significantly more similar to the focal restaurant than the restaurateur's cognitive representation.

Case study three: Fish Fish

We will call the focal restaurant in the third case study 'Fish Fish'. This restaurant had only been opened for about one year at the time of the interview. However, this was the second location of this restaurant that the restaurateur had opened; the other location had been in operation for nearly four years. The restaurateur describes it is as a classic sushi restaurant with a very focused menu: 'sushi, strictly sushi'. Provided this focus, the restaurateur highlights one of their differentiating factors as their homemade sauces that they use with sushi rolls. Because sushi restaurants have a different menu style than do other types of restaurants, we report the median cost of Fish Fish's signature item, so we can most accurately represent comparisons across restaurants (Table 2.3).

The restaurateur highlights that she finds Fish Fish to be comparable to other premium-product restaurants:

> We used to think sushi has a specific demographic but we found that it all comes down to a money thing. It is a financial issue, not a demographic issue, so anybody that has money that could afford to buy a sushi over a hamburger, they buy sushi. Sushi is a premium item. It is a luxury product so people perceive it that way so people have a little bit of spending money, they buy sushi. It is not like a taste thing. Before we also thought it was demographic based 25–35 or women or men, but it turns out everybody from the age of 2–3 years old to like 80–90-year old people, they all buy sushi. Most of the people buy it like a premium product. It is more mainstream now so it's not like, "Oh! Today it is Friday; we're going to have sushi because it is Friday". It is just a regular meal.

Table 2.3 Competitor matrix: Fish Fish

	Categorization by Review Website 1	Categorization by Review Website 2	Categorization by Review Website 3	Median Cost of Signature Rolls or Item	Mean Consumer Evaluation	Distance to Focal Restaurant (Miles)
FOCAL RESTAURANT: Fish Fish	Sushi Bars	Seafood, Sushi, Japanese	N/A	$10	4.25	
		RESTAURATEUR-DEFINED COMPETITOR MATRIX				
Competitor 1	Vegetarian, Sushi Bars, Vegan	Healthy, Sushi, Asian	Vegan	$7	4.6	1
Competitor 2	Japanese, Sushi Bars	Japanese, Sushi, Asian	N/A	$12	4	0.1
Competitor 3	Sushi Bars, Japanese	Japanese, Sushi, Asian	Japanese	$13	4	0.1
Competitor 4	Pizza	Italian, Pizza, Fast food	N/A	$5	4	0.1
Competitor 5	Italian, American (Traditional)	American	N/A	$13	4.25	0.5
Mean (Competitors)				10.00	4.17	0.36
Standard Deviation (Competitors)				3.74	0.26	0.40
		COUNTERFACTUAL COMPETITOR MATRIX				
Competitor 1	Japanese, Sushi Bars	Japanese, Sushi, Asian	N/A	$12	4	0.1
Competitor 2	Sushi Bars, Japanese	Japanese, Sushi, Asian	Japanese	$13	4	0.1
Competitor 3	Japanese, Sushi Bars, Seafood	Sushi	N/A	$14	4.5	0.2
Competitor 4	Sushi Bars, Japanese	Japanese, Sushi, Asian	Japanese	$9	4	0.2
Competitor 5	Japanese, Sushi Bars, Buffets	Japanese, Sushi, Asian	N/A	$13	3	0.2
Mean (Competitors)				12.20	3.90	0.16
Standard Deviation (Competitors)				1.92	0.55	0.05

Note: This table contains the restaurateur-defined (top) and counterfactual (bottom) competitor matrices. For each matrix, five competitors are listed along with information about these restaurants and their relationship to the focal restaurant (*Fish Fish*).

Despite her assertion that Fish Fish does not occupy a narrow competitive space as a sushi restaurant, she then speculates that competition is an unclear construct:

> Competition is a very broad term especially in Manhattan where it is so insane. There are a million restaurants just on this block. [...] Any fast casual place, delivery place would be our competition, but it would be cuisine specific. There are so many people, so many options. Nobody is just eating one thing. It is hardly worth worrying about competition; it is worth worrying about being better than what you are today than trying to figure out what that place across the street is doing, when a month later they will be out of business or maybe you will be out of business. Easier doing your thing well and then you have less competition. Somebody can open sushi place next door, then we really have competition, but the place around the corner selling sushi; are they really our competition?

When the restaurateur was asked to specifically name Fish Fish's competition for the competitor matrix, the restaurateur responded: 'My first go would be [Competitor 1], but they are strictly vegan; they don't have dairy or eggs or anything. They are kind of us if you take the fish out of the sushi. They are pretty interesting like a close gauge to us.' Given her previous comments on competition, it is quite surprising that the restaurateur's first listed restaurant in her competitor matrix is a vegan restaurant, selling a non-fish sushi look-alike. Moreover, this restaurant is one mile away. In total, only two of the restaurants in the restaurateur-defined competitor matrix, Competitors 2 and 3, are (fish-based) sushi restaurants.

Our counterfactual competitor matrix includes five sushi restaurants within 0.2 miles of Fish Fish, yet only two of these appear in the restaurateur-defined competitor matrix. Likewise, the amount of variance in the median cost of a signature item is indicative of a broad interpretation of competition. Since sushi is a particularly narrow niche (i.e. it is relatively clear which restaurants are sushi restaurants and which are not), the lack of clarity in understanding why the manager selected so many non-sushi restaurants says a lot about the infinite dimensionality problem as it relates to competition (i.e. it is not clear on which dimensions the manager establishes similarities and differences amongst potential competitors). Given the fact that there are so many seemingly apparent substitutes to Fish Fish based on external audience categorization that do not make it into the restaurateur-defined set of competition, we again highlight the challenge of defining competitive relationships in this market.

Discussion and conclusion

The previous cases ultimately suggest that the three theoretical perspectives that have been proposed to conceptualize competitive relationships (i.e. the cross-elasticities of demand, strategic groups, and categorical structure of markets perspectives) are only loosely coupled, in the sense that they do not overlap significantly with the restaurant managers' definitions of competitive relationships. Although most of the interview participants cited location and/or cuisine as key dimensions along which they compete, relatively few made explicit mention of price or the restaurant 'concept' or décor. In some instances, participants listed restaurants in the same cuisine category with significantly higher or lower average price points as competitors. In relatively few cases participants cited as competitors were geographically co-located restaurants at roughly the same price point offering a different cuisine type. As such, our interviews revealed both *within* and *between* interviewee variance in mental models of competition.

Our results illustrate how alternative schemas for defining competition can produce remarkably different demarcations in competitive boundaries. In each case, we observe significant heterogeneity in restaurateurs' depictions of competition, though the majority of the participants made reference to location and/or cuisine type when defining competitors. In some cases, this included quite refined comparisons to the extent that one's cuisine might appeal to consumers interested in various substitutes. We find that competition is not entirely a subset of comparable organizations, but at times these two constructs co-mingle. This suggests that managers dimensionalize plausible competitors in a number of ways, and they may seek out comparisons with other market actors on each dimension separately in order to design strategic narratives about their competition (e.g. Rindova and Martins, 2021).

In considering the role of external actors in economic markets, our interviews indicate that organizations may, at times, reject their categorization as defined by external audiences. Nonetheless, these categorical frameworks appear to shape perceptions of competition and help to define competitive boundaries at a more abstract level. In this way, organizations are necessarily assessed with respect to a reference group, and distinctiveness should, therefore, be considered as a collective sensemaking process that extends beyond market exchange partners.

Ultimately, the evidence from these three cases suggests that 'if one looks for clarity in the academic literature measuring competition in markets, one is left even more frustrated' (Cattani et al. 2018: 652). Our qualitative counterfactual analysis, thus, shows that developing a deeper understanding of competition requires one to move beyond isolated transactional, organizational, or categorical analytical perspectives, as no single point of view seems to capture what in essence is the result of a collective attempt to make sense of competitive relationships in markets. A key implication of a sensemaking approach, therefore, is that definitions of competition, and observed competitive relationships, are construed by the actors themselves—whether consumers, firms, external audiences, or even researchers interested in studying competition—rather than simply existing out there as part of the general environment.

References

Arora-Jonsson, S., Brunsson, N., and Hasse, R. 2020. 'Where does competition come from? The role of organization'. *Organization Theory* 1 (1): 1–24.

Allison, G. T. 1971. *Essence of Decision: Explaining the Cuban Missile Crisis*. Boston: Little Brown.

Bain, J. 1952. *Price Theory*. New York: Holt, Rinehart, and Winston.

Baker, J. B. and Bresnahan, T. F. 1985. 'The gains from merger or collusion in product-differentiated industries'. *Journal of Industrial Economics* 33 (4): 427–44.

Baker, J. B. and Bresnahan, T. F. 2008. 'Economic evidence in antitrust: defining markets and measuring market power'. In *Handbook of Antitrust Economics*, edited by P. Buccirossi. Cambridge, MA: MIT Press: 1–42.

Black, J. 2015. *Other Pasts, Different Presents, Alternative Futures*. Bloomington, IN: Indiana University Press.

Bowers, A. and Prato, M. 2018. 'The structural origins of unearned status: how arbitrary changes in categories affect status position and market impact'. *Administrative Science Quarterly* 63 (3): 668–99.

Bresnahan, T. F. 1987. 'Competition and collusion in the American automobile industry: the 1955 price war'. *Journal of Industrial Economics* 35 (4): 457–82.

Berry, S., Levinsohn, J., and Pakes, A. 1995. 'Automobile prices in market equilibrium'. *Econometrica: Journal of the Econometric Society* 63 (4): 841–90.

Berry, S., Levinsohn, J., and Pakes, A. 2004. 'Differentiated products demand systems from a combination of micro and macro data: the new car market'. *Journal of Political Economy* 112 (1): 68–105.

Cattani, G., Porac, J. F., and Thomas, H. 2017. 'Categories and competition'. *Strategic Management Journal* 38 (1): 64–92.

Cattani, G., Sands, D., Porac, J., and Greenberg, J. 2018. 'Competitive sensemaking in value creation and capture'. *Strategy Science* 3 (4): 632–57.

Caves, R. E. and Porter, M. E. 1977. 'From entry barriers to mobility barriers: conjectural decisions and contrived deterrence to new competition'. *Quarterly Journal of Economics* 91 (2): 241–61.

Chamberlin, E. H. 1933. *The Theory of Monopolistic Competition: A Re-orientation of the Theory of Value*. Cambridge, MA: Harvard University Press.

Daniels, K., Johnson, G., and De Chernatony, L. 2002. 'Task and institutional influences on managers' mental models of competition'. *Organization Studies* 23 (1): 31–62.

DiMaggio, P. 1987. 'Classification in art'. *American Sociological Review* 52 (4): 440–55.

Elzinga, K. G. and Hogarty, T. F. 1973. 'The problem of geographic market delineation in antimerger suits'. *Antitrust Bulletin* 18: 45–81.

Froeb, L. M. and Werden, G. J. 1991. 'Residual demand estimation for market delineation: complications and limitations'. *Review of Industrial Organization* 6 (1): 33–48.

Goldberg, A., Hannan, M. T., and Kovács, B. 2016. 'What does it mean to span cultural boundaries? Variety and atypicality in cultural consumption'. *American Sociological Review* 81 (2): 215–41.

Goodman, N. 1947. 'The problem of counterfactual conditionals'. *Journal of Philosophy* 44 (5): 113–28.

Grossman, G. M. and Shapiro, C. 1986. 'Research joint ventures: an antitrust analysis'. *Journal of Law, Economics, & Organization* 2: 315.

Hannan, M. T., Le Mens, G., Hsu, G., Kovács, B., Negro, G., Pólos, L., Pontikes, E., and Sharkey, A.J. 2019. *Concepts and Categories: Foundations for Sociological and Cultural Analysis.* New York: Columbia University Press.

Hannan, M. T., Pólos, L., and Carroll, G. R. 2007. *Logics of Organization Theory: Audiences, Codes, and Ecologies.* Princeton: Princeton University Press.

Horowitz, I. 1981. 'Market definition in antitrust analysis: a regression-based approach'. *Southern Economic Journal* 48 (1): 1–16.

Hsu, G. 2006. 'Jacks of all trades and masters of none: audiences' reactions to spanning genres in feature film production'. *Administrative Science Quarterly* 51 (3): 420–50.

Hunt, M. S. 1972. *Competition in the Major Home Appliance Industry 1960–1970.* Unpublished doctoral dissertation, Harvard University.

Koçak, Ö., Hannan, M. T., and Hsu, G. 2014. 'Emergence of market orders: audience interaction and vanguard influence'. *Organization Studies* 35 (5): 765–90.

Lamont, M., and Molnár, V. 2002. 'The study of boundaries in the social sciences'. *Annual Review of Sociology* 28 (1): 167–95.

Levy, J. S. 2008. 'Counterfactuals and case studies'. In *The Oxford Handbook of Political Methodology,* edited by J. M. Box-Steffensmeier, H. E. Brady, and D. Collie. Oxford: Oxford University Press: 627–44.

Lounsbury, M. and Rao, H. 2004. 'Sources of durability and change in market classifications: a study of the reconstitution of product categories in the American mutual fund industry, 1944–1985'. *Social Forces* 82 (3): 969–99.

Mahoney, J. and Barrenechea, R. 2019. 'The logic of counterfactual analysis in case-study explanation'. *British Journal of Sociology* 70 (1): 306–38.

McNamara, G., Deephouse, D. L., and Luce, R. A. 2003. 'Competitive positioning within and across a strategic group structure: the performance of core, secondary, and solitary firms'. *Strategic Management Journal* 24 (2): 161–81.

Ng, D., Westgren, R., and Sonka, S. 2009. 'Competitive blind spots in an institutional field'. *Strategic Management Journal* 30 (4): 349–69.

Ody-Brasier, A. and Vermeulen, F. 2014. 'The price you pay: price-setting as a response to norm violations in the market for champagne grapes'. *Administrative Science Quarterly* 59 (1): 109–44.

Osborne, J. D., Stubbart, C. I., and Ramaprasad, A. 2001. 'Strategic groups and competitive enactment: a study of dynamic relationships between mental models and performance'. *Strategic Management Journal* 22 (5): 435–54.

Petrin, A. 2002. 'Quantifying the benefits of new products: the case of the minivan'. *Journal of Political Economy* 110 (4): 705–29.

Pleatsikas, C. and Teece, D. 2001. 'The analysis of market definition and market power in the context of rapid innovation'. *International Journal of Industrial Organization* 19 (5): 665–93.

Pontikes, E. G. 2012. 'Two sides of the same coin: how ambiguous classification affects multiple audiences' evaluations'. *Administrative Science Quarterly* 57 (1): 81–118.

Pontikes, E. G. 2018. 'Category strategy for firm advantage'. *Strategy Science* 3 (4): 620–31.

Pontikes, E. G. and Kim, R. 2017. 'Strategic categorization.' In *From Categories to Categorization: Studies in Sociology, Organizations and Strategy at the Crossroads*, edited by R. Durand, N. Granqvist, and A. Tyllström. Bingley: Emerald Publishing: 71–111.

Porac, J. F. and Thomas, H. 1994. 'Cognitive categorization and subjective rivalry among retailers in a small city'. *Journal of Applied Psychology* 79 (1): 54.

Porac, J. F., Thomas, H., Wilson, F., Paton, D., and Kanfer, A. 1995. 'Rivalry and the industry model of Scottish knitwear producers'. *Administrative Science Quarterly* 40 (2): 203–27.

Porter, M. E. 1976. *Interbrand Choice, Strategy, and Bilateral Market Power* (No. 146). Cambridge, MA: Harvard University Press.

Porter, M. E. 1979. 'The structure within industries and companies' performance'. *Review of Economics and Statistics* 61 (2): 214–27.

Porter, M. E. 1980. *Competitive Strategy*. New York: Free Press.

Reger, R. K. and Huff, A. S. 1993. 'Strategic groups: a cognitive perspective'. *Strategic Management Journal* 14 (2): 103–23.

Rhee, E. Y. 2015. 'Strategic categorization: vertical and horizontal changes in self-categorization'. *Academy of Management Proceedings* 25 (1).

Rindova, V. P. and Martins, L. L., 2021. 'Futurescapes: imagination and temporal reorganization in the design of strategic narratives.' *Strategic Organization*: 1–25.

Robinson, J. 1933. *The Economics of Imperfect Competition*. London: Macmillan.

Rosa, J. A., Porac, J. F., Runser-Spanjol, J., and Saxon, M. S. 1999. 'Sociocognitive dynamics in a product market'. *Journal of Marketing* 63 (4): 64–77.

Sands, D. B. 2021. 'Does stylistic similarity to popular competitors affect consumer evaluations of quality? Evidence from online movie evaluations'. In *Advances in Strategic Management: Aesthetics and Style in Strategy*, edited by G. Cattani, S. Ferriani, F. Godart, and S. Sgourev. Bingley: Emerald Publishing: 199–226.

Scheffman, D. T. and Spiller, P. T. 1996. 'Econometric market delineation'. *Managerial and Decision Economics* 17: 165–78.

Slade, M. E. 1986. 'Exogeneity tests of market boundaries applied to petroleum products'. *Journal of Industrial Economics* 34 (3): 291–303.

Smith, E. B. 2011. 'Identities as lenses: how organizational identity affects audiences' evaluation of organizational performance'. *Administrative Science Quarterly* 56 (1): 61–94.

Stoljar, N. 2001. 'Vagueness, counterfactual intentions, and legal interpretation'. *Legal Theory* 7 (4): 447–65.

Tetlock, P. E. and Belkin, A. 1996. *Counterfactual Thought Experiments in World Politics: Logical, Methodological, and Psychological Perspectives*. Princeton: Princeton University Press.

Tilly, C. 2005. *Trust and Rule*. Cambridge, UK: Cambridge University Press.

Triffin, R. 1940. *Monopolistic Competition and General Equilibrium Theory*. Boston: Harvard University Press.

Vergne, J. P. and Wry, T. 2014. 'Categorizing categorization research: review, integration, and future directions'. *Journal of Management Studies* 51 (1): 56–94.

Weintraub, S. 1942. 'The classification of market positions: comment'. *Quarterly Journal of Economics* 56 (4): 666–73.

Werden, G. J. 1992. 'The history of antitrust market delineation'. *Marquette Law Review* 76: 123.

Werden, G. J. 1997. 'Demand elasticities in antitrust analysis'. *Antitrust Law Journal* 66: 363.

White, H. C. 1992. *Identity and Control: A Structural Theory of Social Action*. Princeton: Princeton University Press.

White, H. C. 2002. *Markets from Networks: Socioeconomic Models of Production*. Princeton: Princeton University Press.

Wry, T., Deephouse, D. L., and McNamara, G. 2006. 'Substantive and evaluative media reputations among and within cognitive strategic groups'. *Corporate Reputation Review* 9 (4): 225–42.

Zhao, E. Y., Ishihara, M., and Lounsbury, M. 2013. 'Overcoming the illegitimacy discount: cultural entrepreneurship in the US feature film industry'. *Organization Studies* 34 (12): 1747–76.

Zuckerman, E. W. 1999. 'The categorical imperative: securities analysts and the illegitimacy discount'. *American Journal of Sociology* 104 (5): 1398–438.

3
Competition by mutual adjustment

Patrik Aspers

This chapter looks at competition, asking how it comes about and how it develops. Given this volume's focus on the organization of competition, I zoom in on mutual adjustment. Competition is an important social science concept, as has been shown by numerous reviews of this research field (Chapter 1, this volume; Mantzavinos 1993; Porac and Thomas 1990; Stark 2020; Werron 2015). The argument is that competition can be seen as a state, as spelt out in Chapter 1 of this volume: *'the social construction of a relationship that comprises four core elements: actors, their relationships, desire, and scarcity'*.

States of competition can come about in two ideal-typical ways. They can be the result of decisions for others, that is, organized competition, to create or further competition. Many sport events (Stark 2020), or stock exchanges (MacKenzie and Millo 2003), exemplify this. Even decisions for others that are not aimed at creating states of competition may nonetheless lead to a state of competition and can be seen as examples of organized competition. The other way is that a process of mutual adjustment among actors making decisions for themselves and not for others may lead, eventually and unintentionally, to states of competition. This is the case in many producer markets (White 1981). Competition is then an unintended consequence created by actors who may have different desires and intentions and who are observing, adjusting, mimicking, and relating in different ways to what others are doing. These actions lead to a state of competition. In focus here are cases in which mutual adjustment leads to states of competition.

Analysing competition

The definition presented in Chapter 1 implies that actors must desire something and orient their actions towards it, implying that there is an ambition to obtain it. It is in this mutual adjustment process that some things become 'scarce' (Simmel 1923). The things for which they compete do not have to be identical, it suffices that they compete for the same things.

Regardless of how the state of competition came about, competition requires that actors—individuals, organizations, or states—have agency (Giddens 1984) and are free to make their own decisions. Hence, even if a stock exchange is highly organized, actors' decision-making about buying or not buying (Luhmann 1988) that

Patrik Aspers, *Competition by mutual adjustment* In: *Competition: What It Is and Why It Happens*. Edited by: Stefan Arora-Jonsson, Nils Brunsson, Raimund Hasse, and Katarina Lagerström, Oxford University Press. © Patrik Aspers 2021.
DOI: 10.1093/oso/9780192898012.003.0003

results in the emergence of prices is not determined by the organizer of the exchange. However, the conditions regarding accepted behaviour, the way prices are set, and what can be traded are organized. The decisions of market actors, regardless of whether the conditions of the competition have been organized or not, however, is not the topic of this chapter. Rather the conditions needed for a state of competition are in focus, and, more specifically, how these conditions come about and, to some extent, are maintained. But as will be shown in the case of fashion, mutual adjustment of actors cannot be completely separated from the perpetuation of the initial conditions of competition.

Organized competition

The most clear-cut way to achieve a state of competition is to organize. Organization means that all, or at least one, of the following elements are present and that they are decided: membership, hierarchy, rules, monitoring, and sanctions (Ahrne and Brunsson 2011). Both Werron (2015) and Chapter 1 in this book provide many studies on organized competition, inside and outside of the economy. Much is done and can be done to organize, that is, to try to decide for others, to establish competition (e.g. Brunsson and Jutterström 2018).

There can be no doubt that competition can be organized, and this is perhaps most clearly observed in the case of so-called 'perfect' markets, which I will use here to illustrate my point. Perfect markets are markets in which *competition* is perfect (Knight 1921), because no one can act to improve their situation (Kirzner 1973: 11–13). But this equilibrium can, one may argue, only emerge in an organized market, and many rules and laws are normally implemented to accomplish this 'perfect competition', as noted by Simmel (1955: 78–83). In a practical sense, market organization and organization of competition in markets are intimately linked.

In markets with perfect competition, the roles of seller and buyer are defined by decisions on rules, monitoring, and sanctions, putting constraints on what they can and cannot do. In addition to those competing, it is also possible to speak of those who organize the competition and those who determine what is scarce. It follows that an individual or an organization may hence enact one, two, or even all these roles simultaneously.

Stock exchanges are the most typical example of organized economic competition. In the different markets of an exchange, the objects of trade, such as company shares, are decided to be identical (Carruthers 1996: 161). Membership is controlled and so are rules of trading and information sharing (Abolafia 1996), to take a few examples. These rules are monitored by various governing bodies and sanctions are imposed (Preda 2009: 65–76) by the exchanges. Not only stock exchanges but also markets for carbon dioxide (CO_2) (MacKenzie 2009; Rosenström 2014) or fishing (Dobeson 2019) are to a large extent constructed to have competition, and to make sure that competitors cannot reduce competition. CO_2 emission rights became a 'desired' object of scarcity only when a cap was set in accordance with rules on how much CO_2 a plant was allowed to emit without being fined. But to have market competition for these allowances to emit CO_2 required that these objects of scarcity existed. By decision, these rights were established and issued to firms running the plants emitting CO_2, and an entire system for monitoring CO_2 emissions was put in place. To make sure that the emission rights become scarce, the rights given out had to be adjusted so that they were not too readily available. These markets are actively designed by the decision to be competitive; they are, in other words, performed (Callon 1998; Garcia-Parpet 2007) by market organizers, which in this case at an abstract level, were politicians (MacKenzie 2009).

Related to markets are laws of competition, that is, rules of behaviour that refer to decisions made for others about what market actors are forced to do. They are required to follow laws, be monitored, and accept sanctions. Laws that regulate economic behaviour constitute one way of creating conditions for competition and blocking the formations of cartels (Quack and Djelic 2005). There is no hierarchy regarding the core or market activities—namely actors' right to trade or not—meaning that the actors are in control of their property rights.

There are of course plenty of examples of organized competition that are not markets. There is an abundance of TV shows, for example, in which the best baker or chef is selected according to principles decided by the show. In many cases the winners of such competitions are decided by a jury. Sports competitions are almost always organized, and there are sports, such as figure skating, in which the winners are decided by a jury (Stark 2020).

Organized competition, to sum up, means that decisions for others are made to create, diminish, or alter competition. These decisions include attempts to establish the competitors, the objects of competition, and the rules of the competition.

Competition out of mutual adjustment

In addition to the competition that organization produces, there is competition that results from mutual adjustment; some would call this 'spontaneous competition'. This notion covers decisions that actors make, so to speak, 'for themselves', not for others. A firm in a market may act to reduce the competitive pressure it faces, but the outcome may be the opposite. Thus, such actions—for example launching an advertising campaign—may also affect others' situations and the competitive pressure they face, but the idea is not, for example, to change what is scarce also for others. Furthermore, a single actor may attempt to avoid a rule established to control how to compete—for example by cheating—but this is not done as an attempt to change the rule; this is not organization, because the aim is not to change the conditions for all, nor to make a decision for others. Such behaviour, however, may lead those who organize to react, and to make new decisions for others.

The scientific etymology of the term 'adjustment' leads us to the natural sciences and technology, for example biology, in which it refers to how plants adapt to their environment (Young 1932). A similar type of adjustment is often considered to occur between an actor and the environment, or between a 'race' and its environment, as discussed by, for example, Spencer (1961). Similar ideas are found in the works of Simmel, referred to as *Wechselwirkungen* (1923), but in his work the outcome is due to social actors orienting themselves to one another rather than to 'natural forces'. I follow this Simmelian path. In a wider sense, Gabriel Tarde (1969), Friedrich von Hayek (1976), Peter Berger and Thomas Luckmann (1991), Niklas Luhmann (1995), Robert Axelrod (1984), and Harrison White (1992) are examples of thinkers who make use of the idea of mutual adjustment, most of whom also address competition.

Those who write on mutual adjustment have different points of departure. It is possible to start with 'pure' egos who have interests or preferences—a view characteristic of neoclassical economists—or one can assume that actors are much more institutionalized but nonetheless act with some degree of freedom. Here I start with the assumption that there is an institutional bedrock on which mutual adjustment of competition rests. The idea here is that actors, being social, watch one another, draw conclusions, and act to relate to others and their behaviour. This process is mutual, in the sense that not only 'ego' but also 'alter'—or better, many actors—are involved in this process.

Analytically, mutual adjustment means that competitors, scarce objects, desires, and the conditions of the competition emerge and become established in the process of mutual adjustment (Aspers et al. 2020). It does not have to be clear at the outset, as in the case of organized competition, that the process is competitive. To take one example: when two friends play tennis, for the fun of it, it may eventually turn into a competition if both want to beat the other and win the match. An existing competitive relation may also stop being competitive, for example when one party simply 'drifts away' (that is, ceases to be a competitor) or revolts against the rules ('I don't want to play this stupid game any longer unless we do it my way') or simply sees no value in the 'scarce' object, which then ceases to be scarce, in the eyes of one party at least. This type of change of interest may also lead to a new state of competition, for example who has the most energy or who can hit the ball the hardest, which means that competition is 'moved' to a new arena or to another level.

The main difference from organized competition is that competition out of mutual adjustment is not a result of actors' decisions for others, but it is an unintended outcome of many decisions made by actors to further their own ends. In other words, the difference between mutual adjustment and organization is not a matter of more or less competition but of how we get into a state of competition. I now turn to some examples to develop the ideas of mutual adjustment and competition.

Figure 3.1 A house lit up at Christmas time (Hamrånge, in the municipality of Gävle, Sweden).

Christmas lights on houses

People lighting up their houses on the outside (see Figure 3.1) at Christmas time was originally not a competition in Sweden. For a long time, it was not very common; most people were satisfied with just a Christmas tree in the garden.

The more spectacular approach to Christmas decorations came to Sweden from the USA. This is a clear example of the adjustment (in this case, basically copying) of existing behaviour. Neither the first mover (or movers) in the USA nor the Swedish families who took up this practice stood in any direct relation to one another. It is, in practice, impossible to account for all the steps taken by those involved, which have led unintentionally to the current situation. Here I can do nothing but to offer a highly stylized version of how this process may have unfolded.

The relevant relationships among Swedish house owners begun to be established when at least some of them adjusted their behaviour to one another. In this process, one or several styles of lighting up houses were developed, in which a combination of values were included, such as the number of bulbs used, the level of creativity of the decoration, its attractiveness, and variations on what had already been done. When these styles—which at first were rather tentative—emerged, and actors oriented themselves to others who were 'taking part', it was possible to talk of a relationship between actors. Such a relationship does not have to be, certainly not initially, competitive. Gradually a sense of competition may emerge among some of those who value the practice when the different actors start to act based on what others have done, for example by copying one another. The competitive logic may be noted simply by people who raise the stakes every year, when those in the neighbourhood try to put up better decorations, when people start talking about decorations, or posting on social media, suggesting that some houses look 'better' or some houses have nicer light decorations, or in terms of 'winners'. In this process the criteria gradually become clearer, and scarcity—becoming 'number one' among those involved—is established. In this way a state of competition emerges because many actors who relate to one another—the decorators—begin to want to be the leading Christmas house lighting decorator. This outcome is the result of the actions of many individuals, none of whom necessarily really wanted to engage in competition. Some may indeed 'compete', while others do it only for the fun of it. Once many actors are trying to win out, or who are just trying to put up the most lighting in the neighbourhood, winning becomes something 'scarce'—which is to say that the desire to win, and to act to achieve that end, is formed in the process. But it also becomes clear what it takes to win this contest. Not all decorators orient themselves towards others to become 'winners', but for those who do, this is clearly a competition. And the competition may be more important, and encompass more actors, because those competing may see all decorators, whatever their respective motives, as their competitors.

Eventually a Swedish TV channel (Channel 5) awarded a prize to the winners of 'The Christmas Struggle'—in other words, those with the best Christmas lights. At this stage, then, there was an attempt to organize a competition. But even this decision was not inevitably going to lead to an organized competition. For this to happen the 'competitors' must also orient their activities towards this award. The current situation can perhaps best be described as partly traditional (people are involved but not competing), partly spontaneous competition, and partly organized competition.

Fashion

Fashion is a good example of a phenomenon for which competition is essential: some of the competition is due to organization, some due to mutual adjustment. In the case of Christmas lights, it was shown how competition can emerge out of mutual adjustment. In the case of fashion, it probably originally emerged out of mutual adjustment, but here we claim only that competition maintains fashion. At the same time, fashion propels competition. There are many different actors who try to influence fashion, and some actually manage to do this to some extent. Many firms try, for example, to advertise, or use influencers, and may even join hands to form meta-organizations (Ahrne and Brunsson 2008). Producer firms, designers, influencers, journalists, buyers, trend-spotters, fashion photographers, models, celebrities, makers of fabrics, and fashion organizations are examples of actors who affect fashion, and some of them even try to decide for others. There are, in addition, organized competitions, awards, and rankings (Stark 2020) of different fashion categories that also affect what is in fashion.

However, none of these actors is strong enough to impose, by means of decisions for others, what is in fashion, and this also means that, although many may try to do so, no single actor can organize competition in the field of fashion. Fashion lacks a command centre or a central power to make and implement decisions about what is to be in fashion, and we cannot therefore speak of a 'central organizer' that determines its outcome. Attempts to 'organize' fashion by deciding what is in fashion, which was an active strategy during the Soviet era, have failed profoundly (Gronow 2003). The reason in that instance is that what was valued in terms of fashion was not an inherent characteristic of the mass-produced products selected by the regime to be luxurious and potential candidates for the status of 'fashion', namely champagne and caviar. The result is that neither of these goods could become scarce, in fashion, or even be considered luxurious. Consequently, with no scarcity, there will be no competition over these objects, and they cannot be used for the creation and maintenance of social distinctions. More fundamentally, any decision about what is in fashion negates the entire fashion game, and disables people from making choices.

The Soviet example illustrates an important point, namely, that fashion objects do not possess inherent traits that might explain fashion. This is also evident given the pace at which fashion changes. Instead, the competition to be the first with the latest (Aspers and Godart 2013) is central to all theories since Simmel's (1971) classic formulation of what constitutes fashion. Fashion, moreover, is a type of social game. It is a game based on competition, and here we are interested in how it occurs and unfolds when garments are the material pegs. Fashion garments may of course be— or become—scarce simply out of shortage or because of their price; but not all things that are in short supply or expensive come into fashion—and vice versa, some things that are *not* in short supply or expensive can be in fashion. The reason is that fashion is about attracting attention and stimulating the desires of others, and such attention and the desires of others are scarce. It also tends to fade away, and thus fashion is also about timing; there is scarcity because not everyone can be in fashion at the same time. The rationale for this is that if too many people wear the same thing, inherently it can no longer be in fashion (cf. Rogers 1962).

Because scarcity, a constitutive element of competition, tends to fade away as a result of mass production and diminishing attention and desire, it is not in anyone's control. The scarcity of something's being in fashion is relational, it is about who is producing and wearing what at a certain point in time, and it is the social structure, and above all the status among the actors, consumers, and producers alike, that matter for the emergence and spread of fashion (Aspers 2009). Fashion users can choose from what is available, including recycled products, as well as new items from fashion firms, which means that *what* is in fashion is subject to change. Competition in fashion is ongoing and maintained because there is a permanent quest to attract the attention and desire of (potential) followers. And this maintenance of competition is based on processes of mutual adjustment on both the producer and user sides.

Users of fashion

The social structure relevant to fashion is made up of fashion producers (who sometimes are also the manufacturer, but at least sellers of fashion items) and users, or consumers, of fashion. Both sides of the interface are ordered according to status

(Aspers 2009). Let us begin with the users who compete with one another to 'be in fashion'. Some consumers have more status than others, and what they do is crucial for what is in fashion; other customers—or better ideal-typical consumers, because not every consumer can be known—have less status. Status is inherently relational and is endowed by others; it is not determined by decisions for others (Podolny 1993), because any attempt to affect (cf. Espeland 2020) status by means of organization needs to be co-constituted by audiences. There are many examples of rankings, which indicates that, without being 'verified' by these audiences, attempts to organize or to establish status hierarchies by rankings fail.

Users compete to be fashion leaders, which is a position that is scarce. Though not all take part in the fashion game, even those who try to denounce fashion and develop 'anti-fashion' must be aware of fashion to make sure that they are *not* in fashion. Regardless of which interest actors have, they are part of the fashion competition. The competition for the spot of 'being in fashion' triggers a continuous process of mutual adjustment in which actors orient to one another, for example by trying to wear similar but not identical clothes, and to develop an existing fashion. An example of the latter is the fashion of having ripped jeans: someone may adjust to that by wearing them almost completely torn.

It is in this process of selection of alternatives carried out by prestigious fashion leaders that desires are formed also by others; the use of some high-status actors endows the objects with meaning and makes them, for a relatively short period of time, in fashion. It is in this way that competition may enhance mutual adjustment and vice versa. Even the social position of actors and their identities are constituted or reproduced in the process of mutual adjustment in which actors become competitors.

Being endowed with the status of fashion leader is an outcome of the social competition among members of a group. It is based on attributions by other members of that group, as well as, in some cases, by producers. Status as a fashion leader is not independent of what is seen as in fashion, and often relations with some producers contribute to making these actors fashion setters, in other words, possessing high status. Because users compete for the acceptance of others, some attempts will be taken up by others, whereas many will simply be forgotten. Indeed, one might say that fashion is about being followed by others—that is, about being the first, not just continuing to be the only one. Crucial in this process is the individual actors' decisions to wear a garment or not. Thus, in the strictest sense, fashion is a competition between users to attract the attention and desire of potential followers. Taking a wider view, however, this gives us only half the picture, because producers compete too.

Producers of fashion

What about those sellers of fashion garments that are also the producers—although not necessarily the manufacturers of the garments—of fashion? Producers of, for example, garments try to offer what they believe will make it in the market. Their actions are oriented to both the potential customers and their competitors. To be the 'first with the latest' means that the firms and their designers must offer what will be in fashion before their competitors do so. Consumers react to these offers from firms. Producers react, not only to other producers—as White (1981) says—but also to consumers' choices, preferences and existing 'fashions' (Aspers 2010).

Clearly, fashion sellers position themselves in relation to one another (White 1981), and other sellers offer information about what customers want (Leifer and White 1987). In fashion markets, this is typically a status order (Aspers 2010). As a result of sellers' orientation to one another, in a process in which they try to offer garments to the same set of buyers, they become competitors in the same market. One may thus argue that competition emerges from identifying peers and relating to them by realizing that these peers desire the same scarce thing: high-status customers. But what type of competition is this?

Producers differentiate their offers to reduce the competition they face from competitors with (too) similar products, which corresponds to the differentiation of their identities (Podolny 2005, White and Eccles 1987: 985; cf. Zuckerman 2000). In producer markets this control of a firm's market identity arises mainly from each of them offering a price/quality mix (White 1993). The market, White says, is an unintended consequence of a process in which 'producers watch each other' (1981: 518), while competing for customers and not just reacting to, but actively trying to control, their environment. Competition can emerge as the consequence of producers who are 'jockeying for relative positions' (White 1993: 166). Here, market competition is based on status positions and competition for status. Because social positioning is also reflected in acts of consumers, who operate on the other side of the market and see these producers as comparable peers, consumers are crucial for the social construction of actors and their relations (cf. Furst 2017).

The market structure affects how the competition is played out. Following work by Marshall (1920) and Chamberlin (1948), both of whom wrote on monopolistic competition, White is clear about the fact that firms are 'engaged not in pure competition but in finding and sustaining roles with respect to one another given an environment of discerning buyers' (1981: 520). In contrast to perfectly competitive markets, in which actors switch between being 'seller' and 'buyer', actors in producer markets develop identities as 'producers' in a process of mutual adjustment. However, they become not just producers of fashion but also get involved in niche-making to reduce the economic competitive pressure by means of differentiation to create a type of monopoly, so-called 'monopolistic competition'. The social structure of niches is an outcome of actors facing fierce competition; at the same time it is based on the kind of competition. The aim of finding niches is to face fewer rivals, by offering different product/price combinations. Neither individual sellers nor users (buyers) strive for competition; it is an outcome of many actors making individual decisions, but not decisions for others. But given that they offer fashion garments that are different and that enable consumers to differentiate, the differences cannot be too large, because in that case they would no longer be seen as fashion sellers. However, whether competition is reduced or not—which is a topic that may be of interest to many, because, in the extreme case, it can result in the absence of competition—the potential for competition is unaffected, even though absent competition can re-emerge when niches overlap or when several producers come to populate a niche.

Summing up, competition is a state that can emerge out of social processes of mutual adjustment. House decoration with Christmas lights and fashion are two examples suggesting that mutual adjustment can trigger competition, because preferences emerge in the social mirroring process of people orienting themselves to one another in virtual and real public arenas. With reference to fashion users it can also be shown that mutual adjustment contributes to the maintenance of competition. That the state of competition can, in addition to being organized, be the result of mutual adjustment is the main argument of this chapter. Once such a state is established, it may change and the outcomes may differ considerably and fast—as in the case of fashion.

Concluding discussion

Organized competition is essentially about making decisions for others—using the organizational elements as well as making decisions on them. Hence, decisions have to be made about the competitors, the object of scarcity, and the rules of competition prior to the start of the 'game'. However, the competitive state described by Arora-Jonsson et al. as '*Competition is the construction of a particular relationship (in the Weberian sense and as previously outlined). It covers relationships in which a focal actor desires something that this actor perceives as scarce, because of a belief that other actors have the same desire. Products, money, attention, status, and many other things can become objects of competition.*' (Chapter 1, this volume), may also occur as an unintended outcome of individual actions, for example, by actors who do not make decisions for others but for themselves. This particularly concerns what is desired and how desires are transformed into action. In reality, of course, many processes exhibit examples of both organization and mutual adjustment. Once the conditions for competition are present, in terms of scarce objects and relations, due to either organization or mutual adjustment, there is always mutual adjustment to foster competition between actors over something and this mutual adjustment is crucial for the maintenance of competition.

In processes of mutual adjustment, while pursuing ends, doing things, and reacting to one another, actors gain identities and *become* competitors, the objects of scarcity emerge, and the conditions, as well as the outcomes, of the game can be observed. Taken together, this brings temporality into the equation because the competitive order emerges in a process rather than being a clearly identified condition prior to the 'start' of the interaction.

The difference around which this chapter centres can be summarized with one example. An organized race between two cyclists, each of whom is trying to be the first up a hill, with a prize going to the winner, includes three roles: the competitors, the organizer of the competition, and the one controlling the scarce good. There are then conditions, for example that e-bikes may not compete against ordinary bikes. In this case, 'organizers' and 'those in control of what is scarce' are combined in one actor, whether it be an organization or an individual. But a random situation in which two cyclists who happen to be on the way up a hill start to try to overtake one another, merely for the 'invisible' but nevertheless 'valuable' *prestige*, is also a case of two actors mutually adjusting, and recognizing the same end. A competition may be said to be occurring here, too. This is a kind of competition according to the definition provided in the introduction to this volume, but this state is an outcome of mutual adjustment (cf. Burt 1992: 4, for a similar example on cars).

Reality is likely to be more complex than either of the two ideal-typical processes by which competition comes about, and I therefore suggest that research should look further into how these two are related to one another, over time and in specific cases. How does one go from organized competition to mutual adjustment and vice versa? A second major topic is the fact that scarcity cannot always be decided because it often depends on desires. Fashion is a process in which actors try to make various types of distinctions as the largely unintended outcome of the scarcity of being in fashion and of being the first with the latest, stimulating the desire of others to follow. Distinctions in fashion are based on 'aesthetic' preferences, and these cannot be decided by others. Fashion is thus a case that sheds light on the question of what can be decided by means of organization and what cannot.

References

Abolafia, M. 1996. *Making Markets*. Cambridge, MA: Harvard University Press.

Ahrne, G. and Brunsson, N. 2008. *Meta-organizations*. Cheltenham: Edward Elgar.

Ahrne, G. and Brunsson, N. 2011. 'Organization outside organizations: the significance of partial organization'. *Organization* 18 (1): 83–104.

Aspers, P. 2009. 'Knowledge and value in markets'. *Theory and Society* 38: 111–31.

Aspers, P. 2010. *Orderly Fashion: A Sociology of Markets*. Princeton: Princeton University Press.

Aspers, P. and Godart, F. 2013. 'Sociology of fashion: order and change'. *Annual Review of Sociology* 39: 171–92.

Aspers, P., Bengtsson, P., and Dobeson, A. 2020. 'Market fashioning'. *Theory and Society* 49: 417–38.

Axelrod, R. 1984. *The Evolution of Co-operation*. London: Penguin.

Berger, P. and Luckmann, T. 1991. *The Social Construction of Reality: A Treatise in the Sociology of Knowledge*. London: Penguin Books.

Brunsson, N. and Jutterström, M. 2018. *Organizing and Reorganizing Markets*. Oxford: Oxford University Press.

Burt, R. 1992. *Structural Holes: The Social Structure of Competition*. Cambridge, MA: Harvard University Press.

Callon, M. 1998. *The Laws of the Market*. Oxford: Blackwell Publishers.

Carruthers, B. 1996. *City of Capital: Politics and Markets in the English Financial Revolution*. Princeton: Princeton University Press.

Chamberlin, E. 1948. *The Theory of Monopolistic Competition: A Re-orientation of the Theory of Value*. Cambridge, MA: Harvard University Press.

Dobeson, A. 2019. *Revaluing Coastal Fisheries: How Small Boats Navigate New Markets and Technology*. Cham: Palgrave Macmillan.

Espeland, W. 2020. 'Formalized evaluation: the work that rankings do'. In *The Performance Complex: Competition and Competitions in Social Life*, edited by D. Stark. Oxford: Oxford University Press: 99–122.

Furst, H. 2017. *Selected or Rejected? Assessing Aspiring Writers' Attempts to Achieve Publication*. Uppsala: Uppsala University.

Garcia-Parpet, M.-F. 2007. 'The social construction of a perfect market, the strawberry auction at Fontaines-En-Sologne'. In *Do Economists Make Markets? On the Performativity of Economics*, edited by D. MacKenzie, F. Muniesa, and L. Siu. Princeton: Princeton University Press: 20–53.

Giddens, A. 1984. *The Constitution of Society: Outline of the Theory of Structuration*. Berkeley: University of California Press.

Gronow, J. 2003. *Caviar with Champagne: Common Luxury and the Ideals of the Good Life in Stalin's Russia*. Oxford: Berg.

Hayek, F. A. 1976. *Law, Legislation and Liberty: A New Statement of the Liberal Principles of Justice and Political Economy. Volume 2: The Mirage of Social Justice*. Chicago: University of Chicago Press.

Kirzner, I. 1973. *Competition and Entrepreneurship*. Chicago: University of Chicago Press.

Knight, F. 1921. *Risk, Uncertainty and Profit*. Boston: Houghton Mifflin Company.

Leifer, E. and White, H. 1987. 'A structural approach to markets'. In *Intercorporate Relations: The Structural Analysis of Business*, edited by M. Mizruchi and M. Schwartz. Cambridge: Cambridge University Press: 85–108.

Luhmann, N. 1988. *Die Wirtschaft Der Gesellschaft*. Frankfurt am Main: Suhrkamp.

Luhmann, N. 1995. *Social Systems*. Stanford: Stanford University Press.

MacKenzie, D. and Millo, Y. 2003. 'Constructing a market, performing theory: the historical sociology of a financial derivatives exchange'. *The American Journal of Sociology* 109 (1): 107–45.

MacKenzie, D. 2009. 'Constructing emission markets'. In *Material Markets. How Economic Agents Are Constructed.*, edited by D. MacKenzie. Oxford: Oxford University Press: 137–76.

Mantzavinos, C. 1993. *Wettbewerbstheorie: Eine Kritische Auseinandersetzung*. Berlin: Duncker and Humblot.

Marshall, A. 1920. *Industry and Trade: A Study of Industrial Technique and Business Organization; and of Their Influences on the Conditions of Various Classes and Nations*. London: Macmillan.

Podolny, J. 1993. 'A status-based model of market competition'. *American Journal of Sociology* 98 (4): 829–72.

Podolny, J. 2005. *Status Signals: A Sociological Study of Market Competition*. Princeton: Princeton University Press.

Porac, J. and Thomas, H. 1990. 'Taxonomic mental models in competitor definition'. *The Academy of Management Review* 5 (2): 224–40.

Preda, A. 2009. *Framing Finance. The Boundaries of Markets and Modern Capitalism.* Chicago: University of Chicago Press.

Quack, S. and Djelic, M.-L. 2005. 'Adaption, recombination, and reinforcement. The story of antitrust and competition law in Germany and Europe'. In *Beyond Continuity. Institutional Change in Advanced Political Economies*, edited by W. Streeck. Oxford: Oxford University Press: 255–81.

Rogers, E. 1962. *Diffusion of Innovation.* New York: Free Press.

Rosenström, M. 2014. *Att Skapa En Marknad: Marknad Och Politisk Styrning I Symbios?* Stockholm: Stockholm School of Economics.

Simmel, G. 1923. *Soziologie, Untersuchungen Über Die Formen Der Vergesellschaftung.* München und Leipzig: Duncker und Humblot.

Simmel, G. 1955. *Conflict & the Web of Group-Affiliations.* New York: Free Press.

Simmel, G. 1971. 'Fashion'. In *Georg Simmel on Individuality and Social Form*, edited by D. Levine. Chicago: University of Chicago Press: 294–323.

Spencer, H. 1961. *The Study of Sociology.* Ann Arbor: University of Michigan.

Stark, D. 2020. *The Performance Complex: Competition and Competitions in Social Life.* Oxford: Oxford University Press.

Tarde, G. 1969. *On Communication and Social Influence.* Chicago: University of Chicago Press.

Werron, T. 2015. 'Why do we believe in competition? A historical-sociological view of competition as an institutionalized modern imaginary'. *Distinktion: Journal of Social Theory* 16 (2): 186–210.

White, H. 1981. 'Where do markets come from?'. *American Journal of Sociology* 87 (3): 517–47.

White, H. and Eccles, R. 1987. 'Producers' market'. In *The New Palgrave: A Dictionary of Economic Theory and Doctrine* edited by J. Eatwell, M. Milgate, and P. Newman. London: Macmillan: 984–6.

White, H. 1992. *Identity and Control: A Structural Theory of Social Action.* Princeton: Princeton University Press.

White, H. 1993. 'Markets in production networks'. In *Explorations in Economic Sociology*, edited by R. Swedberg. New York: Russell Sage Foundation: 161–75.

Young, K. 1932. 'Adjustment'. In *Encyclopedia of the Social Sciences*, Vol. 1, edited by E. Seligman. New York: Macmillan: 438–9.

Zuckerman, E. W. 2000. 'Focusing the corporate product: securities analysts and de-diversification'. *Administrative Science Quarterly* 45 (3): 591–619.

4

The origins of competition: institution and organization

Stefan Arora-Jonsson, Nils Brunsson, and Raimund Hasse

Given contemporary society's obsession with competition, a salient question arises: 'How does competition happen?' The preceding chapter outlined the conditions under which competition could emerge in processes of mutual adjustment.* But as indicated in Chapter 1, competition is more pervasive than would be expected if it arose only through such processes. Competition has its basis in institutions and is also the outcome of the organizational efforts of individuals, organizations and states who want to construct a particular situation as competition. In this chapter, we discuss how and when competition results from institutions and organization.

It has always been the human experience that other actors can make a difference in the access to things that are desired and are perceived as being scarce. Initially, these others—the potential competitors—could be individuals, families, or clans. Potential objects of competition have always existed in the form of access to such natural resources as land, water, and food, and, in cases of conflict, to highly motivated allies (Helbling 2006). Nonetheless, several institutions that characterize the rise of modern society have stimulated the propensity to perceive an increasing number of relationships as competition.

This easing of competition into modern society can be illustrated through the grand narrative of Emile Durkheim (1964). According to Durkheim, population density and experiences of scarcity rose in the nineteenth century due to population growth and urbanization. In line with what was later emphasized by organizational population ecologists, this increase in density was viewed as a trigger for competition (Hannan and Freeman 1977; Olzak 1990), and Durkheim argued that the most influential master trend of modernity—the division of labour—was a response to this development.

But in order to understand the contemporary obsession with competition, we need to understand the specific modern institutions that initiate or support

---

* This chapter is an edited and extended version of the section 'Institution and organization' in Arora-Jonsson, S., Brunsson, N., and Hasse, R. 2020. 'Where does competition come from? Organizational and institutional foundations'. *Organization Theory* 1 (1): 1–24.

Stefan Arora-Jonsson, Nils Brunsson, & Raimund Hasse, *The origins of competition: institution and organization*
In: *Competition: What It Is and Why It Happens.* Edited by: Stefan Arora-Jonsson, Nils Brunsson, Raimund Hasse, and Katarina Lagerström, Oxford University Press. © Stefan Arora-Jonsson, Nils Brunsson, and Raimund Hasse 2021.
DOI:10.1093/oso/9780192898012.003.0004

competition and efforts to organize in a way that stimulates competition. By *institutional foundations*, we mean social orders that are taken for granted and do not require efforts for their preservation (Jepperson 1991). With *organization*, by contrast, we refer to decisions that constitute attempts to create a new order or to maintain an established one (Ahrne and Brunsson 2011; 2019). It is noteworthy that this distinction is analytical; in practice, decision-making occurs against the background of institutions, and organization can become institutionalized.

We begin by discussing the institutional foundations of competition. We then discuss how competition can arise through organization. Finally, we point to certain dynamics that tend to facilitate the emergence of competition and then reinforces and stabilizes it.

The institutional basis of competition

Institutions are fundamental for constructing the elements of competition. Actors, their relationships, scarcity, and desire are all heavily shaped—if not created by institutions.

Relationships and actorhood

There are a number of institutions that can foster the construction of relationships and actorhood. One key trend of modern society is expansion of markets (Brunsson and Jutterström 2018), with the help of new technologies for transport and communication, global trade agreements, standardization, and various other forms of soft regulation (Djelic 2006; Djelic and Quack 2003). In line with Durkheim, it can be argued that this expansion has increased the possibility of experiencing novel, potentially competitive relationships. The national expansion of markets at the end of the nineteenth century (Chandler 1977) and the pronounced increase in economic globalization a century later (Chandler 1990) can be viewed as expressions of this development. It has led not only to the discovery of new opportunities for selling products but also to the experience or imagination that others—sometimes in distant parts of the world—desire access to the same customers. In many cases this competition has led to specialization—doing or desiring something specific—just as Durkheim would have predicted.

Globalization has the same effect in other areas. An increasing awareness of a multitude of actors on the other side of the globe increases the likelihood of constructing a situation as competition. Even universities in small European countries claim that they compete for students with Chinese or North American universities (Brankovic et al. 2018; see also Chapter 6, this volume). Globalization also sharpens the identity of nation states as actors and stimulates relationships among them (Jacobsson and Sundström 2016; Meyer et al. 1997). Against a background of seemingly highly institutionalized desires and a sense of scarcity, globalization fosters comparisons with other nation states with respect to a broad spectrum of economic and social criteria, making nation states desirous of achieving favourable positions and outperforming others (Pedersen 2011). Institutions that support globalization in that way render it easier to construct all elements of competition. Consequently, states now compete for 'talent' or 'innovative capability' or the 'ease of doing business' (Porter 1990), and they develop competitive strategies to render them attractive to multinational companies (Kjaer 2015).

The discovery of other actors who desire the same thing is supported by other broad institutional transformations—an example being access to coveted social positions. Top positions are scarce by definition, but in earlier stratified societies, social mobility was typically lower than it is today. Only a few candidates could be considered competitors for the top social positions, and in most cases, a traditional or legal order of succession rendered competition difficult if not impossible. Likewise, two major paths towards social mobility—vocational choice and marriage— were traditionally less likely to be competitive, because they were institutionally circumscribed. Today, by contrast, these choices are less restricted in most societies, as they are no longer limited to members of a privileged group. Current work towards anti-discrimination and compliance with egalitarian norms in employment have further enabled the construction of competition for positions (cf. Besley et al. 2013). And, the institution of meritocracy as the only remaining legitimizer of inequality (Meyer 1977; 2001) can also serve to increase the propensity to interpret more relationships as competition, because it directs attention to a need for outper-forming others (see Chapter 13, this volume).

The trend of considering organizations as actors has created a proliferation of actors that can constitute an element in the construction of competition (Pedersen and Dobbin 1997). This transformation arguably began with the idea that business firms require 'professional' management (Starbuck 2003), a notion closely related to the expansion of markets at the end of the nineteenth century (Hasse and Krücken 2013). Influenced by new professions—engineering and management— firms became objects of design, developed objectives and strategies, and began to identify others they could view as competitors (Davis 2009). A similar develop-ment has occurred since the end of the twentieth century among non-profit organizations (Hwang and Powell 2009) and public organizations—universities, hospitals, and schools (Brunsson and Sahlin-Andersson 2000; Hasse and Krücken 2013). With their enhanced actorhood, these organizations can now experience a greater number of other organizations of the same category that are also imbued with actorhood—as actors that they can see as competitors for fund-ing; for the employment of qualified professionals; and for public support, cus-tomer demand, and stakeholder interests.

A number of institutions structure the agency of individuals and organizations. Of particular importance to competition are social categories (Cattani et al. 2017; Durand et al. 2017; Zuckerman 1999; see also Chapter 2, this volume). The agency of individuals and organizations is drawn partly from the institutionalized categor-ies to which they are ascribed (Durand and Paolella 2012; Hsu and Hannan 2005). To be considered a competitor in sports is usually contingent upon the actor conforming to an institutionalized gender-categorical belonging (Obel 1996). More generally, ambiguity of categorical belonging has been shown to generate questioning of the legitimacy of an actor as a competitor across a wide range of settings, from movie careers to wines to stock markets (Hsu 2006; Roberts et al. 2010; Zuckerman 1999; 2004). If we consider Simmel's example of competition for affection, norms about the appropriateness of same-gender attraction have played a significant role in defining who is considered a legitimate competitor. The actor element of competition is thus institutionally enabled and often circumscribed through social classification.

Scarcity and desire

Institutionalization processes have not only eased the construction of actors and relationships, but have also inculcated a growing sense of scarcity (Xenos 1989), which has further eased the perception of situations as competition. When consumption was related to the fulfilment of 'basic needs'—which is, of course, another social construction—industrialization could be associated with the utopia of bringing scarcity to an end. Since the end of the nineteenth century, there have been similar hopes not only in the early years of the USSR but also among the technocrats and their most visible proponent, Frederick Taylor (Nelson 1980).

Industrialization and economic development have generated the institutionalization of new desires, not all of which are restricted to such basic material needs as nutrition and clothing. Rather, it is taken for granted that people desire cars, computers, or sports watches—a list that may never end and a list that neither Stalin nor Taylor could have imagined. Additionally, consumption of almost any product category has become an opportunity to signal status (Bagwell and Bernheim 1996), and these status aspirations are no longer restricted to the minority that Veblen (2005) has labelled the 'leisure class'. At least in the Western Hemisphere, it no longer seems sufficient for most people to have shoes, cars, and computers. People are expected to desire Nike sneakers, BMWs, and Apple computers. Driven by marketing, people desire more product categories and products of higher status within each category even for the most basic product one may imagine: water—ideally water imported from Switzerland or Japan.

Institutional changes also affect the allocation of status. In the case of organizations, status generally influences survival (Podolny 1993), and competition for status easily arises. As status is partly ascribed in accordance with customers, suppliers, and collaborators with which the organization is associated (Podolny and Phillips 1996), organizations do not compete merely for scarce financiers, suppliers, and customers. Rather, they compete for the most prestigious collaborators, which are, by definition, scarcer. Likewise, universities and researchers do not merely seek funding; they seek funding sources with the highest reputation (Edlund 2020).

These are a few of the ways in which institutions can enable the construction of the four elements of competition. The very idea of competition can also become institutionalized, in the sense that when it is taken for granted that a context is competitive, it is difficult to imagine that an organization active in that context is not involved in competition. It is taken for granted in most societies, for instance, that markets for consumer goods are competitive (Aspers 2011). It is difficult to think of a consumer-goods firm that does not have the actorhood necessary for attempting to attract customers or a political party that is not expected to try to attract votes. Even certain behaviours related to competition may become institutionalized. Strategy researchers use terms like 'industry recipes' (Spender 1989) or 'competitive logics' (Barnett 2008; 2017) to describe such taken-for-granted elements of competitive behaviour.

The organization of competition

The institutionalization of actors, relationships, desire, and scarcity does not mean that competition arises evenly or that it is introduced into any domain of society without resistance. Rather, the construction of competition often requires organization—decisions to construct or decisions that help construct actorhood, relationships, desire, and scarcity. The less these elements are institutionalized, the more organization will be required. We now turn to ways in which competition can be organized using the distinction of four fundamental decisions of organizing— decisions about membership, rules, monitoring, and sanctions (Ahrne and Brunsson 2011)—to structure our discussion.

In order to discuss competition as organized, we extend Simmel's (1903/2008) classic triad of at least two competitors and a third adjudicating party by introducing a *fourth party*: the organizer of the competition. This organizing role has typically been afforded little attention in the literature, which is not strange, given that competition has often been presumed to emerge spontaneously. In some cases, a fourth party has been noted, but this actor has been analysed only cursorily. Dobbin and Dowd (1997), for instance, noted the role of governmental decisions in the introduction of competition among trains operating in the USA. But the attention of their analysis was on the responses of the train operators rather than on the organizational efforts of the government. Likewise, Zuckerman (1999) briefly referred to experts such as security analysts as constituents of what he called 'mediated markets', but these experts are closer to the Simmelian idea of a third party that adjudicates a competition—albeit indirectly through recommendations—than they are to a fourth party that organizes the competition. Cattani et al. (2017; 2018) also made numerous references to significant non-competing actors who categorize organizations and products and argued that this categorization work is crucial for the construction of competition. These studies all point to the fact that competition requires organization, but none of these researchers treat the organizer as a fourth party of competition, with intentions, plans, and the capacity to act.

Competition by design: contests and reforms

Contests offer a clear illustration of the ways in which competition can be organized. Contests are an instance of episodic competition, characterized by a restricted time window during which competition is legitimate; it is distinct from continuous competition, which is more often discussed as a way of organizing competition in relation to markets (Chadwick 1859). Contests are typical in sports, but they are commonly organized in other areas as well. Product development contests, for example, are used for initiating competition (Rao 1994). In democratic political systems, the competition among parties is organized as contests in the form of elections. In many countries, public procurement is organized as contests, wherein firms are invited to compete by bidding for contracts, but these firms do not necessarily compete once the contract has been allocated (Hood and Dixon 2015; Le Grand 2009).

Contests are a highly organized way to determine the *outcome* of an existing competition among such actors as sport teams, established political parties, or firms. They build on decisions about membership by determining who can participate in the contest, clear rules, active monitoring of behaviour and results, and such positive sanctions as prizes and contracts or such negative sanctions as fines for breaking the rules.

The organization of contests can also *contribute to* competition. By deciding on the membership in a contest, an organizer can stimulate relationships among actors who were not previously related. The European Union (EU) rule that public procurement projects must be published in a way that firms within the entire EU can apply is intended to stimulate competition beyond the individual member state. Predictability in deciding the result of contests—by clear rules and active monitoring by referees or others—is likely to attract more participants, thus increasing the number of those with which a competitive relationship can be established.

Contest organizers are sometimes involved in creating actors for their contests, which they can do by such methods as stipulating that those eligible to bid for a contract must represent a consortium of firms or be of a minimum size. In international sports contests, it is common to form the participants of many existing club teams into a national team. Election laws often presume that contenders organize into political parties, and elections sometimes stimulate the creation of new parties or alliances among parties. Organizers can also select actors by limiting participation to those actors that have a chance to win or even assist in the creation of such actors. In sports, decisions about divisions or pre-contests for seeding participants and rules for drafting new team members sometimes are made in a way that ensures that teams are sufficiently similar to guarantee close competition.

Contest organizers create scarcity by restricting the number of winners to fewer than the number of participants. In order to stimulate the construction of competition, the organizer also needs to stimulate desire by creating positive sanctions: by connecting the outcome with parliamentary seats, contracts, or prize money, for instance.

Contests constitute just one way of organizing competition. Organizers may strive for continuous competition and must handle situations more complex than contests— as when markets or organizations are reformed in order to establish competition. We know from studies of the introduction of competition among railway service providers that such initiatives may require considerable organizational effort and time (Castillo 2018; Dobbin 1994). The organizer must convince others that they are actors who should relate to other actors and that both parties share a desire for something scarce. To achieve this situation a combination of decision-making and legitimating discourse is often required, and it can be accompanied by legal changes that legitimize or circumscribe actions in relation to competition. Where there are no actors that are legitimate competitors, a first organizational task is the creation of such actors. In a monopoly situation, new organizations must often be carved out by splitting up a monopolistic producer (Barnett and Carroll 1993; Castillo 2018; see also Chapter 5, this volume): transforming incomplete organizations such as state agencies or subsidiaries of a corporation into more complete organizations with their own management, clear boundaries, and identity (Arora-Jonsson et al. 2018; Brunsson and Sahlin-Andersson 2000). Where actors are already institutionalized, their legitimacy as competitors needs to be established. And support for the legitimacy of state agencies as competitors can be found in the economic literature, which is rife with arguments for the intrinsic value of public choice in service provision (see for instance Le Grand 2009; Shleifer 1998).

The organizer may also need to define a good that can be the object for competition and ensure the desire for this good among those who are to compete. One strategy is to invoke third parties that are equipped with the ability to control a desired good. Such examples include citizens with the right to vote or parents of school children whose choice of school involves a money transfer to the school chosen. In many cases, this means turning former users of a public service into consumers whose choice adjudicates among potential providers (cf. Le Grand 2009). When there are no third parties, such as consumers, 'imagined publics' can serve as equivalents (Werron 2015); they do not control money transfers, but their imagined attention or appreciation is desirable. For example, producers of a ranking or those being ranked may nurture the idea that the ranking has a large, interested readership that act upon the information.

Relationships among competitors cannot be directly created by the organizer but need to be stimulated, as they result from sensemaking (cf. Cattani et al. 2018; Porac and Baden-Fuller 1989; see also Chapter 2, this volume). Several organizational techniques can be used to kindle a relationship among organizations—by making them members of a list of would-be competitors, for instance, and systematically monitoring them, their desires, their capacity to influence future access to a desirable good, and their recent actions. Porac et al. (1995) have demonstrated how an industry association of Scottish knitwear manufacturers stimulated and reinforced such relationships by obtaining a list of members, monitoring sales and products from a specific set of producers, and publishing the data. Similarly, Anand and

Peterson (2000) illustrated how the top-of-the-chart lists compiled by record stores stimulate artists to think of specific other artists as their competitors. Decisions to create lists or collect sales data can be combined with talk about the threats that competitors imply. In the early 1980s, Japan was singled out as a competitor to the USA in a series of reports and books about the Japanese industrial threat (cf. Teece 1987). Then, China has become the looming threat (Broomfield 2003).

Scarcity may require organization. One example is the persistent, albeit not always successful, attempt by 'guardians' in state budget processes to decide on a fixed total budget and to defend their decision against 'advocates' for more money for their departments—an attempt to show that money is indeed scarce, that one department's desire cannot be fulfilled merely by expanding the budget, and that more money to one department does in fact mean less money to another (Wildavsky 1980). Another example is provided by historian E. P. Thompson (1967), who discussed the significant organizational efforts required to establish competitive labour markets in early industrializing Britain. A major obstacle was the cultural meaning of time. In agrarian societies, time was conceived of in a non-standardized task-oriented manner, like the time taken to plough a field, which prevented calculations of its scarcity. Only after significant organizational efforts that spread the use of watches and clocks and led to the acceptance of 'merchant time' or 'clock time' could labour be considered scarce and form the basis of a competitive labour market. Clock time is now deeply institutionalized in most societies, illustrating the fact that organizational efforts can become institutionalized over time and require no further organization in order to be maintained.

Competition as a side effect

The illustrations presented so far describe situations in which organizers intend to create and maintain competition. Competition may, however, result from organization even when this was not its purpose as it may inadvertently contribute all the elements of competition, or may add one or two missing elements. Alternatively, organizers may provide a few elements that inspire others to create the missing ones.

Organizations that have similar identities or engage in similar activities often organize by using membership to form a common meta-organization (Ahrne and Brunsson 2005)—a business association, for example. The purpose of a business association may be restricted to public relations or lobbying for the industry as a whole. Yet, membership can fuel the construction of the situation as competition, because it clarifies who can be seen as competitors, and those competitors may be more numerous than the average manager could have imagined. For the same reason, as argued in Chapter 1, membership in a cartel may stabilize or even sharpen competition, rather than reducing or abolishing it, as is often presumed.

The awarding of a prize, which is a form of positive sanction, constitutes another type of organizational effort that can unintentionally give rise to competition. The people or organizations that establish prizes may want to initiate competition, but they often have no intention other than rewarding superior achievements, pointing to good examples, or attracting attention to themselves (Edlund et al. 2019). But a prize may initiate competition if it is scarce, for instance limited to one person or organization, at least during a specific period; if it is sufficiently attractive to be desired; and if the rules are formulated in such a way that it is easy to imagine that others could possibly receive the prize. A prize will also more likely create competition if it is combined with membership, thereby defining who can possibly win the prize—and in retrospect, all of those who have not won it, even though they could have done so. Such a case makes it easy to identify and relate to specific other competitors, thereby constructing relationships that can be competitive.

Relationships can be inadvertently organized as competition by monitoring people or organizations and comparing them. These comparisons often include rankings, whereby someone decides which are the best and perhaps the worst of that category. Ranking is an old tradition in sports, but actors can be compared and ranked without any contests or prizes. Firms are ranked with respect to customer satisfaction; local governments—not unlike restaurants—are ranked with respect to the quality of their service; universities are ranked with respect to their contributions to research or to the level of competence of their staff; and states are ranked with respect to their level of democracy or development.

Rankings are conducted by various types of organization, and, like prize givers, rankers may have no intention of initiating competition. Several prominent rankers of universities argue that their only purpose is to inform prospective students of their choice of universities (Wedlin 2006). Yet, rankings may produce competition (Brankovic et al. 2018) because, by definition, positions in rankings are scarce, and by listing actors, rankings can initiate relationships among those actors. It is far from certain, however, that people have strong reasons to desire a high position on the list (see Chapter 6, this volume.) And a large number of rankings can reduce the desire to rank highly on a given ranking; if the result in one ranking is disappointing, it is possible to focus on another ranking (see Chapter 7, this volume).

Even if those creating a meta-organization, initiating a prize, or creating a ranking table are not interested in promoting competition, others who want to construct competition can try to complement with the missing elements. Membership can be complemented by scarcity and desire by deciding which member has the best practice or by introducing different levels of membership, for instance. When a prize generates little desire, people other than the prize givers can try to boost its status. Those who are interested in using rankings to initiate competition may need to create relationships by informing people that they or their organizations are ranked. They must also convince people that the ranker's categories signify entities that can be considered actors, which is not always an easy task. Not every academic would necessarily believe that universities—their own or others—are actors capable of coordinating researchers and teachers according to a plan to compete, for instance.

Furthermore, proponents of competition can try to convince people to desire a prize or a high position in a ranking, by arguing that those distinctions are not only signs of status but also likely to have such further positive effects as making it easier to generate money, for instance.

Asymmetries as motives for organizing competition

Summing up, there are three types of actors that can construct competition: two or more *competitors*; *third parties*, who adjudicate between the competitors; and *fourth parties*, who are interested in seeing competition or who have other interests, such as celebrating achievements, in which case these interests result in competition as a side effect. Construction of the four elements of competition may differ among these parties, and they may therefore have different views about whether competition actually exists. Where competition is institutionalized and therefore unquestioned, it is likely that all three actor types agree in their constructions of the situation as competition. Agreement across constructions is only one of the possible cases, however. In some cases, only the competitors construct the situation as competition; in other cases, only the organizer sees competition (which can be what economists and strategy scholars call 'diffuse competition'), or it can be that only the third party believes that there is competition. Likewise, there are cases in which all but one party believe that there is competition. In any situation in which competition is not institutionalized, we suspect that the constructions among the three actor types are often asymmetric.

Asymmetries in construction is a strong motivator for the organization of competition. Government officials who are not sure that schools or healthcare units are actually constructing the situation as competition need to intervene and reorganize so the managers of these units can begin to construct competition (see Chapters 5 and 11, this volume.) Similarly, if parents or pension savers do not believe that they are customers who should be actively selecting among providers, the government must inform them of their rights or even compel them by law to become actors who make choices (Ball 1993; Jutterström 2018). A further example is that firms in business-to-business markets often seek to help in the creation of new actors at an earlier stage in the value chain, in order to stimulate competition at this stage (Porter 1991).

Interrelations and dynamics

For those wanting to see competition, the modern institutions we have pointed to come in handy. Some elements of competition may already be institutionalized, and organizers must merely add missing elements. But promoters of competition are also helped through self-reinforcing dynamics of two types. The elements of competition can reinforce each other and thus increase the likelihood of competition being constructed, and the construction of competition may reinforce and stabilize its elements.

As for the type 1, there are relatively trivial cases of interrelationships among the elements of competition, such as when the desire of many actors for a certain good creates scarcity and scarcity creates relationships (Shah et al. 2015). Perhaps an increase in demand for metal creates relationships among recycling organizations and those who need metals, or individuals who have never shopped online decide to do so during a pandemic, thereby entering into a relationship with online shops worldwide because local stores have run out of face masks.

There are also more intriguing cases in which scarcity may evoke or reinforce desire, as marketers of luxury goods know well. If a good is produced in a limited edition, even more people want to buy it and have to compete for it. Desire is a common reason to create or reinforce actorhood—to create a new political party or a consortium of firms capable of bidding for a large project, for instance. As described in some Shakespearean dramas, relationships based on friendship can result in the imitation of desires, which nurtures competition for the affection of the same person (Girard 1991).

And, not least, actorhood and the categorization of actors may create desire and scarcity. Individuals, organizations, and states are expected to have goals and to strive towards something they want to achieve (and thus, per definition, do not yet have), but the goals and aspirations of actors are far from arbitrary (Cyert and March 1992). A company is expected to desire profits, sport teams are expected to desire game victories, political parties are expected to want to gain political power, and so on. Goal achievements with respect to these expectations often form the basis for comparing companies, sport teams, or political parties. They determine the status of a given actor, and status can be an end in itself or a means to other ends (see Chapter 6, this volume). Consequently, actors of a given type tend to strive for the same achievements, and scarcity of what is desired may increase due to such overlapping desires.

Once a situation has been constructed as competition, there are dynamics that tend to stabilize and reinforce it (type 2). Instead of a simple cause–effect relationship, we need to consider the processes of mutual self-enforcement of competition and its elements. Actors are not only necessary for the construction of competition, but competition also has a profound influence on the images and identities of these actors (Hasse and Krücken 2013). The introduction of a status competition among universities contributes to a transformation of universities into actors or expands their actorhood (see Chapter 6, this volume). Firms in competitive markets have also transformed themselves from mere profit-making instruments into management-based economic actors. Hospital managers who believe that their organization is in competition strengthen their actorhood and abandon the belief that their hospitals are mere opportunity structures for physicians or scientists.

Competition may also result in the ascription of more generalized actorhood. Nobel Prize winners are thought to be experts in fields of expertise far beyond their own; financially successful firms are considered generalized role models; and the fastest runner in the world can be considered a candidate for goodwill ambassador for disadvantaged children, competing, in this respect, with artists or retired politicians who also may desire that position. Thus, competition does not merely require actors; it helps to constitute them and affects their identity.

Similarly, competition may reinforce relationships and move them into areas other than the competitive one, as when competitors begin cooperating, only to discover that they can learn from each other—as touched upon in our discussion of industry associations and further discussed in Chapter 11. And competition may reinforce scarcity and desire, so that competitors gradually get a stronger desire for a good over time or come to think that it is scarcer than they thought at the beginning of the competition. Leblebici et al. (1991), for instance, show that as radio stations began to finance their programming through advertising, resources such as marketers, which had previously been considered surplus in the industry, became increasingly scarce, as more radio stations competed for the advertisers' money.

To conclude, our conceptualization of competition implies that anyone who wants to convince others that they are involved in competition—or observe it—must specify for which good the competition exists, that it is scarce, and that there are competitors with relations to each other. They can be helped by institutions or organization that support any of the elements of competition. Both reformers and researchers can benefit from the distinction we have made here of the four elements of competition, the three actor types, and the interrelationships of these two categorizations. These distinctions make it possible to theorize in a more nuanced and specific manner about the ways in which competition happens—more than if competition is conceptualized as a whole and seen from the perspective of only one observer. It also explains that competition can be a side effect, and facilitates an analysis of how to resist or abolish competition. In the following chapters, these—and other questions concerning the organization of competition—are explored across a wide variety of settings.

References

Ahrne, G. and Brunsson, N. 2005. 'Organizations and meta-organizations'. *Scandinavian Journal of Management*, 21 (4): 429–49.

Ahrne, G. and Brunsson, N. 2011. 'Organization outside organizations: the significance of partial organization'. *Organization* 18 (1): 83–104.

Ahrne, G. and Brunsson, N. 2019. *Organization outside Organizations: The Abundance of Partial Organization in Social Life*. Cambridge: Cambridge University Press.

Anand, N. and Peterson, R. A. 2000. 'When market information constitutes fields: sense-making of markets in the commercial music industry'. *Organization Science* 11 (3): 270–84.

Arora-Jonsson, S., Blomgren, M., Forssell, A., and Waks, C. 2018. *Att styra organisationer med konkurrens* (To govern organizations using competition). Lund: Studentlitteratur.

Arora-Jonsson, S., Brunsson, N., and Hasse, R. 2020. 'Where does competition come from? Organizational and institutional foundations'. *Organization Theory* 1 (1): 1–24.

Aspers, P. 2011. *Markets*. Cambridge: Polity Press.

Bagwell, L. S. and Bernheim, B. D. 1996. 'Veblen effects in a theory of conspicuous consumption'. *American Economic Review* 86 (3): 349–73.

Ball, S. J. 1993. 'Education markets, choice and social class: the market as a class strategy in the UK and the USA'. *British Journal of Sociology of Education* 14 (1): 3–19.

Barnett, W. P. 2008. *The Red Queen among Organizations: How Competitiveness Evolves*. Princeton: Princeton University Press.

Barnett, W. P. 2017. 'Metacompetition: competing over the game to be played'. *Strategy Science* 2 (4): 212–19.

Barnett, W. P. and Carroll, G. R. 1993. 'How institutional constraints affected the organization of early US telephony'. *Journal of Law, Economics, and Organization* 9 (1): 98–126.

Besley, T. J., Folke, O., Persson, T., and Rickne, J. 2013. 'Gender quotas and the crisis of the mediocre man: theory and evidence from Sweden'. *American Economic Review* 107 (8): 2204–42.

Brankovic, J., Ringe, L., and Werron, T. 2018. 'How rankings produce competition: the case of global university rankings'. *Zeitschrift für Soziologie* 47 (4): 270–88.

Broomfield, E. V. 2003. 'Perceptions of danger: the China threat theory'. *Journal of Contemporary China* 12 (35): 265–84.

Brunsson, N. and Jutterström, M. 2018. *Organizing and Reorganizing Markets*. Oxford: Oxford University Press.

Brunsson, N. and Sahlin-Andersson, K. 2000. 'Constructing organizations: the example of public sector reform'. *Organization Studies* 21 (4): 721–46.

Castillo, D. 2018. 'Creating a market bureaucracy: the case of a railway market'. *Organizing and Reorganizing Markets*, edited by N. Brunsson and M. Jutterström. Oxford: Oxford University Press: 32–45.

Cattani, G., Porac, J., and Thomas, H. 2017. 'Categories and competition'. *Strategic Management Journal* 38 (1): 64–92.

Cattani, G., Sands, D., Porac, J., and Greenberg, J. 2018. 'Competitive sensemaking in value creation and capture'. *Strategy Science* 3 (4): 632–57.

Chadwick, E. 1859. 'Results of different principles of legislation and administration in Europe; of competition for the field, as compared with competition within the field, of service'. *Journal of the Statistical Society of London* 22 (3): 381–420.

Chandler, A. D. 1977. *The Visible Hand*. Cambridge, MA: Harvard University Press.

Chandler, A. D. 1990. *Strategy and Structure: Chapters in the History of the Industrial Enterprise*. Cambridge, MA: MIT Press.

Cyert, R. M. and March, J. G. 1992. *A Behavioral Theory of the Firm*. Cambridge, MA: Blackwell Business.

Davis, G. F. 2009. *Managed by the Markets: How Finance Re-shaped America*. Oxford: Oxford University Press.

Djelic, M. L. 2006. 'Marketization: from intellectual agenda to global policy-making'. In *Transnational Governance. Institutional Dynamics of Regulation*, edited by M. L. Djelic and K. Sahlin-Andersson. Cambridge: Cambridge University Press: 53–73.

Djelic, M. L. and Quack, S. 2003. *Globalization and Institutions: Redefining the Rules of the Economic Game*. Cheltenham: Edward Elgar.

Dobbin, F. 1994. *Forging Industrial Policy: The United States, Britain, and France in the Railway Age*. Cambridge/New York: Cambridge University Press.

Dobbin, F. R. and Dowd, T. J. 1997. 'How policy shapes competition: early railroad foundings in Massachusetts'. *Administrative Science Quarterly* 42 (3): 501–29.

Durand, R., Granqvist, N., and Tyllström, A. 2017. 'From categories to categorization: a social perspective on market categorization'. In *From Categories to Categorization: Studies in Sociology, Organizations and Strategy at the Crossroads*, edited by R. Durand, N. Granqvist, and A, Tyllström. Bingley: Emerald: 3–30.

Durand, R. and Paolella, L. 2012. 'Category stretching: reorienting research on categories in strategy, entrepreneurship, and organization theory'. *Journal of Management Studies* 50 (6): 1100–23.

Durkheim, E. 1964. *The Division of Labour in Society* (1893) (translated by G. Simpson). Glencoe: Free Press.

Edlund, P. 2020. *Science Evaluation and Status Creation. Exploring the European Research Council's Authority*. Cheltenham: Edward Elgar Publishing.

Edlund, P., Pallas, J., and Wedlin, L. 2019. 'Prizes and the organization of status'. In *Organization outside Organizations: The Abundance of Partial Organization in Social Life*, edited by G. Ahrne and N. Brunsson. Cambridge: Cambridge University Press: 62–83.

Girard, R. 1991. *Shakespeare: A Theater of Envy*. New York: Oxford University Press.

Hannan, M. T. and Freeman, J. 1977. 'The population ecology of organizations'. *American Journal of Sociology* 82 (March): 929–64.

Hasse, R. and Krücken, G. 2013. 'Competition and actorhood: a further expansion of the neo-institutional agenda'. *Sociologia Internationalis* 51 (2): 181–205.

Helbling, J. 2006. *Tribale Kriege. Konflikte in Gesellschaften ohne Zentralgewalt*. Frankfurt/Main: Campus.

Hood, C. and Dixon, R. 2015. *A Government that Worked Better and Cost Less? Evaluating Three Decades of Reform and Change in UK Central Government*. Oxford: Oxford University Press.

Hsu, G. 2006. 'Jacks of all trades and masters of none: audiences' reactions to spanning genres in feature film production'. *Administrative Science Quarterly* 51 (3): 420–50.

Hsu, G. and Hannan, M. T. 2005. 'Identities, genres, and organizational forms'. *Organization Science* 16 (5): 474–90.

Hwang, H. and Powell, W. W. 2009. 'The rationalization of charity: the influences of professionalism in the nonprofit sector'. *Administrative Science Quarterly* 54 (2): 268–98.

Jacobsson, B. and Sundström, G. 2016. 'The Europeanization of the Swedish state'. In *The Oxford Handbook of Swedish Politics*, edited by J. Pierre. Oxford: Oxford University Press: 515–28.

Jepperson, R. L. 1991. 'Institutions, institutional effects and institutionalism. The new institutionalism in organizational analysis'. In *The New Institutionalism in Organizational Analysis*, edited by W. W. Powell and P. J. DiMaggio. Chicago/London: University of Chicago Press: 143–63.

Jutterström, M. 2018. 'Markets as open systems: organizing and reorganizing a financial market'. In *Organizing and Reorganizing Markets*, edited by N. Brunsson and M. Jutterström. Oxford: Oxford University Press: 115.

Kjaer, P. F. 2015. 'Context construction through competition: the prerogative of public power, intermediary institutions, and the expansion of statehood through competition'. *Distinktion: Journal of Social Theory* 16 (2): 146–66.

Le Grand, J. 2009. *The Other Invisible Hand: Delivering Public Services through Choice and Competition*. Princeton: Princeton University Press.

Leblebici, H., Salancik, G. R., Copay, A., and King, T. 1991. 'Institutional change and the transformation of interorganizational fields: an organizational history of the U.S. radio broadcasting industry'. *Administrative Science Quarterly* 36: 333–63.

Meyer, J. W. 1977. 'The effects of education as an institution'. *American Journal of Sociology* 83 (1): 55–77.

Meyer, J. W. 2001. 'Comment: reflections: the worldwide commitment to educational equality'. *Sociology of Education* 74: 154–8.

Meyer, J. W., Boli, J., Thomas, G., and Ramirez, F. 1997. 'World society and the nation state'. *American Journal of Sociology* 103 (1): 144–81.

Nelson, D. 1980. *Frederick W. Taylor and the Rise of Scientific Management*. Madison: University of Wisconsin Press.

Obel, C. 1996. 'Collapsing gender in competitive bodybuilding: researching contradictions and ambiguity in sport'. *International Review for the Sociology of Sport* 31 (2): 185–202.

Olzak, S. 1990. 'The political context of competition: lynching and urban racial violence, 1882–1914'. *Social Forces* 69 (2): 395–421.

Pedersen, J. S. and Dobbin, F. 1997. 'The social invention of collective actors: on the rise of the organization'. *American Behavioral Scientist* 40 (4): 431–43.

Pedersen, O. K. 2011. *Konkurrencestaten*. Copenhagen: Hans Reitzels Forlag.

Podolny, J. M. 1993. 'A status-based model of market competition'. *American Journal of Sociology* 98 (4): 829–72.

Podolny, J. M. and Phillips, D. J. 1996. 'The dynamics of organizational status'. *Industrial and Corporate Change* 5 (2): 453–71.

Porac, J. F. and Baden-Fuller, C. 1989. 'Competitive groups as cognitive communities: the case of Scottish knitwear manufacturers'. *Journal of Management Studies* 26: 397–416.

Porac, J. F., Thomas, H., Wilson, F., Patson, D., and Kanfer, A. 1995. 'Rivalry and the industry model of Scottish knitwear producers'. *Administrative Science Quarterly* 40 (2): 203–27.

Porter, M. 1990. *The Competitive Advantage of Nations*. New York: Free Press.

Porter, M. E. 1991. 'Towards a dynamic theory of strategy'. *Strategic Management Journal* 12 (S2): 95–117.

Rao, H. 1994. 'The social construction of reputation: certification contests, legitimation, and the survival of organizations in the American automobile industry: 1885–1912'. *Strategic Management Journal* 15 (Winter special): 29–44.

Roberts, P. W., Simons, T., and Swaminathan, A. 2010. 'Crossing categorical boundaries: the implications of switching from non-kosher wine production in the Israeli wine market'. In *Categories in Markets: Origin and Evolution*, volume 31, edited by G. Hsu, G. Negro, and Ö. Kocak. Bingley: Emerald: 153–73.

Shah, A. K., Shafir, E., and Mullainathan, S. 2015. 'Scarcity frames value'. *Psychological Science* 26 (4): 402–12.

Shleifer, A. 1998. 'State versus private ownership'. *Journal of Economic Perspectives* 12 (4): 133–50.

Simmel, G. 1903/2008. 'Sociology of competition'. *Canadian Journal of Sociology/Cahiers Canadiens de Sociologie* 33 (4): 957–78.

Spender, J.-C. 1989. *Industry Recipes*. Oxford: Basil Blackwell.

Starbuck, W. H. 2003. 'The origins of organization theory'. In *The Oxford Handbook of Organization Theory*, edited by C. Knudsen and H. Tsoukas. Oxford: Oxford University Press: 143–82.

Teece, D. J. 1987. *The Competitive Challenge: Strategies for Industrial Innovation and Renewal*. Cambridge, MA: Ballinger.

Thompson, E. P. 1967. 'Time, work-discipline, and industrial capitalism'. *Past & Present* 38 (1): 56–97.

Veblen, T. 2005. *Conspicuous Consumption*. London: Penguin Books.

Wedlin, L. 2006. *Ranking Business Schools: Forming Fields, Identities and Boundaries in International Management Education*. Cheltenham: Edward Elgar.

Werron, T. 2015. 'Why do we believe in competition? A historical-sociological view of competition as an institutionalized modern imaginary'. *Distinktion: Journal of Social Theory* 16 (2): 186–210.

Wildavsky, A. B. 1980. *How to Limit Government Spending: Or, How a Constitutional Amendment Tying Public Spending to Economic Growth Will Decrease Taxes and Lessen Inflation*. California: University of California Press.

Xenos, N. 1989. *Modernity and Scarcity*. London/New York: Routledge.

Zuckerman, E. W. 1999. 'The categorical imperative: securities analysts and the illegitimacy discount'. *American Journal of Sociology* 104 (5): 1398–438.

Zuckerman, E. W. 2004. 'Structural incoherence and stock market activity'. *American Sociological Review* 69 (3): 405–32.

5
Convincing others that they are competing: the case of schools

Niklas Bomark, Peter Edlund, and Stefan Arora-Jonsson

Arguably, one of the master trends of the past decades has been the increasing eagerness of governments across the world to introduce competition into sectors of society where competition has not been present earlier (Djelic 2006; Kjaer 2015; Werron 2015).* Since the late 1980s, governments have sought to introduce competition into education, healthcare provision, and other public services. However, while researchers have begun to examine the effects of this spread of competition into new areas of society (Björklund 2005; Bloom et al. 2015; Hood and Dixon 2015; Propper et al. 2004), little is known about the process by which competition is introduced. This is the focus of this chapter.

As argued in Chapter 1, competition can be studied as a collective construction made up of four constitutive elements. A situation is constructed as competitive when there are *actors* involved in a *relationship* that centres on something thought to be both *scarce* and *desirable*. These four elements are, in themselves, generic to almost any organizational context. For instance, an organization could have relationships with other organizations, but this does not mean that the situation which the organizations are part of is constructed as competition. Likewise, an organization can desire something that it considers scarce, but this organization may do so without constructing the situation as competition. An important qualification for competition in Chapter 1 is that the four elements are constructed *in relation to one another*. Introducing competition into a new setting may thus require organizational efforts in two steps: first, the elements need to be constructed (if they do not already exist), and second, they need to be related to one another in a meaningful way.

In this chapter, we focus on how organizers of competition attempt to introduce competition for students by constructing the four constitutive elements in relation to one another. Empirically, we develop a historical case study of the organizing efforts by a Swedish municipality that sought to introduce competition for students among its upper secondary schools following a national reform in the early 1990s. The core idea behind the reform was to provide students with increased

* The authors gratefully acknowledge financial support from Handelsbanken, grant P18–258.

Niklas Bomark, Peter Edlund, & Stefan Arora-Jonsson, *Convincing others that they are competing: the case of schools*
In: *Competition: What It Is and Why It Happens.* Edited by: Stefan Arora-Jonsson, Nils Brunsson, Raimund Hasse, and
Katarina Lagerström, Oxford University Press. © Niklas Bomark, Peter Edlund, and Stefan Arora-Jonsson 2021.
DOI:10.1093/oso/9780192898012.003.0005

choice in terms of schooling. Choice would, in turn, lead to competition for students and therefore spur schools to improve their quality, efficiency, and innovation as they competed for students (Björklund 2005). We examine the municipality's efforts to introduce competition for students over a span of twenty years. Specifically, we analyse the transition from a situation that neither municipal officials nor school principals experienced as competitive to a situation that both officials and principals viewed as competition. Our analysis suggests that the introduction of competition was a gradual process that involved continuous efforts from organizers as they attempted to construct and configure the elements of competition in relation to one another.

Reforms towards competition among schools

Along with Chile, Sweden has been one of the most active countries in introducing competition throughout its school system. The idea of competition among schools in Sweden was presented in the 'freedom of choice reform' (*Swe. valfrihetsreformen* (Prop. 1992/93: 230, 1992)). As the name suggests, one central tenet of this reform was that students would have the possibility to choose where to be schooled. Another important feature was that it opened up the Swedish educational system for different forms of ownership, including private for-profit schools. Launched by the Swedish government in 1992, the reform was directed at the entire school system: pre-schools, compulsory grades 1–9, and two- or three-year voluntary upper secondary schools.

While called a choice reform, it was in its essence a competition reform. Conceived of in an era when public choice was highly valued (Hood and Dixon 2015; Le Grand 2009), a core expectation behind the reform was that student choice would function as a competitive feedback and incentive mechanism for schools to improve and diversify their educational offerings (Björklund 2005). These expected effects were in line with the common understanding of competition as augmenting quality, efficiency, and innovation (e.g. Dennis 1975; McNulty 1968; Vickers 1995).

Because Swedish schooling, since the 1991 'municipalization law' (*Swe. kommunallagen* (SFS 1991: 900)), is organized and funded at the municipal level under guidelines from the National School Inspectorate, it was the municipalities that were charged with introducing competition among their schools. In our case, we investigate the efforts to introduce competition among upper secondary schools in Alpha, a mid-sized municipality with approximately 200,000 inhabitants and close to 2,500 new students applying for upper secondary schooling every year. We use a fictive name for our studied municipality in order to preserve the anonymity of our informants. Our focus is on the efforts of the education board at Alpha as the focal organizer of competition, and on how its decisions shaped the construction of the four constitutive elements of competition over a span of two decades after the reform was implemented. Our data include interviews with past and present municipal officials and school principals, academic reports, practitioner memoirs, municipal archive documents, and National School Inspectorate statistics.

Trials and tribulations of the introduction of competition

Competition among upper secondary schools in Alpha would, along the lines of the model presented in Chapter 1, mean that principals come to view themselves and other schools as actors involved in a relationship that influences their opportunities to attract scarce and desirable students. On the basis of this, our analysis proceeds as follows. First, we describe the situation in Alpha prior to the reform, with respect to how school principals and municipality officials understood and interpreted the constitutive elements of competition at the time. This serves as our baseline, against which we compare subsequent developments that result from the municipality's organizing efforts. Second, we analyse how the elements of competition were constructed and configured in relation to one another over a period of twenty years of reform implementation in Alpha. This enables us to trace a transition where principals and officials gradually start to understand and interpret the four constitutive elements as existing and being relevant in relation to one another, thus constructing their situation as a competition over students.

Pre-reform: Schooling without competition

Prior to the reform, there was no coherent set of ideas or rules that supported the notion of upper secondary schools competing against one another for students and their associated resource flows. Students were allocated to schools according to a 'proximity principle' (*Swe. närhetsprincip*), that is, they were placed at schools in close proximity to their homes (Böhlmark and Lindahl 2012). While students chose the educational programme to attend, they could not choose a specific school, and this also meant that the schools could not influence their student inflow in any significant way. Through demographic analyses of incoming student cohorts, Alpha's education board allocated seats in different educational programmes to schools on the basis of projected demand in different areas of the municipality. Privately owned schools were, generally, not allowed, and schools received funds based on what they needed to fulfil their educational tasks, as set by the Swedish government and operationalized by the municipality.

Schools were not seen as actors in terms of their management; instead, these were run as an extension of Alpha's education board and were consequently more like agents of the municipality than actors in their own right (cf. Brunsson and Sahlin-Andersson 2000). The schools desired to have students, but in a generalized sense; students were not desired as tokens for an inflow of funds to the school. What is more, students were not seen as particularly scarce because the capacity and funding of each school was adjusted in accordance with demographic forecasts.

To the extent that competitive relationships existed, these revolved around long-standing status concerns between the two oldest schools in Alpha. This competition primarily concerned having the 'best' natural sciences programme, the 'most rigorous' training in the social sciences, the 'most prominent' legacy of former students, and other academic superlatives that functioned as status symbols for upper secondary schools. Although these schools competed for status and, in the course of this, attempted to develop distinct identities, much of their status was already determined by the schools' location as residential segregation determined the socioeconomic background of students and thereby, to a great extent, their academic achievements (Holmlund et al. 2014). The outcome of this status competition was also not connected to any additional resources. In this period, the four constitutive elements of competition—actors, relationships, desirability, and scarcity—were thus generally not seen as relevant in relation to one another. These elements had been organized in a way that did not lead Alpha's school principals to construct their situation as one of competition for students and resources.

As discussed in Chapter 4, competition most often originates from institutions and organizational efforts. The first organizational effort to introduce competition for students among schools was undertaken in 1992 at the national level when the Swedish parliament sanctioned a regulatory framework that would link the educational choice of students with the resources allocated to schools.

Because Swedish schooling would remain publicly funded after the reform, this had to be taken into consideration when attempting to link resource flows with student choices. The effort therefore took the form of a municipality-funded educational voucher system for students (Böhlmark and Lindahl 2012). Each student was allocated a voucher that would be credited to the student's chosen school, regardless of whether it was a municipality owned or a privately owned school. While school funding had previously been based on the total number of students educated across any municipality school, the voucher system was meant to make individual schools directly responsible for their own funding situation by connecting their resources to the number of students attracted.

This national regulatory framework needed translation and implementation at the municipality level. In what follows, we trace the organizational efforts to enable and encourage Alpha's schools to understand themselves and other schools as actors enmeshed in relationships where students were perceived as desirable and scarce. As will become evident, municipal officials initially proceeded with these efforts reluctantly and emphasized the different constitutive elements of competition at different points in time.

1992–2001: constructing choice without competition
Several key features that marked Alpha's initial implementation of the competition reform made this a slow process. Swedish municipalities were still in the midst of

implementing another major national reform that concerned the general responsibilities of municipalities in relation to the state (SFS 1991: 900). The content and structure of education in Swedish upper secondary schools was also being reformed, which, by 1994, resulted in the establishment of seventeen national programmes that determined what combinations of courses a school could offer (Lpf 1994).

In Alpha's elected municipal council, there were ongoing ideological discussions regarding the organization of the activities that the municipality was responsible for. A neo-liberally inspired way of providing public services was becoming popular in Sweden (Blomgren 2003; Hood 1995), which was most evident in the enactment of the competition reform that the liberal and conservative government had promoted at the national level. A neo-liberal way of providing public services contrasted radically with the beliefs of the Social Democratic party that had dominated politics in Alpha for long periods of time. Municipal officials and school principals were used to approach the schooling of students as a duty and a social mission, and not as an arena for competition within which students were seen as resources. While there was a right-wing majority in the municipal council from 1990 to 1994, most of the officials and principals were deeply familiar with a system where schools were not supposed to compete. Throughout most of our interviews, informants talked about the competition reform as an event that broke with old traditions and ways of understanding schooling. Many spoke of long-standing efforts to provide equal education and of the uncertainty about how a 'market-based' system would affect those efforts. Taken together, after the competition reform was launched, the first years showed relatively little efforts undertaken to implement it.

A key question of the choice reform was the possibility of students to choose where to be schooled. The municipality did, however, not change the system by which it allocated students to schools at this time. It retained the earlier system of seeking to match supply of seats to student demand and to allocate students to schools by the 'proximity principle'. This limited the construction of the situation as competition because it curtailed the actorhood of schools in the sense that they could do little to influence their number of students. In 1994, a national re-regulation allowed—but did not mandate—municipalities to abandon the proximity principle so that students could choose both programme and school (Bet. 1992/93: UBU17, 1994; Rskr. 1992/93: 406, 1993). This allowed the construction of schools as actors that could seek popularity through educational programme offerings, as well as by other means such as attractive lunches and buildings, or free laptop computers. While many Swedish municipalities removed the proximity principle in the allocation of students, Alpha responded with caution.

Alpha's officials decided that students should be guaranteed seats in their chosen educational programmes, but that all programmes would not be offered at all schools. This decision opened up for certain student choice by relaxing the use of the proximity principle. However, as most educational programmes were only offered at one school, students, in practice, only chose a programme and, thus, not a school. Because the municipality decided what educational programmes different schools should offer, school attractiveness among students remained in the hands of Alpha officials. Although there was a voucher system in place and students could exert certain choice, the actorhood of schools in relation to students as something desirable and scarce was very limited. As offered programmes, and the number of seats per programme, were controlled by the education board, the allocation of students did not develop into a focal point for any meaningful competitive relationships. While schools upheld a number of relationships with one another, such as sharing pools of substitute or part-time teachers, these relationships were not focused on scarce and desirable students.

More generally, although the competition reform had been officially implemented in Alpha, we saw little real change in comparison to our baseline throughout the decade following the 1992 reform. The constitutive elements of competition were still not constructed in relation to one another, and there was, to the best of our knowledge, no sense of competition among the principals of Alpha's upper secondary schools. A key reason for this was the reluctance of the education board to alter the system by which students were allocated to schools.

2002–2012: energized attempts at constructing competition

As a result of several interrelated events and decisions in Alpha, the four constitutive elements of competition were reorganized in relation to one another during the second decade after the reform. To begin with, there were important political forces within the municipality that shaped the construction of competition. Broadly speaking, the municipality comprised two political camps that represented different standpoints on the value of the choice reform. On one side, there was a coalition consisting of the Social Democratic, the Green, and the Left parties, which were hesitant about the reform. On the other side, the Liberal, the Conservative, and the Christian Democratic parties had formed a political alliance that advocated for a wholesale implementation of the reform.

Despite these political differences, Alpha had, since the late 1980s, made various attempts to optimize and increase the efficiency of its organizational structure. In 2003, a decision was made across all local political parties to organize the municipality's public services—for example, schooling, transportation, and healthcare—according to a 'purchaser–provider' model (*Swe. beställar-utförarmodell*), inspired by the New Public Management movement that was popularized in the UK and the USA during the 1980s (Hood 1991; 1995; Pollitt et al. 2004). In brief, this meant that a set of opposing units was created within each of Alpha's public service sectors. One unit would act as a purchaser of services in its respective sector, while the other unit would act as the provider of the service. The idea was to create internal markets within the municipality for the purchase and provision of public services so that also intra-municipal transactions were contractual. As is often the case with internal markets, Alpha's purchasing units were also allowed (and often encouraged) to contract external providers if they could offer better and/or cheaper services than the municipal providers.

For Alpha's school sector, the new purchaser–provider model meant that the education board was designated as the purchaser and a new production committee was created from which the purchaser could procure schooling services. Because it provided most of the upper secondary schooling in Alpha, this committee, in practice, shaped how schools were run. Archival data show that the production committee was presented early on as a 'school market-oriented' unit that would operate as a 'business area' within Alpha. In interviews, we also learnt that the committee recruited managers with extensive experience from the private sector. Not long after, a vision was presented in which the production committee would be transformed into an agile and responsive organization that ran schools as consumer-focused divisions. Activities to implement this vision included the creation of business plans, marketing schemes, and performance indicators that were mimicked from the private sector. Other activities encompassed courses and seminars in which principals were encouraged to approach their role and their schools as organizations located in a competitive schooling market. Terminology such as 'market shares' and 'competitive strengths and weaknesses' was integrated into the reporting system for each school. Alpha's schools would operate as subsidiaries in a municipal 'corporation', forging relationships with one another as competitors on an internal municipal 'market' for students. To further reinforce this vision, the production committee expanded the scope of autonomy for schools, thus allowing them certain leeway in matters associated with the profiling and advertising of their educational programmes.

An annual school fair, which was established in the early 2000s, became an important arena for schools to embody and manifest Alpha's new vision. Once every year, all municipality-owned schools exhibited their school to potential students. This was not a fair in the traditional sense because students did not choose schools then and there. The idea behind the fair was instead to inform prospective students so that they could make a well-grounded schooling choice. Alpha principals knew about the promotional role of fairs from others settings that were characterized by market competition. Principals could thereby hope to raise awareness of the features of their respective schools and, hopefully, begin to see themselves as actors. Over time, this fair grew into a platform where competitive relationships between schools were expressed in very tangible ways. The large conference centre, filled with students, school representatives, and carefully decorated pop-up booths, made the fair a bazaar-like setting where the notion of competition appeared real and consequential. Among prospective students, the colourful candy handed out by different schools was a topic of discussion alongside vivid discussions about what grade point average (GPA) different schools could boast with among their students.

At the same time as Alpha launched its new purchaser–provider organization, vision, and fair, the establishment of privately owned upper secondary schools began in earnest, which most likely helped the production committee's efforts to inculcate a sense of competition among schools. Until 2001, all schools but one were

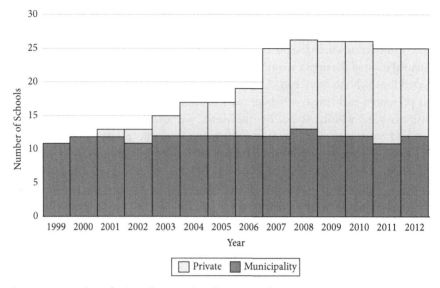

Figure 5.1 Number of privately owned and municipally owned upper secondary schools in Alpha, 1999–2012.

municipality-owned, and they were dimensioned according to demographic analyses on the expected number of future students, which limited most concerns among principals about student scarcity. As can be seen in Figure 5.1, fifteen privately owned schools were established in Alpha between 2002 and 2008, in addition to the already established twelve municipal schools. This likely increased the perception of student scarcity among the principals in the municipality.

While the number of students also increased between 2002 and 2008, the number of new upper secondary schools outstripped the increase in demand for seats. Effectively, this meant that the number of students each school could hope to attract in each cohort diminished. In the early 2000s, each school could potentially attract about 200 students from the new cohort (assuming that schools shared equally); in 2012, this number was down to about 100 students. We show the development of this ratio in Figure 5.2.

This inflow of new privately owned schools that drew on public resources would only create scarcity for municipal schools if students chose to attend a private alternative. As can be seen in Figure 5.3, between 2000 and 2012, the students that chose privately owned schools increased from less than 1 per cent to almost 30 per cent. Further analysis shows that the privately owned schools grew in a relatively even way; the 30 per cent market share of these schools is thus not the result of a few successful entrants.

While all principals faced the possibility of losing students to another school ever since the competition reform was launched in 1992, the entry of privately owned schools significantly changed the meaning of Alpha's school choice system. Prior to

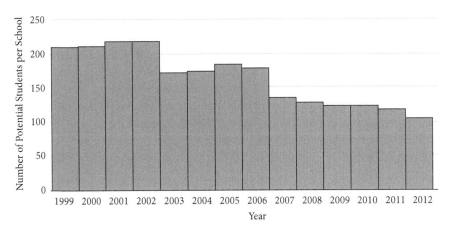

Figure 5.2 Number of potential students per upper secondary school in Alpha, 1999–2012.

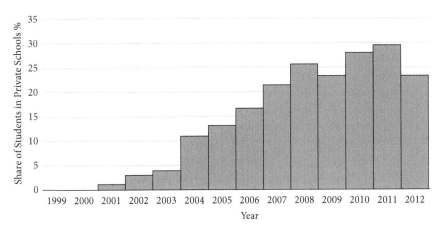

Figure 5.3 Percentage of students choosing privately owned upper secondary schools in Alpha, 1999–2012.

the expansion of privately owned schools, student scarcity was not necessarily palpable for principals. Although some upper secondary schools were able to attract larger contracts from the purchaser unit than did other schools, municipal officials evened out the resulting student number disparities in two ways: active levelling of school attractiveness and post-choice redistribution of resources. From interviews with officials, we know that their aim was to provide as equal schooling as possible throughout Alpha. Schools that lost attractiveness were therefore compensated by the educational board with the allocation of popular educational programmes, such as sports-profiled programmes, with the hope that this would raise the schools' attractiveness. Evening out disparities across schools also made economic sense for Alpha's production committee as each school carried a fixed cost in the medium term because of its infrastructure and personnel, and a school that did not fill its capacity would be unnecessarily costly. Moreover, the committee also re-shuffled resources on the basis of annual targets that dictated what schools should deliver. Schools that excelled received higher targets, whereas those that ailed received lower targets.

With the expansion of privately owned schools, the ability of the production committee to even out disparities among municipally owned schools was drastically reduced. When privately owned schools attracted close to one-third of all students in Alpha, a third of the resources was beyond the control of municipal officials; this directly curtailed the redistribution of resources. The possibility of improving the attractiveness of a particular school by allocating educational programmes was also undermined as privately owned schools could offer similar and competing programmes, and this would thereby reduce the relative attractiveness of the programme allocated to an ailing school. The convergence of these changes transformed competition into a tangible phenomenon for principals, who now faced a non-negligible number of privately owned upper secondary schools that attracted a significant share of the students. Many of the principals we interviewed spoke about this marking a turning point that heightened their sense of student scarcity and, thereby, competition. After this point, privately owned schools would be regarded as competitors to be reckoned with.

This rapid expansion was not necessarily unexpected for municipal officials in Alpha. In other, larger municipalities where privately owned schools entered in the mid-1990s, these schools had attracted up to half of the local students. It was not until 2008 that privately owned schools attracted more than 20 per cent of Alpha's students, but the production committee had already launched some pre-emptive initiatives in 2005 to increase the attractiveness of the municipally owned schools. One important initiative was the establishment of an 'elite' school that would spearhead the municipality's educational offerings and keep attracting high-performing students. Although the establishment of this school was meant as a strategic countermove against the anticipated rise of privately owned schools, it also encouraged municipally owned schools to look at one another as potential competitors—particularly when Alpha's old, top-status schools experienced difficulties in recruiting students with the highest GPA.

The establishment of a new municipally owned school soon provoked managerial issues within the production committee. On the one hand, municipally owned schools were asked to compete against all upper secondary schools—both private and municipal. On the other hand, they were also obliged to support municipal expansion initiatives. The elite school's principal struggled to gain acceptance among other principals who did not want another competitor in a school sector whose density was increasing at a fast pace. The establishment of this new school rearranged the relationships among municipally owned schools because those upper secondary schools that already targeted high-performing students now had to identify other student segments and develop new educational programmes. It was thus not only the private alternatives that could be competitors, but also other municipally owned schools.

In 2008, after the Conservatives, Liberals, and Christian Democrats won a majority in the municipal council, Alpha officials took further steps that would relate the elements of competition closer to one another by changing the allocation of students to allow for student choice of both programme and school, as well as deciding entry to popular schools by student ninth-grade GPA. While this did not affect student scarcity per se, it enabled actorhood among schools in relation to student flows, and each school would now be more closely tied to its fate in terms of its attractiveness to students. To further enhance school actorhood in relation to being attractive to students, schools were allowed to differentiate themselves on the basis of educational programmes with special 'profiles'. That is, a school could take any of the seventeen national programmes from 1994 and 'profile' it by adding special features. For instance, by offering additional classes in German, schools could launch a 'profiled' natural science programme with emphasis on the German language, or by providing additional classes in media analysis, schools could offer a social science programme with a media profile.

Another step to introduce competition following the change in the political majority was an experiment in 2009 where municipally owned schools could operate as autonomous schools in relation to the production committee. This meant that they operated outside the municipal resource redistribution system. It was highly appreciated by some of the participating schools, but the experiment ended after only a few years in 2012, allegedly because the autonomy that these schools enjoyed made it difficult for officials to maintain an equal level of schooling quality across Alpha.

At this time the expansion of privately owned schools had reached a plateau. In order to adjust the total schooling capacity of Alpha, the municipality had closed down two of its schools. In addition, there was a forecasted negative demographic shift—that is, fewer upper secondary students were projected to enter the system in the upcoming period. As our informants told us, most principals by now experienced their situation as one of competition—mainly constructed between private and municipal schools but also among municipally owned schools. This shift seems to have been brought about by concerted efforts from municipal officials to construct and configure the four constitutive elements of competition in ways that would shape a perception of competition for students and resources, combined with an increase in privately owned schools and a reduction in the number of students.

A piecemeal introduction of competition

In this chapter, we studied the efforts at introducing competition into a societal sector where competition was not common before. We used a national competition reform and its implementation in a municipality to trace a two-decade-long process by which the municipality, acting as a fourth party, constructed the four constitutive elements of competition—*actors*, their *relationships*, and the *scarcity* of and *desire* for something—in a stepwise and hesitant and fragmented manner.

Throughout the first post-reform decade, the constitutive elements of competition were constructed in a piecemeal manner. Our informants suggest that most school principals did not see their situation as one of competition for students. Although the elements of competition existed in a generic sense—that is, in many respects, schools were already legitimate *actors* that had *relationships* with one another, circling around students that had always been *desirable*, and, in some cases, even *scarce*—these were not related to one another in ways that formed the basis for constructing the situation as competitive. While students could choose educational programmes, the programmes offered by each school were planned by the education board, which meant that schools were not really actors in the sense of being able to influence student choice. Thus, schools did not need to take each other's expected actions into consideration when planning their own courses, nor did they have too many other parameters to plan either. Student choice did not affect the flow of resources to individual schools directly because of the redistributive system that was in place within Alpha. This was a period of student choice that was generally not perceived as inter-school competition.

In the second decade after the reform, following a change in Alpha's political leadership, school principals increasingly began to construct their situation as competitive. There were several reasons for this, including a change in the student allocation system, an expansion of privately owned schools that undermined the municipal resource redistribution system, and a conscious effort by a new production committee to re-cast itself as a business-like organization. Altogether, these developments seems to have constructed competition as a palpable phenomenon for principals in Alpha. The relationship between school principals changed, and one of our informants likened the regular meeting of municipal principals to a poker game where they all held their cards close to their chest. Promotion of the individual school was seen as more important than the collective development, and the practice of advertising towards prospective students became more common than before. Other studies show that, at this time, the role of teachers was expanded to also include marketing of the school (cf. Lundström and Parding 2011).

Our chapter contributes with three insights that advance our understanding of competition. First, competition does not necessarily result just because it forms part of a national or a local policy. Earlier studies of the introduction of competition have worked from the assumption that there is a single (often implicit) organizer, such as a state or some other form of government, that wants competition to occur (see, for example, Dobbin and Dowd 1997). In our context the national government and the municipality were both, in a sense, fourth parties, but at different levels. In the translation between the national and municipal levels, there was room for policy slippage, in the sense that Alpha organized its upper secondary schools through a system of student choice, although very few of the principals who were supposed to compete thought of the resulting situation as competition.

Furthermore, our findings inform large-scale evaluation studies that seek to examine the effects of competition reforms in various sectors (for instance, Bloom et al. 2015; Propper et al. 2004). In the case of Sweden, several national-level evaluations have sought to establish the effect of competition among schools on student achievement. These evaluations have shown unexpectedly weak results, which has been interpreted as implying that the presence or absence of competition only marginally affects student achievement (cf. Böhlmark and Lindahl 2012; Hinnerich and Vlachos 2017; Söderström and Uusitalo 2010). Our findings suggest that an explanation for these weak effects may be the research designs, where a situation is labelled as 'competitive' if there is more than one school present in a particular geographical area. As is evident from our study, such designs can mask significant variation in how school principals construct their situation. Those research designs would have classified Alpha as a municipality where there was 'competition' already from 1992, whereas most principals did not think of themselves as competing until around 2008. In terms of the discussion on asymmetries in the construction of competition (see Chapters 2 and 4), our findings suggest an asymmetry between what school principals understand as competition, on the one hand, and what school researchers understand as competition, on the other hand. Raising awareness about, and considering the implications of, this potential asymmetry could aid future research.

The second insight is that the introduction of competition requires extensive and sustained efforts on behalf of the organizer of competition. The national government created legal room for competition among schools by introducing a voucher system and relaxing the proximity principle, and by allowing privately owned schools to enter the municipally funded schooling system. At the municipal level, several decisions were made on how students were allocated to schools, the relative remuneration to schools in relation to their attractiveness, the role of officials with respect to the educational programmes offered by schools, and the degree of autonomy that schools would be able to enjoy. Furthermore, a new school was founded, two schools were closed, and an annual student fair was created. We have not detailed the various marketing schemes that were organized by Alpha's officials with the purpose of shaping a common identity for the municipally owned schools; however, principals suggested that their responsibility for arranging open houses and similar publicity events increased markedly during the second period of our study. An implication of this is that the construction of a situation as competition does not occur lightly or without cost. Changing a context and constructing it as competitive requires, in some cases, extensive resources. Evaluations of the effects of introducing competition need to consider not only the effects once competition is 'up and running', but also the effects of the organizing required in order to introduce it in the first place.

A third insight is that competition and choice do not necessarily go hand-in-hand. In societal debates about whether or not competition should be introduced, it is often implied that competition is a prerequisite for choice. Our study shows otherwise. In this respect, the development of actual possibilities for student choice alongside the construction of competition in Alpha is interesting. When we looked at the number of students that were granted access to their first choice, the trend was quite clear. By the year 2000, when Alpha operated on the principle that students would get their choice but school principals did not see themselves as enmeshed in competition, almost 95 per cent of the students were granted their first choice. In 2012, when principals sensed that they were involved in competition for students, the share of students who received their first choice was around 85 per cent. In the twelve years in between, about fifteen new schools were founded, and the number of applying students per school dropped from over two hundred to about a hundred. Hence, there can be choice without competition, and competition does not always lead to increased choice.

Rounding off, we note that, in relation to the model in Chapter 1, our study only covers two of the three actor types that can meaningfully construct competition. In this chapter, we have focused on Alpha as an organizer and upper secondary schools as competitors, but we have ignored parents and their children, who, as the third actor, are supposed to adjudicate between competing schools. From previous studies on school choice (Ball 1993; Hsieh and Urquiola 2006; Östh et al. 2013), it is well known that the will and capability to be a 'consumer' of education varies significantly throughout society. Some 'consumers' are eager and active, while others pay little attention to their role as a third actor. Moreover, these studies suggest that the construction of the self as a third actor may be closely related to socio-economic status. There are many important and intriguing questions that remain open for further research on the construction of competition in educational systems and elsewhere.

References

Ball, S. J. 1993. 'Education markets, choice and social class: the market as a class strategy in the UK and the USA'. *British Journal of Sociology of Education* 14 (1): 3–19.

Bet. 1992/93: UBU17, 1994. *Valfrihet i skolan*. Stockholm: Sveriges Riksdag.

Björklund, A., Clark, M. A., Edin, P.-E., and Fredriksson, P. 2005. *The Market Comes to Education in Sweden: An Evaluation of Sweden's Surprising School Reforms*. New York: Russell Sage Foundation.

Blomgren, M. 2003. 'Ordering a profession: Swedish nurses encounter new public management reforms'. *Financial Accountability & Management* 19 (1): 45–71.

Bloom, N., Propper, C., Seiler, S., and Van Reenen, J. 2015. 'The impact of competition on management quality: evidence from public hospitals'. *Review of Economic Studies* 82 (2): 457–89.

Böhlmark, A. and Lindahl, M. 2012. 'Independent schools and long-run educational outcomes: evidence from Sweden's large scale voucher reform'. Working Paper, IFAU-Institute for Evaluation of Labour Market and Education Policy.

Brunsson, N. and Sahlin-Andersson, K. 2000. 'Constructing organizations: the example of public sector reform'. *Organization Studies* 21 (4): 721–46.

Dennis, K. G. 1975. *Competition in the History of Economic Thought*. Oxford: University of Oxford.

Djelic, M. L. 2006. 'Marketization: from intellectual agenda to global policy-making'. In *Transnational Governance: Institutional Dynamics of Regulation*, edited by M. L. Djelic and K. Sahlin-Andersson. Cambridge: Cambridge University Press: 53–73.

Dobbin, F. R. and Dowd, T. J. 1997. 'How policy shapes competition: early railroad foundings in Massachusetts'. *Administrative Science Quarterly* 42 (3): 501–29.

Hinnerich, B. T. and Vlachos, J. 2017. 'The impact of upper-secondary voucher school attendance on student achievement. Swedish evidence using external and internal evaluations'. *Labour Economics* 47 (C): 1–14.

Holmlund, H., Häggblom, J., Lindahl, E., Martinson, S., Sjögren, A., Vikman, U., and Öckert, B. 2014. *Decentralisering, skolval och fristående skolor: resultat och likvärdighet i svensk skola*. Uppsala: Institutet för arbetsmarknads-och utbildningspolitisk utvärdering (IFAU)).

Hood, C. 1991. 'A public management for all seasons?' *Public Administration* 69 (1): 3–19.

Hood, C. 1995. 'The "New Public Management" in the 1980s: variations on a theme'. *Accounting, Organizations and Society* 20 (2–3): 93–109.

Hood, C. and Dixon, R. 2015. *A Government that Worked Better and Cost Less? Evaluating Three Decades of Reform and Change in UK Central Government*. Oxford: Oxford University Press.

Hsieh, C.-T. and Urquiola, M. 2006. 'The effects of generalized school choice on achievement and stratification: evidence from Chile's voucher program'. *Journal of Public Economics* 90 (8): 1477–503.

Kjaer, P. F. 2015. 'Context construction through competition: the prerogative of public power, intermediary institutions, and the expansion of statehood through competition'. *Distinktion: Journal of Social Theory* 16 (2): 146–66.

Le Grand, J. 2009. *The Other Invisible Hand: Delivering Public Services through Choice and Competition*. Princeton: Princeton University Press.

Lpf 1994. *1994 års läroplan för de frivilliga skolformerna*. Stockholm: Regeringskansliet. Available at: https://gupea.ub.gu.se/bitstream/2077/30768/1/gupea_2077_30768_1.pdf (accessed 2 September 2020).

Lundström, U. and Parding, K. 2011. 'Lärares upplevelser av friskolereformen-effekter av marknadiseringen av den svenska gymnasieskolan'. *Arbetsmarknad & Arbetsliv* 17 (4): 59–77.

McNulty, P. J. 1968. 'Economic theory and the meaning of competition'. *Quarterly Journal of Economics* 82 (4): 639–56.

Östh, J., Andersson, E., and Malmberg, B. 2013. 'School choice and increasing performance difference: a counterfactual approach'. *Urban Studies* 50 (2): 407–25.

Pollitt, C., Talbot, C., Caulfield, J., and Smullen, A. 2004. *Agencies: How Governments Do Things through Semi-autonomous Organizations*. Basingstoke: Palgrave Macmillan.

Prop. 1992/93: 230, 1992. *Valfrihet i skolan*. Stockholm: Sveriges Riksdag.

Propper, C., Burgess, S., and Green, K. 2004. 'Does competition between hospitals improve the quality of care? Hospital death rates and the NHS internal market'. *Journal of Public Economics* 88 (7): 1247–72.

Rskr. 1992/93: 406, 1993. *Valfrihet i skolan*. Stockholm: Sveriges Riksdag.

SFS 1991: 900. *Kommunallag*. Stockholm: Sveriges Riksdag.

Söderström, M. and Uusitalo, R. 2010. 'School choice and segregation: evidence from an admission reform'. *Scandinavian Journal of Economics* 112 (1): 55–76.

Vickers, J. 1995. 'Concepts of competition'. *Oxford Economic Papers* 47 (1): 1–23.

Werron, T. 2015. 'Why do we believe in competition? A historical-sociological view of competition as an institutionalized modern imaginary'. *Distinktion: Journal of Social Theory* 16 (2): 186–210.

6
Constructing competition for status: sports and higher education

Nils Brunsson and Linda Wedlin

Over the past few decades many people have argued for various benefits of competition and have promoted the introduction of competition in new areas, such as higher education, schooling, health care, correctional treatment, and employment services. It is sometimes clear that competition is desired but less clear what good should be the target of the competition: what people or organizations in these areas should be competing for.

Competition can concern almost any type of good: money, attention, status, and affection constitute some examples. In order to act as a competitor, it is crucial to know what good one is competing for. The same is true for observers trying to understand competition and its behavioural consequences. In the literature on competition, it is often stated that competition is for 'resources'. But such a general term hides large variation, and we believe that greater precision is necessary. Different goods vary in how often, when, and how they are scarce and desired and in who can acquire them. All these factors are in turn dependent on the way goods are allocated among people in society. Money in a market context, for instance, is allocated differently than are prizes for excellent achievements, creating different conditions for constructing competition in these areas.

Furthermore, if we take the concept of resource seriously, we can define it as a good that is desired, because it is a means for acquiring another desirable good. Arguably, money is almost always seen as a resource (at least normatively), whereas attention or love from others may sometimes be perceived as desirable in itself and not merely a resource for acquiring something else. The extent to which a good is seen as a resource influences the level of competition for it. On the one hand, desire for a good is likely to be more intense if it not only has a value in itself but is also seen as resource for acquiring another desirable good. On the other hand, desire for a resource that has no value in itself can easily evaporate if it can be replaced by another resource that more effectively leads to the attainment of the valuable good. When goods are perceived as resources, they easily connect to other goods, and competition for one good may become intertwined with competition for another. The intertwining of competitions for two different goods should not lead us to

Nils Brunsson and Linda Wedlin, *Constructing competition for status: sports and higher education* In: *Competition: What It Is and Why It Happens*. Edited by: Stefan Arora-Jonsson, Nils Brunsson, Raimund Hasse, and Katarina Lagerström, Oxford University Press. © Nils Brunsson and Linda Wedlin 2021. DOI: 10.1093/oso/9780192898012.003.0006 confuse the competitions with each other, however; rather it makes it essential to distinguish between them analytically.

In this chapter, we are interested in competition for status and how that type of competition can be constructed. We investigate the case of an organized allocation of status in the form of prizes, ratings, rankings, and the like, and we analyse the effects of that allocation on competition among organizations. We argue that there is no automatic link between organized status allocation and competition. Rather it is useful to think of organized status allocation as providing more or less convincing arguments in a discussion among proponents and sceptics of the idea that an organization is or should be involved in status competition. We illustrate our arguments with examples from sports and higher education.

We begin with a discussion of special features of status as an object for competition. In the next section, we address the organization of status allocation and its relationship to competition, using contemporary sports as our primary illustration. In the third section, we use the example of European higher education in order to illustrate processes in which status competition is constructed with the help of an organized status order. And we conclude with a discussion on strategies that competitors for status can use and the risks that status competition imply for organizations.

Status and status competition

In the early days of social science, status referred to the roles and values connected to social classes, professions, or other groups within which different levels of privilege and different access to valuable goods existed (Ulver-Sneistrup 2012). The concept of status was commonly connected to such concepts as respect, prestige, and honour (Goode 1978). Status was seen as a relative phenomenon: groups vary in their status, and one can speak of a status order in which each group experiences a different degree of status, ranging from virtually none to extremely high (Mills 1963; Weber 1970). Under modern conditions, however, striving for status can become an individual project. People strive for higher status, and such strivings can be found almost anywhere (Simmel 1957). Individuals can move among professions and groups with varying levels of status and can also influence their status within these professions and groups.

Status can also be attributed to organizations. Firms are compared, and some are thought to have 'best practices', implying better practices than those of other firms. States are divided into categories, ranging from well-functioning to 'failed'. Some universities are considered more prestigious than others. Some types of organizations appear to have higher status than others; firms in the IT industry, for instance, currently seem to enjoy higher status than do firms in the foundry industry. Public-sector organizations have sometimes enjoyed higher status than have organizations in the private sector, but the opposite has been true during other periods (Czarniawska 1989).

Status is basically a social concept that is attributed by an audience that can determine what is high and low status, and a status seeker must consider the values of that audience (Garfinkel 1964). This real or imagined audience (Werron 2015) influences the attributes that confer status or that are assumed by the status seeker to confer status. There may be considerable uncertainty. Which attributes will give status is often difficult to know beforehand. And there are no ownership rights connected to status: status seekers have little control over their status; having been allocated high status once is no guarantee of maintaining it. Although there can be considerable inertia in changing status, stability is not a given.

Actorhood, relationships, scarcity, and desire

Competition for status appears only if there is a combination of actorhood, relationships, scarcity, and desire. Actorhood is not a given. Status can be allocated to collectives that are not actors. A group of scholars such as all the world's physicists may enjoy high status, but they do not constitute an actor that is able to compete. The same is true for neighbourhoods or regions with high status. Similarly, there were no individual actors in a pre-modern system of fixed status order among social classes, because it was almost impossible to change one's status by moving to a higher social class.

People do not compare themselves to just anyone; they are selective. If they do not relate to others who have the potential of gaining high status, there is little room for competition.

Status is not necessarily perceived as scarce. Rather, a status seeker may find an affluence of status, meaning that many people or organizations, including the status seeker itself, can enjoy high status at the same time. Driving an expensive car may give status in some circles, and many people can afford such cars. Breakthroughs within research in physics may give all scholars in that field higher status. Newcomers to a high-status profession are likely to acquire the same status as existing members of that profession without reducing the status of the existing members. A failed state that turns into a functioning one does not take away the high status of other well-functioning states.

Nor is the desire for status a given. People may strive for things other than status. And it may be difficult to argue that status should be a key goal for an organization; profits and the effective achievement of the primary task are more immediately legitimate goals in most organizations.

Competition for status

But sometimes actorhood, relationships, scarcity, and desire combine, creating a situation in which competition for status becomes possible. Modern individuals are constructed as actors (Chapter 4, this volume). But actorhood may also be created: groups of individuals, such as physicists, can join forces, creating a professional organization, for instance, just as groups of organizations can form a trade association or other forms of meta-organization with the purpose of defending their common interests, partly in relation to other meta-organizations.

Expanding one's relationships to others with high status favours competition. Even if one organization has a stable high-status position in the national context, global status comparisons may widen its range of relevant others and open for a new competition.

Status is likely to become scarce when people think in terms of fine-grained status orders with exclusive positions in a continuous scale of status. Then only one person or organization can be Number 1, and few can belong to the top 10 per cent. In such situations, one may begin to think of status not only in terms of 'successful and failed states' but as more finely graded degrees of success, so that non-failed states can also differ in status. Similarly, people with insight in the field of physics may be able to define, say, the ten most successful scholars in the field and even differentiate among them.

Although people tend not to admit their desire for status (Mason 1981), it is likely to be a common desire. Reaching and maintaining high status can be values and goals in themselves—in fact, an implicit or explicit argument in much of the scientific literature on status (Ulver-Sneistrup 2012). But people may also see status as a resource for achieving something else. On a personal level, for example, high status in society at large may increase a person's chances in a competition for affection. Or status can be perceived as a resource for obtaining money. In consumer markets with relatively few producers, the producers tend to be perceived by customers as having different degrees of status, and the producer with the highest status enjoys some advantages, such as the ability to charge a higher price (Podolny 1993). Status becomes more attractive if more money is a likely side effect.

The reverse is also true. Not only can status provide money, but money can also provide status, which early thinkers like Marx and Weber presumed. This is a common theme in the status literature from Veblen (1899/1994) onwards. By demonstrating one's affluence, by engaging in 'conspicuous consumption' (Veblen 1899/1994) for instance, one can increase one's status, at least among certain audiences. Competitions for status and money then become intertwined.

The organization of status allocation and its implications for competition

Status may arise and disappear in emergent processes that lie outside the control of any specific person. The allocation of status can also be *organized* (Chapter 4, this volume), being the result of decisions, not by thousands of individual decisions by thousands of people in the audience but by some specific organizers who make and communicate decisions for others. It is organized status allocation that interests us in this chapter. As an illustration we use public sports, which is perhaps the most evident example of a strong and successful organization of status allocation. Organization is used to determine which person or team should be considered the best in a certain region, in a country, or in the whole world.

Most public sports have organizations at the local, national, and international levels in a complex pattern where local organizations belong to national meta-organizations and these national organizations belong to what can be called international meta-meta-organizations (cf. Ahrne and Brunsson 2008). All these organizations allocate status by making decisions on membership, rules, monitoring, sanctions, and hierarchy (cf. Ahrne and Brunsson 2011). They arrange contests; set rules for the contests; decide who can participate in them; monitor achievements; register and keep track of contestants, results, scores, and achievements; compile tables that compare contestants across time and space and rank them according to the quality of their achievements; and distribute prizes. The organized status order is clear and easily accessible to others. There are sports—boxing and wrestling, for instance—in which organizations compete for the right to organize contests legitimately, but in most cases sports organizations have a monopoly in organizing status allocation.

Contemporary sports represent a highly successful case of an organized status allocation that creates actual status. The organized status allocation has become virtually the only route to status. It is extremely difficult to obtain status in a more traditional way. It does not help to interact every day with the leading athletes; it is only list ranking or medals that count for status in sports (cf. Jensen 2006; Sharkey 2014). And it is rare for anyone to claim that someone who ranked in eighteenth place is the champion. The organization of sports has failed to determine global status order clearly only in the few cases in which there is more than one world organization arranging contests (which may be interpreted as an unclear hierarchy).

Status allocation is organized in sports in a way that helps to construct and sustain competition. The essence of contests and sport tables is scarcity: the position of winner in an individual contest is scarce, as are the positions in the tables. There is also much work being conducted on who can be an actor in contests. Individual athletes are divided into classes according to gender or past achievements—classes that make it more likely that they see each other as serious competitors able to win the scarce positions. Collective actors in the form of teams are actively constructed in order to be competitive, and sometimes the organizers have rules for constructing teams that are supposed to be relatively evenly matched, as are the teams in North American ice hockey.

Elite sports have piqued the interest of millions of people, resulting in an audience that is knowledgeable about the organized status order and, in many sports, contributing large amounts of money. Until the 1960s, status was seen as the key motivation for participation. The possibility of using one's status as a resource for earning money was forbidden. This notion changed upon the abolishment of the so-called amateur rules, and successful athletes can now win large sums of money. And they can earn even more, based on their sport achievements, through sponsor contracts. The money involved is likely to increase both the number of people willing to participate in sports and their desire for high-ranking table positions once they do participate.

Because of the enormous (and highly astonishing) salience of sports in contemporary society, this way of organizing a status order is well known to almost everyone. Status allocation is organized in similar ways in other fields as well, although normally not to the same extent as in sports. There is an increasing number of prizes distributed across diverse sectors of society for scientific achievements, artistic activities, beer production, and entrepreneurship, for example (Edlund et al. 2019). There are ranking tables for almost any aspect of public life: which companies are best known for their social responsibility, which states have the lowest unemployment rate, and which municipalities have the best schools (Werron 2015). And contests are sometimes arranged even in such fields as music or inventions. Membership in prestigious organizations, such as various forms of academies or exclusive meta-organizations, is another way of organizing status order.

But not all efforts to organize status allocation are as successful as they are in sports. The efforts may not be convincing: the connection between organization in the form of rankings or prizes and actual status is often weaker than it is in sports.

Furthermore, there is no guarantee that status organization in contexts other than sports produces or stimulates competition in the same way. Nor may they be intended to. Prizes may be designed in such a way that many actors can receive them once they have reached a certain level of achievement; one does not have to relate to other possible prize winners just because one wants a prize. Positions on tables may not be scarce, as exemplified by credit rating: one organization attaining an AAA+ rating does not exclude others from achieving the same designation. Membership, even in prestigious organizations, may be open to anyone in the appropriate category—organizations that organize professionals in high-status jobs, for example. The desire for prizes, table positions, or membership may be low because people are sceptical about their connection to status and they have few other positive effects. Or actorhood may be lacking: a ranking table of the most beautiful region in a country does not produce competition because there is no actor that can change the beauty and thereby change the position. The Ibrahim Prize for Achievement in African Leadership, intended for state leaders, has been awarded only twice so far because of lack of acceptable candidates.

Arguing for competition

Within the context of formal organizations, the relationship between the organization of status allocation and competition becomes even more complex. As long as competition has not become institutionalized, organization members are likely to have different propensities to perceive a situation as competitive and to be more or less willing to do so. Some members may argue for the view that the organization is competing, whereas others are not convinced or may even argue for the opposite view. And there is no guarantee that people agree on what good should be the target for the competition, who are or should be the competing actors, whether the good is scarce, or whether it is desirable.

An organized status allocation does not automatically create competition among organizations. People who see a situation as competitive must therefore convince other organization members to agree with their view—not least the organization's managers but perhaps other key external parties as well—by directing their attention to the organized status order and convincing them that it is relevant.

The key question is when, how, and why the organization of status allocation stimulates status competition. Historical studies can demonstrate how organized status allocation and competition was created and became institutionalized in such areas as sports (Ljunggren 2020). It is also promising to study fields in which the idea of competition is newer, more controversial, or part of reforms—deliberate attempts at introducing competition in new areas. European higher education offers a case in point. Whereas the basic organization of most sports was established more than a century ago, the organization of status allocation in European higher education is a more recent phenomenon. Discourse in this sector has contained more and more references to competition; in fact, the idea of competition was even part of an extensive reform to transform the field of Swedish higher education. Yet, it is far from clear who shall compete and what good they should compete for.

Also in this sector, reformers or others aspiring to create competition must find or construct actors, relationships, scarcity, and desire for a good of their choice, and they must try to convince others that these factors exist and should be considered important. They can be helped by various forms of organized status allocation, as we explain in the next section.

Constructing status competition in higher education

For almost two decades, contemporary global policy debates about higher education have been rife with competition discourse and references. An expansion of higher education, specifically, a focus on 'competitive' higher education systems, is now considered one of the 'core elements of successful participation in global progress' among nations (Ramirez and Meyer 2013: 257). In the national context of Sweden, the idea of competition among universities entered the debate with the higher education reform of 1993, in which one of the primary arguments was that '[a]dvanced knowledge development […] requires freedom, independence and competition' (Prop. 1992/93: 1, 9). In a 2011 reform that made Swedish universities more 'autonomous' from state legislation, the associated documents are laden with competition discourse. The argument is that this development would make universities more prone to respond to 'market forces' and to take part in international competition.

'State universities and university colleges need to be autonomous in order to meet the new challenges and the increasing demands for both collaboration and competition [in the global playing field]' (Prop. 2009/10: 149, 16).

This competition rhetoric is echoed in the university strategy and policy documents of Swedish universities that we have studied, as the following example illustrates:

A starting point for our strategy work is that all of the university's activities are increasingly subject to competition, and significant effort has been invested to increase the awareness of this [...]. The goal is to ensure that the culture inherent in the university reflects this awareness of the increasing significance of competition and the partly changing conditions [of higher education].

(Strategic Plan for Linköping University 2012: 4–5)

Competition is described here as being necessary. And it seems already to be there: it is claimed that the goal of the strategy work is to 'increase awareness' of competition in the organization.

The rhetoric fosters a generalized notion of international or global competition among universities and the need for creating and enhancing competitiveness and devising competition strategies. Universities are clearly the entities that are supposed to be competing, but it is unclear for which good they should be competing – there are few, if any, details provided: what desired and scarce good is at stake?

One could argue that the global competition among universities is about students, faculty, and research funding—significant goods for these organizations. We suspect, however, that university competition is more about status. We view status as the relevant good for three reasons: the global perspective, long-standing status issues, and the increasing visibility of status allocation.

Although the competition rhetoric is all about *global* competition among universities, the allocations of students, faculty, and resources are largely national, at least in Swedish universities. Although Swedish universities are allowed to charge tuition to the relatively few students originating outside the EU/EES area, the vast majority of students and faculty come from Sweden, and almost all the money involved comes through the Swedish government, directly through block grants or indirectly through research councils and other state funding bodies (see Engwall and Weaire 2008). It is difficult to argue that global competition for Swedish universities can concern these goods, except in an extremely limited way. Status, however, is a good that can be imagined to have global scope.

Status concerns and status struggles are common and long-standing in higher education and science (Hammarfelt et al. 2017). In many national contexts there are firmly established status orders among universities, with Ivy League universities at the top in the USA and Oxbridge in the UK. The Swedish context has had two divisions that reflect status differences and struggles: the division between the 'old' and the 'new' universities and the division between universities and university colleges. But the competition rhetoric implies new relationships: universities are expected to relate not only to their national peers but to all universities on the globe.

There is a third reason that status is easily constructed as the good in university competition: it is easy to imagine status to be salient because the allocation of status among universities is increasingly *organized* on a global scale and is highly visible. If people at a contemporary university would like to increase the status of their university globally, this organized status allocation comes in handy; they meet an organized world where they can try to connect to various organized elements for status allocation, and some of them are designed in a way that fosters competition. Although there are no prizes for universities as there are for participants in sports, there are other forms of organization that can be used for constructing competition: a university can seek the positive sanction of certification, it can seek to become a member of prestigious meta-organizations, and it can use the monitoring performed by ranking organizations.

We now move to a description of the organization of status allocation in the sector and a discussion of how that organization can help construct competition by not only providing a basis for global relationships but also providing scarcity, reinforced actorhood, and a desire for status. How can the organization of status help someone inside or outside universities who wants to argue that there is or should be competition?

Constructing scarcity

University status is not necessarily perceived as scarce. Status can be perceived as high for many universities and can simultaneously increase for many. If individual universities try to increase their status, it may have no effect on other universities or may even increase the status of all universities rather than reduce the status of others. Some forms of organized status allocation may be used to support the construction of scarcity, however.

University *certifications*—often called 'accreditations' in the field of higher education[1]—have become abundant. A certification is given based on the monitoring of the university's compliance with a set of rules. The certification is used as a sign of quality, and it is often broadcast in public communications from the certified university. It is a form of positive sanction, whereas the not-uncommon refusal to award certification is a clear negative sanction. When this type of certification was introduced, a certification was seen as creating scarcity of status; it was expected that only the best universities would be certified. But there was nothing inherent in the instrument that produced scarcity, and as more and more universities have become certified, the value of this certification as a status marker has decreased. Because it has become clear over time that any university able to comply with the rules can be certified, certifications no longer help to create scarcity and are no longer a useful form of status allocation for those who want to argue that universities should compete.

---

[1] Here we use the more established term, 'certification', which is the accepted term for this type of activity in other fields, in which 'accreditation' roughly means certification of certifiers (cf. Gustafsson and Tamm Hallström 2019).

But some forms of status allocation in higher education do still provide scarcity. Scarcity is constructed in one of two ways: by *restricting membership*, as with prestigious meta-organizations to which universities can apply, and by monitoring universities, comparing them, and presenting the comparisons in the form of continuous orderings in *ranking tables* in which only a few universities can have top positions.

Membership in prestigious meta-organizations is common among universities, and many meta-organizations have restricted membership. Uppsala University, for example, is proud to announce on its webpage that it is a member of both COIMBRA and MATARIKI, two international meta-organizations. COIMBRA is described as 'an association of long-established European multidisciplinary universities of high international standard' with forty members. MATARIKI is a global organization for old universities with high status within their countries. LERU (League of European Universities) is another example: it was founded 2002 and now has twenty-one of Europe's 'leading' research universities as its members. Membership can be obtained by invitation only, and one of the criteria is 'peer-recognised academic excellence'. Lund University is a member of Universitas 21, a global twenty-seven-member meta-organization with the aim to create a network of leading global universities.

By strictly limiting membership, these meta-organizations try to increase status for themselves and their members. They build on an old mechanism for status: gaining status by creating the perception of being connected to other high-status entities (Sharkey 2014). The meta-organizations recruit their members based on status, with such expressions as 'leading within its country'. Membership is not based on function or role; membership is useful primarily for publicity purposes. Members can exploit the status and position of other members, while excluding others from enjoying the same opportunity. Similar meta-organizations exist for more specialized areas, such as management schools. One example is CEMS, which allows only one business school per country into its membership, and this school is selected based upon one criterion: that it has the highest status within its own country (Ahrne and Brunsson 2008).

Another form of status organization developed over the past two decades is the ranking tables of universities, which basically perform a monitoring system for universities. The number of ranking tables has increased; they have recently received greater attention and are including more universities. The development of the international rankings for European business schools, for instance, was driven largely by the desire to create scarcity. Rankings provided them with elite and distinctive status as 'leading business schools' (Wedlin 2006), thereby offering a distinguishing tool alongside the established forms of certifications—one that could supposedly help to define status position as a scarce good. Today, the two status allocation systems interact because certification is a sorting mechanism for ranking: only certified European business schools are ranked by the most prestigious rankers in the field.

Since the early 2000s, ranking tables have proliferated, particularly those that rank universities worldwide. Among the most-cited global ranking systems are the Times Higher Education Supplement; the QS Top Universities ranking; and the Academic Ranking of World Universities, produced by Shanghai Ranking Consultancy, and also known as the Shanghai Ranking. These rankings each employ different measures and systems to assess and compare universities and their offerings, and they focus on different aspects of education, research, and other features. The rankings create an order among a small, elite of existing universities—the 'leading' universities. Most of them rank between 100 and 500 universities out of a total of some 26,000 universities worldwide. Most of the ranked universities are European, North American, and, to a lesser extent, Asian. There are also regional or national rankings as well as rankings for specific fields or educational programmes. Business school rankings are among the most prominent, featured in such international business magazines as *Financial Times*, *Business Week*, and other media outlets.

Many university rankings are created with the official purpose of providing information to potential students in the process of choosing a university for their studies. But rankings can also contribute to the construction of competition. A ranking by its very nature defines status as something scarce: only one entity can have the highest position and the other positions may also be scarce (Brancovic et al. 2018). Rankings directly and indirectly determine who is an appropriate actor—directly by including some and excluding other universities from being ranked (by ranking the top hundred for instance) and indirectly by restricting the ranked into those that fit the model that the ranking represents. This restriction gives higher status to those being ranked compared to all others. Many rankings resemble contests; they are repeated annually, and the results vary over time.

In conclusion, some forms of organized status allocation in higher education are useful for constructing competition by making status scarce. These forms also offer concrete operationalization of the notion of status, and thereby facilitate the decision on what exactly one should compete for when competing for status—namely membership positions and ranking table positions. People who want to argue that universities are or should be competing for status can thus point to these positions. Scarcity is a necessary but not a sufficient argument for competition, however. Those arguing for competition must also convince others that there are actors capable of competing.

Constructing actorhood

In the policy discourse referenced here, higher education is often reduced to the concept of *university*; it is universities that expand and reflect all the positive aspects of higher education. Changes in professional activities are expected to happen through universities, which are perceived as organizations capable of following global models of organization and management (Frølich et al. 2019). In this discourse, universities are treated as a type of actor that brings competition to the field of higher education (Ramirez and Meyer 2013: 270).

It is not a given, however, that universities are actors able to compete. A modern conception—or even definition—of organizations is that they are actors and autonomous, coordinated units able to produce coordinated actions affecting their environments (Meyer and Jepperson 2000). But it is far from clear that traditional European universities constitute organizations in this sense. Their internal organization has traditionally been weak. They cover heterogeneous activities with little central control and seldom represent a meaningful category in terms of coherence and unitary organization. Rather, universities have been described as arenas for professional activities consisting of many disconnected and uncoordinated units and people; the key role of its management is not to control activities but to provide administrative service to other units (Brunsson and Sahlin-Andersson 2000; Hasse and Krücken 2013). It is harder to imagine that such units, compared to centralized industrial firms or sports teams, could be competitors with the ability to affect their status positions. Scholars, managers, and outside observers may doubt that their own or any other university can do something about their status positions. If quality of scholarship is a criterion for status enhancement, scholars may believe that they can try to do something as individuals, but that does not mean that the university as a whole can do anything.

Arguing for university actorhood has become easier, however. More and more societal entities are constructed as organizations; examples include state administrative units and 'professional arenas', such as schools, hospitals, and universities (Brunsson and Sahlin-Andersson 2000). In fact, the policy documents we have studied seem to take the actorhood of universities for granted. In the Swedish higher education reform of 1993, one of the primary arguments was that '[a]dvanced knowledge development [...] requires freedom, independence and competition' (Ds 1992:1: 3). This argument formed a starting point for a continuing and escalating discourse on the need for freedom and responsibility of *university organizations*, culminating, one might suspect, in the 2011 reform that made Swedish universities more 'autonomous' from state legislation and allowing them to participate in international competition.

Similar developments have been noted in other European contexts (Seeber et al. 2015). Reformers tend to give universities greater autonomy, and their administrations are to a greater extent seen as if they were serving a management function, controlling the organization, and being responsible for its results (Krücken and Meier 2006). As illustrated in our last long quotation in this section, our investigation of Swedish universities shows that they are even performing strategic planning exercises. Such changes make it easier to convince people that universities are actors with the ability to compete.

Constructing desire

Desire is a necessary prerequisite for competition, but in higher education it seems to be more complicated to argue for desire than it is to argue for scarcity or actorhood. Desire for a ranking position or membership in a meta-organization is not a given—particularly a desire that is strong enough to lead to complicated or expensive actions. Personal desire is not enough in an organizational setting; even top managers must argue for why a certain position is desirable for their organization. Why would an 'autonomous' university pay attention to, let alone participate in, exclusive meta-organizations or rankings created by journalists or others, and what arguments could convince people that they should?

In the field of sports, the argument of status is highly legitimate. For universities, the situation is not as simple. A desire for status is far from self-evident and must be explained—both by scholars and by practitioners who demonstrate this desire. The task of universities has traditionally been considered as providing a place for academic professionals to produce high-quality research and teaching, and it is not obvious how that task would give rise to the goal of reaching the status of a meta-organization member or a position in a university ranking. And we can, in fact, assume that many researchers and teachers have no significant interest in their universities becoming meta-organization members or being highly ranked—at least if it involves a significant cost in money, time, or energy.

Those who want to emphasize the salience of table and membership positions must therefore argue for their cause and should probably use arguments that are more closely connected to the main purpose of university activities. One way of linking these positions to more legitimate purposes is to construct them as resources. The argument can be that positions provide status, but that status is important only because high status is a resource for achieving such higher and non-controversial ends as recruiting the right personnel, attracting the right students, and obtaining more money. This was how European business school managers argued for their engagement in and attention to the proliferating global rankings of the early 2000s (Wedlin 2006). The rankings came to be seen as defining the 'international business school market', and participating in these rankings was considered a means of recruiting students, faculty, and financial resources to what was argued to be an increasingly global and competitive market.

Like all organization, the organization of status invites challenges (Ahrne and Brunsson 2011), and challenges may reduce desire and create problems for those who want to construct competition. It is possible to argue that decisions about rankings or membership are unfair and do not really reflect the qualities that show one university to be better or worse than others. In fact, the existence of several ranking tables and meta-organizations with different memberships provides a clear indication that decisions are not necessarily 'right' (cf. Sauder and Espeland 2006). What can be questioned is the relationship between decisions about these positions and what a relevant audience considers high status. They may not believe in the idea that a highly ranked university that is a member of a certain meta-organization is actually better than other universities. People with such views are difficult to mobilize in the quest to construct competition.

Furthermore, organized status orders may be challenged by other options to allocate status. Even for university managers who are interested in the status of their universities, there may be other ways of gaining status—by demonstrating its excellence in research or teaching or its past achievements and historical legacy. They could even argue—as managers of leading business schools have done—that positions in meta-organizations and ranking tables are valuable only for universities with lower status that want to challenge the current status orders (Wedlin 2006).

Finally, status organizers in higher education have long had to imagine much of their audience. It was uncertain who and how many know of or care about the organized status positions of universities. And even if they did, their interest may have no practical implications, because most people do not interact with or have a relationship with universities as a whole—but rather with certain disciplines, education programmes, scientific communities, or specific professionals, which can all vary widely in quality or in other relevant respects.

But over time, a real audience may emerge. There are recent signs that at least rankings have begun to influence the perceptions and actions of students and other stakeholders. Some students use rankings to shortlist their applications to universities. Other groups, such as graduate student recruiters, sometimes use rankings to make their recruitment decisions. Governments, governmental boards, sponsors, alumni, and other groups increasingly use rankings to influence their relationship with universities, primarily in terms of decisions about investments, funding, or support (Hazelkorn 2014).

The signs that 'others care' is, in fact, a common argument among university managers for the salience of organized status and for its function as a resource for other ends. Many university managers have now responded in a way that reveals beliefs both in global status competition and in the organized allocation of status. For instance, university managers seek certifications, create and participate in meta-organizations, devise strategies, spend money, and employ 'ranking personnel' in order to participate in global rankings and improve their ranking (Hazelkorn 2007; Wedlin 2006).

Competition strategies and the risks of competing for status

We have used the field of higher education to illustrate the complexities of constructing a status competition, even in cases in which there are organized forms for status allocation. An organized status allocation is far from a guarantee that people will think of a situation as competitive. Nor is it obvious that those who do perceive competition would be able to convince others to share their views. There is no automatic link between the organization of a status allocation and the construction of competition. And even if a researcher or other observer believed that all elements of competition were present in a field, it is far from certain that other people would believe the same. If we are to understand the successful or non-successful construction of competition in various fields, we have to consider all these complexities.

Once people see their organization as competing for status, they may react in different ways. What types of behaviour are generated by a competition for status and what are the possible positive or negative outcomes of that behaviour? We end this chapter by analysing some possible strategies for status competitors and some of the risks that they run.

Strategies for status competitors

People who seek to increase the status of their organizations can use various strategies, alone or in combination: 1) improving their organization in salient criteria, 2) influencing perceptions of which group their organization belongs to, 3) influencing the status of their group, or 4) influencing the audience to change the criteria for status.

At one level, perhaps the most obvious one, competitors can seek to influence their status within the group to which they are seen as belonging by *improving on the salient criteria* for status in that group. A business school may improve its status relative to all business schools in the world by improving its education or by cooperating with other high-status schools or high-status firms. When status is scarce, an individual or organization increases its status at the cost of others, which may be accomplished by convincing audiences of its own merits or by convincing them of the faults of other organizations (Douglas and Isherwood 1979). If everyone strives for higher status when status is scarce, the relative status of the passive actor deteriorates over time—a factor that may mobilize even the unwilling. A constant race for status may arise, allowing no one to ever rest.

A second strategy is to *influence the perceptions of others about which group the organization belongs to*. A business school may be able to obtain higher status if it is seen as belonging to the global category of universities or if it is compared with educational organizations only within its own country. If another category has higher status, to be merely counted in that category increases status. Or if there is competition for status within that group, there may be a chance of a higher ranking there than in the former group.

A third strategy is to try to *influence the status of the group to which the organization belongs*; if business schools in general are awarded higher status than other educational organizations are, the status of one's own school increases: increasing the status of the group becomes the way of increasing status for oneself. But again, there is no guarantee that one can avoid competition. For instance, a meta-organization for business schools that tries to increase the status for their members can meet competition from meta-organizations for other types of universities.

A status seeker can also use a fourth strategy: trying to influence the criteria that audiences use to allocate status—to have the criteria changed to *attributes on which the status seeker can receive a high score*. Like all decided orders, a status order that is based on organization opens itself up for criticisms and challenges: it can be argued that the criteria are not the correct ones and new criteria can be suggested.

A competing organization may even, alone or with others, introduce its own ranking or rating systems, new meta-organizations, or new prizes that fit its own profile. Yet, success is far from guaranteed. Competition is likely at this level as well: a newcomer in the business of organizing status will probably meet competition from the established organizers in gaining attention and acceptance of audiences for this new way of organizing status allocation.

Risks of status competition

Competition for status among organizations and the strategies used for handling it may provide opportunities, but it may also involve risks. We now point to four of these risks: 1) status competition can decrease status, 2) organizations are turned into actors, 3) organizations can lose their autonomy, and 4) status may come at the expense of other values.

The strategies used to increase status may, in fact, be counterproductive. Status competition may actually reduce the status of a group of organizations. Individual organizations may concentrate on seeking status by the first strategy rather than by the second and third. An organization may too easily accept the decision by the status organizers that it belongs to a category, thereby neglecting the opportunity to increase its status by trying to be seen as belonging to another category or by trying to increase the status of their old or new category as a whole. A strong focus on competition among organizations within a certain category runs the risk of reducing the status of the entire group. Although there are winners, there are also losers, demonstrating that a category is diverse, and membership in it is no guarantee of quality or whatever measure is being used. Intense status competition among universities can therefore create a lower status for universities in general.

The assumption that organizations have status and that they can compete implies a threat to organizational structure. Competition implies that organizations are perceived as actors. For firms competing in a market context and for sport teams, this is a standard construction. But for other entities with little resemblance even to the standard idea of formal organization, that assumption implies a fundamental change. Universities and other professional arenas provide cases in point. One aspect of organizational actorhood is the need for a clear hierarchy, normally in the form of strong and responsible management that can create status for the organization by adapting it to relevant criteria for status. The risk is that internal structure and power relations become adapted to the task for status competition and not to other, more fundamental tasks. Even when a high degree of decentralization has proved successful for these fundamental tasks, competition for status may lead to centralization. Universities constitute perhaps the clearest case in point. Furthermore, this change may easily stabilize or reinforce status competition, because status competition provides a lasting argument for top management to justify its role and interventions.

In competing for status according to an organized status order, *organizations may lose another part of their actorhood—their autonomy*. They easily become victims to other organizations that organize status allocation. Instead of following their own route, they may start adapting their activities to the key criteria of success used by others. For instance, many university rankings place strong emphasis on research production that may, ironically, imply that rankings intended to help students in their choice of university may lead universities to prioritize research over teaching. In addition, the loss of autonomy reduces the money that can be spent on both research and teaching, because personnel and money have to be allocated to attempts at improving the possibility that the university will obtain high rankings or become and remain members in the right meta-organizations or adapt to certification rules.

Whether this loss of autonomy is good or bad can be discussed, and the evaluation should differ for different organizations and situations. Lack of autonomy can be seen as a sobering reminder that the construction of organizational actorhood is unrealistic, but for some organizations the claim for autonomy is nevertheless a salient part of their identity. Auditing and certifying organizations, courts, and universities constitute examples of organizations that refer to autonomy, integrity, and independence as their key values (Gustafsson and Tamm Hallström 2019). Their legitimacy can be eroded by joining a competition and investing in an attempt to obtain high values on criteria for status allocation formulated by other organizations.

This problem can be handled, although not fully solved, by the affected organizations taking some control of the status allocation, normally by joining forces in meta-organizations that make those decisions. As described previously, in most sports, international meta-meta-organizations consisting of national sport meta-organizations have taken complete control over such criteria. And in most cases, these meta-meta-organizations have a monopoly on these decisions. Similar attempts have been made in the case of universities, but much of the status allocation is still performed by other organizations, such as newspapers and magazines. There is an irony in the fact that many universities make a point of being independent from state authority but are willing to be dependent on journalists.

Fourth, there is a risk that *status competition comes at the expense of other more fundamental values and purposes* of organizations—that the situation in other fields comes to resemble the situation in contemporary sports, in which competition is the essence. Can that happen to European higher education? One can only speculate about the long-term development. In contrast to the situation within contemporary sports, the organization of status allocation and competition are far from institutionalized in the field of European higher education. But the present situation may be an early phase of a process, the result of which may be that most people take for granted that there is global status competition among universities. Hopefully, it will not lead to anything like the obsession with competition that is characteristic of sport. Competition in sports is salient for creating its special form of entertainment. But we hope that entertainment does not become a key purpose of higher education.

References

Ahrne, G. and Brunsson, N. 2008. *Meta-organizations*. Cheltenham: Edward Elgar.

Ahrne, G. and Brunsson, N. 2011. 'Organization outside organizations: the significance of partial organization'. *Organization* 18 (1): 83–104.

Brancovic, J. Ringel, L., and Werron, T. 2018. 'How rankings produce competition: the case of global university rankings'. *Zeitschrift für Soziologie* 47 (4): 270–88.

Brunsson, N. and Sahlin-Andersson, K. 2000. 'Constructing organizations. the example of public sector reform'. *Organization Studies* 21 (4): 721–46.

Czarniawska, B. 1989. 'The wonderland of public sector reform'. *Organization Studies* 10: 531–48.

Douglas, M. and Isherwood, B. 1979. *The World of Goods*. New York: Routledge.

Ds 1992:1. "Fria Universitet och Högskolor" (Independent Universities and University Colleges"). Swedish Government: Sveriges Riksdag, Utbildningsdepartementet.

Edlund, P., Pallas, J., and Wedlin, L. 2019. 'Prizes and the organization of status'. In *Organization outside Organizations: The Abundance of Partial Organization in Social Life*, edited by G. Ahrne and N. Brunsson. Cambridge: Cambridge University Press: 62–83.

Engwall, L. and Weaire, D. 2008. *The University in the Market*. London: Portland Press.

Frølich, N., Christensen, T., and Stensaker, B. 2019. 'Strengthening the strategic capacity of public universities: the role of internal governance models'. *Public Policy and Administration* 34 (4): 475–93.

Garfinkel, H. 1964. 'Studies of the routine grounds of everyday activities'. *Social Problems* 11 (3): 225–50.

Goode, W. J. 1978. *The Celebration of Heroes: Prestige as a Social Control System*. Berkeley: University of California Press.

Gustafsson, I. and Tamm Hallström, K. 2019. 'Organizing for independence'. In *Organization outside Organizations: The Abundance of Partial Organization in Social Life*, edited by G. Ahrne and N. Brunsson. Cambridge: Cambridge University Press: 155–76.

Hammarfelt, B., de Rijcke, S., and Wouters, P. 2017. 'From eminent men to excellent universities: University rankings as calculative devices'. *Minerva* 55: 391–411.

Hasse, R. and Krücken, G. 2013. 'Competition and actorhood: a further expansion of the neo-institutional agenda'. *Sociologia Internationalis* 51 (2): 181–205.

Hazelkorn, E. 2007. 'The impact of league tables and ranking systems on higher education decision making'. *Higher Education Management and Policy* 19: 87–110.

Hazelkorn, E. 2014. 'Reflections on a decade of global rankings: what we've learned and outstanding issues'. *European Journal of Education* 49 (1): 12–28.

Jensen, M. 2006. 'Should we stay or should we go? Accountability, status anxiety, and client defections'. *Administrative Science Quarterly* 51 (1): 97–128.

Krücken, G. and Meier, F. 2006. 'Turning the university into an organizational actor'. In *Globalization and Organization: World Society and Organizational Change*, edited by G. S. Drori, J. W. Meyer, and H. Hwang. Oxford: Oxford University Press: 241–57.

Ljunggren, J. 2020. *Den Svenska Idrottens Historia*. Stockholm: Natur & Kultur.

Mason, R. 1981. *Conspicuous Consumption: A Study of Exceptional Consumer Behaviour.* Farnborough: Gower.

Mills, C. W. 1963. 'The sociology of stratification'. In *Power, Politics, and People*, edited by C. W. Mills. New York: Oxford University Press: 305–23.

Meyer, J. W. and Jepperson, R. L. 2000. 'The "actors" of modern society: the cultural construction of social agency'. *Sociological Theory* 18 (1): 100–20.

Podolny, J. M. 1993. 'A status-based model of market competition'. *American Journal of Sociology* 98 (4): 829–72.

Prop. 1992/93: 1. 'Om universitet och högskolor: frihet för kvalitet'. Regeringens proposition 1992/93:1 (About universities and university colleges: freedom for quality).

Prop. 2009/10: 149. 'En akademi i tiden: ökad frihet för universitet och högskolor'. Regeringens proposition 2009/10:149 (An academy of our time: increased freedom for universities and university colleges).

Ramirez, F. O. and Meyer, J. W. 2013. 'Universalizing the university in a world society'. In *Institutionalization of World-Class in Global Competition*, edited by J.C. Shin and B. Kehm. New York: Springer: 257–73.

Sauder, M. and Espeland, W. N. 2006. 'Strength in number? The advantages of multiple rankings'. *Indiana Law Journal* 81 (1): 205.

Seeber, M., Lepori, B., Montauti, M., Enders, J., de Boer, H., Weyer, E., and Reale, E. 2015. 'European universities as complete organizations? Understanding identity, hierarchy and rationality in public organizations'. *Public Management Review* 17 (10): 1444–74.

Sharkey, A. 2014. 'Categories and organizational status: the role of industry status in the response to organizational deviance'. *American Journal of Sociology* 119 (5): 1380–433.

Simmel, G. 1957. 'Fashion'. *American Journal of Sociology* 62 (6): 541–58.

Strategic Plan for Linköping University 2012. 'Forsknings- och innovationsstrategi för Linköpings Universitet 2013–2016' (Research and innovation strategy, Linköping University). Linköping University.

Ulver-Sneistrup, S. 2012. *Status*. Malmö: Liber.

Veblen, T. 1899/1994. *The Theory of the Leisure Class*. New York: Dover Thrift Editions.

Weber, M. 1970. 'Class, status, party'. In *From Max Weber: Essays in Sociology*, edited by H. H. Gerth and C. W. Mills. New York: Oxford University Press: 180–95.

Wedlin, L. 2006. *Ranking Business Schools: Forming Fields, Identities and Boundaries in International Management Education*. Cheltenham: Edward Elgar.

Werron, T. 2015. 'Why do we believe in competition? A historical-sociological view of competition as an institutionalized modern imaginary'. *Distinktion: Journal of Social Theory* 16 (2): 186–210.

7
Avoiding competition: the effects of rankings in the food waste field

Nadine Arnold

Our society is permeated by a strong belief in the positive effects of competition (Arora-Jonsson et al. 2020; Hartmann and Kjaer 2015; Werron 2015).* Based on this belief, ranks are introduced in many fields to induce competition by means of organization (see Chapter 4, this volume). Ranks compare and evaluate quality and performance in a hierarchical manner (Busch 2011)—classically, ranging from good to bad. The rankers, who aim to stimulate competition, thereby expect that the 'exposure of poor performers will lead to a general raising of standards' (Smith 1993, as cited in Dorn 2019: 329). For example, corruption ranks should encourage competition between nation states so that their performances will improve towards a 'very clean' rating (Warren and Laufer 2009), while environmental ranks should induce competition for the most ecological products (Bullock 2017). Indeed, social scientists confirm that ranks are pivotal drivers for the rise in competitive relations (Brankovic et al. 2018; deRijcke et al. 2015; Kornberger and Carter 2010). But although scientists themselves are great believers in competition (deRijcke et al. 2015), the link between hierarchical ranks and the induction of competition has yet to be critically examined.

The aim of this chapter is to shed light on the ways in which ranks encourage the formation of competitive relations within societal fields. To do so, I use the theorization of competition proposed by Arora-Jonsson et al. (2020), as it is particularly well suited to interrogating and problematizing the establishment of competition. Scholars of organization argue that competition refers to the 'construction of a relationship among actors that centres on something scarce and desired' (Arora-Jonsson et al. 2020: 2). In line with this theory, and cross-fertilizing it with insights from the literature on ranks, status, and fields, I will argue that ranks render status scarcity visible and thereby manifest status hierarchies among the actors operating in a particular field. My central argument is that the status hierarchies manifested by these ranks are not equivalent to competitive relationships because that would require that all the actors involved desire the status-laden positions at

* This work was supported by the Lucerne research committee [grant number 19-013].

Nadine Arnold, *Avoiding competition: the effects of rankings in the food waste field* In: *Competition: What It Is and Why It Happens.* Edited by: Stefan Arora-Jonsson, Nils Brunsson, Raimund Hasse, and Katarina Lagerström, Oxford University Press.

the top of the hierarchy. Against this background, I consider whether all those being ranked do in fact desire these high-status positions and why this may or may not be the case.

Guided by these questions, I examine the role of the food waste hierarchy in establishing competitive relationships in the field of food waste. This ranking arranges the food waste performances of actors in a hierarchical order, creating new populations of varying status. I use qualitative data to study how the member organizations of both the 'winning' and 'losing' populations respond to their ranks. The data reveal that organizations from both populations reflect on whether they truly desire the status-laden position and wish to compete for it; however, they each draw different conclusions. While the winners actively fuel the establishment of competition, along with the rankers, the losers show no interest in the status competition and divert their attention to other fields. This study thus reports on an empirical case where competition fails to take hold throughout a field, further deepening our understanding that competition is not a 'natural given' (Arora-Jonsson et al. 2020; Kornberger and Carter 2010). Instead, it supports the concept that ranks do not necessarily trigger a desire to achieve the highest, status-laden positions—as those doing the ranking intend and social scientists often assume. Ranks only trigger desire when the actors believe they can achieve a high-ranking position and that attaining such a position will benefit them. If these opportunities are not seen, they accept their position with indifference and turn instead to those competitions that promise better prospects.

The first section clarifies what ranks are and details why we can consider them as drivers for status competition. The second section presents the empirical study, focusing firstly on the discrete ranking being considered and secondly on the responses of the organizations in the winning and losing populations. Based on the empirical findings, I summarize in the third section that actors are always involved in the induction of competition across multiple fields and conclude with a brief discussion of the implications of this multiplicity.

Ranks as potential drivers of competition in fields

I build on the proposition of Arora-Jonsson et al. (2020) that competition depends on four constituent elements: actors, relationships, desire, and scarcity. Therefore, in this section, I disentangle the link between ranks and competition with regard to each of these elements. Firstly, I define ranks and explain that they encounter *actors* and *relationships* in a particular field; I then focus on the link between ranks and *scarcity*, highlighting the good that is rendered scarce by the ranks; thirdly, I problematize *desire*. The section ends by summarizing the function of ranks as potential drivers for competition.

Ranks in fields

With a focus on quality and performance, ranks arrange social actors and inanimate entities into a hierarchical order that is either continuous or discrete (Busch 2011). *Continuous ranks* attribute an individual value, usually numerical, to each entity being ranked. Social scientists show great interest in the study of continuous ranks that place organizations, individuals, or even cities and nation states into a simple list of positions, which is then called a 'ranking'. The best-examined rankings are probably those in the field of higher education, such as the rankings of business schools (Wedlin 2011) and law schools (Sauder and Espeland 2009). *Discrete ranks*, on the other hand, place those being ranked into groups, thus establishing new populations (Kette 2018). In everyday life, we refer to these types of rank as 'ratings' and/or 'grades'. For example, grades rank the quality of different types of food (e.g. the size of an egg as S, M, L, or XL) while ratings rank the performance of companies (e.g. credit risk from AAA down to D). Hence, discrete ranks tend to make use of letters (or symbols, such as the famous stars in the ranks of gastronomy and the hotel industry) to label the populations, which together form a hierarchy with a limited number of positions. In contrast, continuous ranks rely upon numerical measures that afford the establishment of a more detailed and potentially unlimited list of positions.

According to Foucault (1984: 234), ranks perform two functions. Firstly, they mark the 'distance' between the parties being ranked. For example, the 'distance' between the performance of a company ranked by a rating agency as AAA (top position) and AA+ (second-highest position) is smaller than the 'distance' between a company ranked as AAA and D (lowest position). Secondly, ranks reinforce positions through rewards and punishments, thereby creating order. Typically, a high position offers rewards, as it functions as a positive endorsement (e.g. companies rated highly are perceived as extremely capable of meeting financial commitments). In contrast, a low position is a reprimand, and must be considered as a punishment (e.g. low-graded eggs command low prices and retailers might decide not to sell them). Yet, low positions do not necessarily connote punishment or stigma. For example, an individual with a low rank in the military has the opportunity to demonstrate progress, in order to advance to a higher rank (Busch 2011). Furthermore, we must consider that high positions are also used as a means of punishment—as when, for example, the air quality in a series of countries is ranked and the most polluted country occupies the top position. Independently of the way in which ranks punish and reward, however, they always evaluate and compare the entities being ranked (Busch 2011; Kette 2018).

Influenced by these characteristics, ranks appear in various fields, from medicine and education to tourism, sport, and cuisine. In each field, the ranks encounter two fundamental elements of competition: relations and actors. They do so directly or indirectly. If the ranks assign positions to actors (e.g. business school rankings, company ratings), they impact the actors and their relations directly. If the ranks focus on inanimate entities (e.g. grades of eggs, movie ratings), they affect the actors and their relations indirectly because there are usually actors behind the entities—for example behind the graded eggs are producers and behind the ranked movies are directors and writers. Whether they are evaluated directly or indirectly, all these actors may be depressed or delighted by the ranks they receive. Yet, the combination of a rank with a web of relations among actors is not sufficient in itself to establish competition. To do that, scarcity and desire are needed too.

Ranks and (status) scarcity

Ranks are often instrumental in portraying status as a desirable scarcity. Status involves esteem, admiration, and deference that is given to or achieved by an actor (Boudon and Bourricaud 1992). This means that status is a relational concept and that an actor cannot achieve status on its own. Status can result from networks because it depends on the perceived quality and performance of others (Podolny 1993). Organizations derive status by demonstrating quality, connecting with high-status actors, and belonging to status-laden social categories (Sharkey 2014). The resulting perceptions of quality and performance are rendered visible by the ranks, which also shape these perceptions in turn. For example, if a rank gives a company's creditworthiness the lowest rating (D), this position can be viewed as a reflection of low esteem. At the same time, the firm's lowly D rating can also shape future perceptions of it, as stigmatizing positions can enforce negative perceptions (Warren and Laufer 2009). However, the status manifested by particular ranks may be regarded either positively or negatively, as ranks display and influence all types of status perceptions.

Like rank, status has hierarchizing effects. With a focus on markets, Podolny (1993) argued that status processes result in a hierarchization, by which market players obtain different positions of status that can be used to make inferences about the quality of their goods and services. Yet status is also relevant beyond market fields, as the study of organizational status generally implies the analysis of social hierarchies between organizations (Sauder et al. 2012). Due to the hierarchizing nature of status, ranks inevitably portray it as a positive scarcity, for which the members of a particular field can strive.

The scarcity of status will be emphasized to varying degrees, depending on the type of rank. In the case of continuous ranks, the scarcity of status is strongly accentuated because only one actor can occupy the top spot. For example, even though the 'distance' between the evaluated competitiveness of Singapore (score 84.8/100) and the USA (83.7/100) is small, according to the competitiveness ranking of the World Economic Forum, Singapore is still awarded the most status (Schwab 2018). Conversely, in the case of discrete ranks, status manifests as being less scarce because these ranks confer status on populations rather than singular entities. This means that many individual entities can achieve the best, highest-status position—as in the case of company credit ratings, for example, where many enterprises can occupy the top tier (Kette 2018). Some discrete ranks even ensure that almost every actor attains the highest grade. This occurred in the case of an environmental rank for cars, which gave most cars the best grade, despite the fact that they did not meet the climate targets (Zehnder 2020).

Various actors can operate as rankers, including regulators, policymakers, donators, scientists, rating agencies, and certifiers. Rankers can play a mediating role between those who are being evaluated and those who consult the information provided by the ranks. Significantly for this study, research has shown that intermediaries redefine status hierarchies in societal fields (Sauder 2006; Sauder et al. 2012). This means that the intermediaries, who are not themselves the subject of the ranks, form hierarchies through the establishment of certain ranks. Intermediaries have attracted intense attention in particular markets, where they mediate between the organization and the valuation of the exchange of goods and services, without selling or buying them (Ahrne et al. 2015; Arnold and Hasse 2016). However, intermediaries also operate in other fields, such as education or health, and often operate in more than one field (Fligstein and McAdam 2012).

When examining the scarcity of status manifested by ranks, we must remember that status is shaped by institutional patterns. To capture these patterns, literature suggests the concept of *field frames*. These frames, by definition, impart meaning to a field and define what activities and beliefs are more appropriate than others within a field (Lounsbury et al. 2003). The notion of frames originates from Goffman (1986), who argued that frames are culturally determined definitions of reality that enable individuals to make sense of situations, events, and objects. To examine frames at field level, we must capture the agreed-on values that shape perceptions of what constitutes high or low status (Sauder et al. 2012). For example, Lounsbury et al. (2003) showed how recycling organizations, which had previously been marginalized, steadily gained more status than waste-to-energy organizations due to shifts in field frames. Importantly, status depends on whether certain types of performance and quality are perceived as appropriate and expedient. Consequently, status-laden positions are given to those organizations that demonstrate the most appropriate (and not necessarily efficient or effective) qualities and performances with regard to the dominant field frame.

Ranks and desire for status-laden positions

In terms of the rankers, we can observe that some create ranks with the aim of inducing a trend, in order that the actors being evaluated and compared will desire the top positions and start competing for them. These intentions of stimulating competition have led Arora-Jonsson et al. (2020) to conceptualize the rankers as organizers of competition. The intention to trigger a desire for status-laden positions makes most sense in the context of environmental ranks. Bullock (2017) explains that rankers have developed a wide range of ranks that reward those actors who demonstrate environmentally friendly practices and punish those deemed to be causing harm to the environment. In so doing, the rankers aim to encourage an upward shift towards better treatment of the environment. For example, the global footprint measurement of humans and companies, which is a continuous rank, aims to stimulate the desire—and, with it, the competition—for the smallest footprint. Discrete ranks in this area also aim to motivate actors to produce and buy the most environmentally friendly products. One example is the EU energy label, which grades the electricity consumption of white goods and other products from A to G, along with a colour coding (from green to red), inducing competition among both producers and consumers for the 'best' white goods.

Interestingly, the desire for status-laden positions anticipated by rank creators is also assumed by social scientists. In this vein, Werron (2015) argues that today's modern forms of competition no longer centre around financial and material resources but focus on immaterial 'audience goods', such as status. He claims that status-laden positions are, nowadays, worth striving for. With regard to organizations, we can assume that they strive for status because status gains are associated with advantages; they can reduce costs while simultaneously increasing revenues and access to survival-enhancing opportunities and assets (Sauder et al. 2012). Indeed, studies have shown that organizations are eager to ensure high positions and benefit from the associated status gains because they are apparently willing to manipulate the ranks in their own favour (Luca and Zervas 2016; Sauder and Espeland 2009). Anchored in these considerations, social scientists assume, in the same way as the rankers, that actors desire and fight for high-status positions manifested by ranks. In this view, a ranking is conceptualized as an 'engine that produces social situations of competition' (Brankovic et al. 2018: 276) or 'the battleground on which [actors] compete with each other' (Kornberger and Carter 2010: 326).

Taking inspiration from Berger and Luckmann, we can summarize that actors' desire for status-laden positions reflected in ranks is reified in public and scientific discourse. This means that the desire takes the form of 'a strange facticity, an *opus alienum* over which [one] has no control' (Berger and Luckmann 1991: 106). Yet, we should bear in mind that, in practice, actors may have no real desire for the status-laden top positions. This may be because they regard achieving a higher position as irrelevant, because the higher positions are beyond their reach, or because they do not see any opportunity to improve their own position. In these cases, competitive relations do not develop, as actors must show a desire for the status-laden positions, and shifts between the actors must be initiated to create competition (Arora-Jonsson et al. 2020; Simmel 1895). Consequently, we must consider ranks as *potential* drivers of competition.

The food waste hierarchy and how the winners and losers respond to it

The literature differentiates between surplus (food produced beyond our nutritional needs) and food waste (the product of food surplus), the latter being further subdivided into avoidable and unavoidable food waste (Papargyropoulou et al. 2014). As this chapter is interested in the organizational relations formed around the issue and less interested in the issue itself, I use a broad understanding of food waste that refers to all edible material that is discarded, lost, degraded throughout the chain, or fed to animals and eliminated as a by-product of food processing.

Food waste is a proliferating issue, and we know that such burning issues can initiate the formation of fields (Hoffman 1999). Due to food waste activism, shifts in policy and regulations, and the global food and environment crises, organizations have increasingly engaged in addressing this issue (Evans et al. 2012). On an international level, attention was focused on food waste when the United Nations' (UN) Food and Agriculture Organization (FAO) estimated that a third of the food produced globally every year for human consumption—approximately 1.3 billion tons—is lost or wasted. In 2015, the urgent need to tackle the food waste issue was cemented when the UN dedicated one of its sustainable development goals (SDG) to food waste: 'By 2030, halve per capita global food waste at the retail and consumer levels and reduce food losses along production and supply chains, including post-harvest losses' (United Nations 2018). Formalized goals such as these create new meso-level orders by connecting various organizations in new ways.

Switzerland is home to a growing number of actors who share an understanding about the need to reduce food waste. This federal country is committed to the UN's SDGs while still being one of the largest producers of waste in Europe. According to Eurostat (2020), municipal waste per capita was 703 kg in Switzerland. Only Norway produces more waste, with 739 kg municipal waste per capita. Switzerland opened a field-level conversation on food waste when the Federal Office for Agriculture called for a stakeholder dialogue on the topic in 2013. This stakeholder dialogue can be considered as a major field-configuring event, as various actors have exchanged their ideas and perspectives on the issue and started to build relationships (Lampel and Meyer 2008). Specifically, the actors involved (i.e. scientists and policymakers, consumer and environmental organizations, food banks, retailers, agricultural associations, and political authorities) re-examined food-dating practices, quantified Swiss food waste, improved cooperation among food banks, and conducted the first awareness-raising campaign to bring the issue into the wider public sphere (Projektgruppe Food Waste 2015). Indeed, the topic of food waste has continuously gained momentum, such that in 2018 a politician from the Swiss green-liberal party called for more coordination among the many organizations dealing with food waste (Postulate 18.3829, 25 September 2018). To date, the tasks involved in this coordination are mainly performed by non-governmental organizations that organize public food-saving banquets throughout Switzerland, support political actions relating to food (e.g. a national 'fair food initiative' in 2019; a national 'food is politics' demonstration in 2020), develop teaching materials, and have recently launched the 'save food' campaign to raise awareness about the problems of food waste. This latest campaign is broadly supported by the government and municipalities, as well as by private organizations from various sectors (agriculture, energy and waste disposal, retail, catering). These linkages formed around the food waste issue strengthen relations within the field and simultaneously increase the field's visibility in the wider public sphere.

A discrete ranking operates in the Swiss food waste field; it is the so-called *food waste hierarchy*, which evaluates and compares the individual and collective actors' approaches to food waste. I used rich qualitative data to analyse the connection between this rank and the possible emergence of competition in the Swiss food waste field. As a first step, I worked through newspaper articles and websites and participated in several field-configuring events to identify those organizations that, together, form a relational space concerned with food waste. The resulting list totalled 106 organizations. As a second step, I conducted twenty-two semi-structured interviews with members of intermediary organizations (political parties, scientific laboratories, city administrations, umbrella organizations) and organizations that have established a clear approach to fighting food waste. These interviews provided information about the organizations' performance and how they themselves perceive it. Furthermore, they revealed field frames and status hierarchies in the field of food waste and the role of the food waste hierarchy therein. Participant observations in a range of organizational settings, detailing the effects of the varying performance in everyday life, provided additional data. As a final step, I identified the member organizations of the winning and losing populations and examined their (non-) desire for achieving the status-laden position and the reasons for this. Information from interviews and written, public statements in newspapers and press releases was useful in this respect.

The food waste hierarchy

The European Union (EU) has developed a policy that 'ranks the desirability of different waste-management approaches according to their environmental impact' (Hultman and Corvellec 2012: 2413). This discrete rank has also been applied to food waste. The result is the food waste hierarchy, which captures the approval ratings assigned to the actors' food waste performances (Papargyropoulou et al. 2014). While each organization's performance has a different value according to the food waste hierarchy, all the organizations share a need for food waste, which they depend on so they can introduce interventions to reduce it. In doing so, they do not eradicate food waste but rather reform it such that it is made reusable. The impact of such actions is unknown, because it is unclear whether these organizations actually contribute to a reduction in food waste or whether they trigger a rebound effect—namely, the negative impact of increased consumption, which can accompany the improvement and might outweigh the benefits of the interventions (Papargyropoulou et al. 2014; Sorrell and Dimitropoulos 2008). In this sense, food waste organizations are analogous to prisons, which, according to Foucault (1984), require prisoners to fight against ever-present criminality and help reform other prisoners with unknown impact. Drawing on these parallels, and because Foucault argued that prisons 'discipline' prisoners, we can, therefore, consider food waste organizations as organizations that 'discipline' food waste. The manner in which they discipline it is rewarded with a certain level of status by the food waste hierarchy.

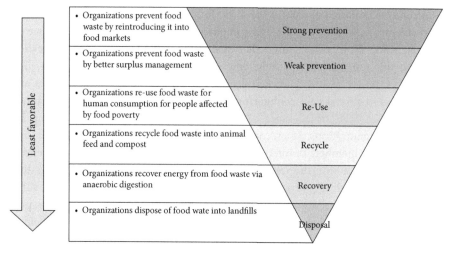

Figure 7.1 The food waste hierarchy.
(**Sources:** compiled from Mourad 2016; Papargyropoulou et al. 2014)

Just like the winners' podium at sports competitions, the food waste hierarchy embodies the fact that the top position is difficult to attain. Figure 7.1 demonstrates that the apex of the hierarchy is occupied by those organizations that engage in the prevention of food waste throughout production and consumption. According to the food waste scientist Marie Mourad (2016), this position should be divided into strong and weak prevention. *Strong prevention* generates a demand for food waste and contributes to transforming food exchange in markets by reintroducing food waste as a marketable product. Strong prevention thus sits at the very peak of the hierarchy, being held in the highest esteem by scientists and policymakers alike. *Weak prevention*, meanwhile, refers to better surplus management, which involves efficiency-driven corporate policies that target the optimization rather than the transformation of food markets. Weak prevention occupies second place. The third-best position comprises those organizations that *re-use* food waste for human consumption, such as food banks and other redistribution networks that pass surplus food to those affected by food poverty. The fourth position is awarded to organizations that *recycle* food waste into animal feed and compost. The *recovery* of energy from food waste via anaerobic digestion is ranked fifth, while *disposal* in landfill sites is positioned at the sixth and lowest level. Since no urban waste is sent to landfill sites in Switzerland, the lowest position is awarded to recovery performances. Overall, the more food waste that is 'disciplined' and reformed into marketable food for human consumption, the higher the status conferred by the food waste hierarchy.

The food waste hierarchy reflects the environmental-economic field frame that dominates the field of Swiss food waste. The environmental dimension of the frame may be observed when field actors outline the negative consequences of food waste on the environment. The slogans on the posters of the food waste association are instrumental in raising awareness of this topic, and claim that 'avoiding food waste in Switzerland would have the same effect on the climate as taking 1–2 million cars off the road' or emphasize that 'about half of the environmental impact of food waste [...] is caused by food that we throw away in households and restaurants' (Infographics, foodwaste.ch 2019). This environmental frame is layered with economic considerations, when field actors claim that food waste is senseless from an economic perspective. For example, an environmental organization calculates that the average Swiss citizen currently loses CHF 620 by wasting food (Foodsave campaign, Pusch 2020). The resulting environmental-economic frame is summarized succinctly by a politician who explained that food waste is an 'environmental and economic concern' (Interview, 30 May 2018). The frame is also put forward by other field members, such as food waste consultants, scientists, and non-governmental organizations, who claim in a leading educational brochure that food waste is an environmental sin as well as economic nonsense:

> The prevention of food losses can alleviate two problems at the same time. Firstly, we save unnecessary expenditure on products from which we get nothing. In terms of Switzerland as a whole, this amounts to several billion Swiss francs, which society could invest more sensibly than in discarded food. Secondly, we can effectively reduce environmental pollution and the waste of resources.
>
> (Brochure, *Food losses in Switzerland—Scope and options for action*, WWF, foodwaste.ch, October 2012)

In summary, the data show that the food waste hierarchy and the environmental-economic field frame support one other, conferring the highest status on those organizations that convert food waste into marketable food for human consumption. In other words, they esteem those performances that create not only environmental but also economic value. Less status is given to those organizations that pass food waste to the needy free of charge or at a symbolic price, because these food banks fail to turn waste into economic value. Even less status is accorded to organizations that transform food waste into animal feed, compost, or biogas. Their low position and status are justified by the considerations that recycling and recovery are of little economic value and also environmentally problematic because food should be consumed by people.

The responses of the winners

The best performers, who contribute to keeping food waste within consumption markets, form the newest population, having been in existence since around 2016. This population consists of seventeen organizations, all but three of which are profit-oriented. Typically, these organizations have just a handful of employees and describe themselves as start-ups that are aiming to tackle the food waste issue with their business ideas. In particular, they 'discipline' food waste by reselling it (e.g.

collecting surplus bread from bakeries and reselling it), processing new goods from it (e.g. bouillon, terrine, marmalade, snack chips made from bread, beer brewed from food waste), or developing software applications, typically mobile apps, that bring market participants together for the economic exchange of food waste. In doing so, they emphasize the economic value of food waste and do not consider it as something that can be used to fight food poverty and help the poor. This is a new vision that is being brought into the field, which is why these organizations can be regarded as challengers (Fligstein and McAdam 2012). In contrast to the expectation that challengers 'occupy less privileged niches within the field' (Fligstein and McAdam 2012: 13), we know that this population enjoys strong approval, because its member organizations conform to the economic-environmental frame and occupy the top position in the food waste hierarchy.

These challengers make an effort to secure and maintain their high position. In particular, they emphasize the 'distance' between themselves and those organizations that are ranked closest to them in the hierarchy—namely, food banks. For example, the founder of a start-up insists that the population of challengers has greater value for society than the food banks: 'It makes no sense that a growing proportion of the population eats for free because we produce too much. [...] We have to try to get what we produce into the market, so that you buy it' (Interview, 7 February 2018). Another interviewee, well positioned at a superior level of the hierarchy, is opposed to the food banks:

> I particularly like the initiatives in which the person concerned can do something. I find the food banks difficult, because they have to give [the food] to people who have little money and are in poverty, I say it now with exaggeration, it is a waste that sloshes out of the wasteful luxury society. I am just more interested in efficiency [...]. Where we don't solve other people's problems, but try to solve our own together with others.   (Interview, 12 February 2018)

A third interviewee underlines the inferior status of the food banks by emphasizing their close proximity to the population at the very bottom of the hierarchy (biogas plants; see next section). She explains that '[she does not] think that [the performance of food banks] is solving the issue. The food banks have far too much [food waste], and they give so much to the biogas plants' (Interview, 25 April 2018). The chef at a food waste restaurant explains that he does not 'want to participate in that [charitable food bank] system. That doesn't change the system' (Interview, 22 March 2018). Hence, the challengers demonstrate their desire to occupy a status-laden position in the food waste hierarchy by highlighting the 'distance' between themselves and other populations in the hierarchy—particularly food banks, which occupy the adjacent position. As the quotes show, this distancing requires great rhetorical and persuasive effort because the food banks enjoy a high degree of legitimacy by taking responsibility for others (Meyer and Jepperson 2000).

Furthermore, the challengers underpin their desire by declaring themselves the winners of the status hierarchization, who have no fear of competition. For example, the founder of a food waste restaurant states in a newspaper: 'I hope to get competition everywhere soon' (*Tages-Anzeiger*, 8 September 2017). With this quote, he invokes the idea that competition will contribute to tackling the food waste issue (the more organizations that tackle food waste, the better), while also boasting that he is ready to fight competitors. In this ostensibly competitive environment, the challengers cement their status-laden position by participating in prize competitions and displaying the prizes they have won. For example, at a public food waste event, organized by the non-government organization WWF, three organizations pitched their food waste business models (food waste catering, food waste bread chips, a food waste app) and received resounding applause from the audience (field notes, 31 January 2019). In these situations, the winning population demonstrates its desire to achieve the status-laden position. This may be observed when they list their achievements. For example, the website of one challenger reads: 'At the "Battle of SDG Ideas", [...] 12 initiatives, start-ups and companies outlined how their work contributes to the SDGs. [Our organization] was able to win the "Battle"' (Ässbar website, 30 November 2019).

For the challengers, achieving the status-laden position is important for three reasons. Firstly, the organizations that process food waste into new products operate as suppliers of food products in conventional market fields. The data show that the organizations face one particular challenge in these fields: justifying their prices. As the processing of misshapen and damaged food waste is labour-intensive, and a standardized procedure cannot be employed, food waste products cost more than conventional products. Justifying these prices is a challenge, because customers expect lower prices, assuming that entrepreneurs receive food waste free of charge. An interviewee explains that 'the customer has the feeling that when cooking with waste, it must be free of charge' (Interview, 12 February 2018). Since status distinctions can cross over and have implications for other fields (Podolny 2005: 15), the challengers can use the status achieved in the food waste field to justify the price and quality of their products in conventional food markets. For example, the producer of food waste beer highlights that approximately a quarter of all bread remains unsold after closing time and therefore explains how their comparatively expensive 'Damn Good Beer' (twenty-four 33-cl bottles cost CHF 44.00) contributes to tackling the issue (Breadbeer website, 20 February 2020). This quote illustrates how the challengers use the status gained in the food waste field to sell their products in market fields. However, we can also assume that the challengers use their status to improve their chances of survival (Sauder et al. 2012).

This brings us to the second reason, which relates to the fact that the challengers form the newest population and have entered the food waste field only recently. Consequently, their life cycle is still short. Following Stinchcombe's (1965) pioneering concept of the liability of newness, we must therefore expect that these new organizations are more likely to fail, due to their relative lack of experience and trustworthy relationships compared with the older populations that inhabit the field. In this context, the entrepreneurs could benefit from status gains to overcome this liability.

Thirdly, the challengers are usually small start-ups with few employees, as previously outlined. Like newness, smallness has also been identified as a further liability that increases the chances of failure (Aldrich and Auster 1986). As a consequence, we could suppose that challengers also desire high positions and their associated status gains to overcome their liability of smallness. Overall, the organizations of the winning populations have good reason to desire status-laden positions, as they might use them to overcome their liabilities of newness and smallness while simultaneously enhancing their survival chances in the price-sensitive food-market fields.

The responses of the losers

Biogas plants are the poor performers of the food waste hierarchy. They transform large quantities of food into energy and are mostly organized as profit-oriented businesses. Often, the biogas plants also recycle food waste into compost—a performance that achieves a better position in the food waste hierarchy. For simplification and to avoid confusion, I limit the focus to recovery performance. More than 80 per cent of the thirty biogas plants identified are organized as stock corporations. These organizations were mainly established in the 1990s and form the oldest population. In alignment with the food waste hierarchy, the intermediary parties of the food waste field (i.e. scientists, the media, and politicians) agree that biogas plants have the worst and least esteemed approach to fighting food waste. For example, a city administrator argues: 'I'd like to make it very clear. Fermentation is the last resort' (Interview, 14 November 2018). The low position of biogas plants becomes particularly evident in the context of meat, where it is considered a success if biogas plants play no part at all. An excerpt from a newspaper highlights this aspect in the context of discarded laying hens:

> It is a success story that egg producers can announce: 70 percent of the discarded laying hens—around 1.2 million hens—were processed into charcuterie products or marketed as soup hens last year. Seven years ago, this share was a low 20 percent. Instead of 80 percent as in 2010, 30 percent of the old hens currently end up in the biogas plant. [A] poultry expert says that it is important for the industry's image that more discarded chickens end up on the plate again.
> (Agricultural Information Service Nr. 3317, 31 March 2017)

This excerpt shows that the status of biogas plants in the food waste field is so low that their very *raison d'être* is called into question.

Interestingly, the biogas plants show little concern over the humble status ascribed to their performance. They accept their low position and show no ambition to climb up the hierarchy. This is exemplified by a public letter of the association of biogas plants, which was published as a response to a parliamentary initiative regarding the absurdity of the incineration of food waste (Initiative 15.418, 13 March 2015). In the letter, the biogas plants highlight that their performances are environmentally more beneficial than conventional incineration practices but admit that food waste actions should target human consumption. In doing so, the losers cede status to the other field inhabitants (food banks and challengers):

> We firmly believe that every ton of food waste that goes into incineration is one too many. First and foremost, food should be used to feed people instead of wasting it; secondly, it should be used as animal food. [...] If those uses are not possible, we must aim for a utilization that leaves the organic matter in the cycle. [That is fermentation here...] During incineration, both valuable energy in the form of biogas and digestate as fertilizer and soil improver are lost.
>
> (Public letter from Biomasse Schweiz, 14 October 2015)

This public statement demonstrates that the poor performers agree with the dominant environmental-economic frame, which anchors their positions at the very bottom of the hierarchy. From the standpoint of the biogas plants, there is consequently no possibility of improving their position. As a result, they do not have a desire to achieve a higher position. But how can this population afford to accept its low position of little status? Of course, the biogas plants benefit from being older and usually also larger than the other field inhabitants, which improves their chances of survival (Aldrich and Auster 1986; Stinchcombe 1965). Yet, the data show two more specific reasons why the biogas plants can accept the stigmatization of a low rank and do not desire to improve it.

Firstly, the biogas plants can shift their attention to additional fields that they also inhabit, beyond food waste. Specifically, they can focus on the gas-market field, where they operate as suppliers of biogas in competition with sellers of natural gas. In this market field, the biogas plants are accorded high status, as biogas is categorized as a renewable gas. The Swiss federal office concludes that the consumption of natural gas must be reduced, and the biogas plants' potential for extracting gas should be better exploited with a view to meeting climate targets (UVEK 2019). In the gas-market field, biogas plants are thus held in high esteem and are ranked as the winning population, just as the challengers are ranked as the winners in the food waste field. It is no surprise that the biogas plants claim their high position in this field, typically by invoking the myth of a circular economy, in which waste is turned into a valuable resource (Gregson et al. 2015). However, for the focus of this study—the food waste field—it is important to highlight that the losing population can afford their disinterest, as they are the winners in other fields. In other words, it makes no sense for the biogas plants to desire and compete for status-laden positions in fields in which they have little chance of success, particularly as they can easily position themselves as winners in other fields.

Secondly, the biogas plants dissociate themselves from the food waste field by creating their own sub-field centred on food waste recovery. In doing so, they divert the attention from the broader food waste field and channel competition into their own sub-field, which is known to be positioned at the bottom of the hierarchy. To create their own sub-field, the biogas plants make use of language and discourse. To clarify this, I should briefly explain the meaning of the term 'waste' and its German and French translations. According to the dictionary, the term 'waste' carries two meanings: 1) an unnecessary or incorrect use of substances, time, money, and so on and 2) unwanted matter of any type. In both French and German, there are different terms for these two varying meanings. Unnecessary use (meaning 1) is captured by *Verschwendung/gaspillage*, while unwanted material (meaning 2) is called *Abfall/ déchets*. The biogas plants use these linguistic nuances to shape field relations. While the organizations of the winning populations and the intermediaries, (i.e. scientists, policymakers, journalists) predominantly use the English term ('food waste') or occasionally refer to the term *Verschwendung/gaspillage*, the biogas plants avoid the English term 'food waste', preferring *Abfall/déchets* instead. With this usage (*Abfall/ déchets*), the biogas plants highlight the message that they transform unwanted and worthless materials, because this meaning is associated with these terms (Heinich 2017). At the same time, they distinguish their food waste performance from that of other field actors, who are portrayed as working with avoidable and unnecessary food waste. In practice, however, the biogas plants and the challengers often process the same type of food. For example, the organization that produces jams from food waste processes fruit that could not be redistributed by the food banks and would otherwise have been sent to the biogas plants (field notes, 3 October 2019). This means that the materials with which the various field actors work do not necessarily differ in practice. At a discursive level, however, the biogas plants create a distinction by invoking the term *Abfall/déchets* and constructing their own sub-field around it. Inhabitants can then strive for status within this sub-field— as when, for example, the association Biomasse Schweiz gives its green award to those that 'demonstrate excellent work in the recovery of organic waste' (Press release, 3 April 2019). Recourse to a sub-field is, therefore, another option for the losing population, giving them the scope to accept a low rank with little status in the higher-order field.

In summary, the losers of the status hierarchy (the biogas plants) show hardly any interest in their stigmatizing position. They do not consider themselves players in such a competitive game and direct their attention away from the food waste field. As a result of this, the hoped-for competition has failed to engage the biogas plants, and competitive relationships therefore remain absent in the food waste field.

Conclusion

My study indicates that the actors being ranked reflect on whether and how they wish to respond to ranks. More precisely, the actors reflect on whether they truly desire the top position and the status gains associated with it. Since fields are always nested (Bourdieu and Wacquant 1992; Fligstein and McAdam 2012), the actors take into account their positions in other fields. Their reflections then either inflame or dampen their desire for the ranks' status-laden position. These field-spanning considerations might explain why competition is not a 'natural fact' (Arora-Jonsson et al. 2020; Kornberger and Carter 2010). Specifically, they might show us why competition may not develop consistently throughout a field, because actors reflect on which competitions they wish to participate in, and which they consider worthwhile, from the choice available to them.

The multiplicity of competitions has two major implications. Because actors are involved in the construction of multiple competitions, we can expect that their desires for competition can diffuse, as well as focus on selected competitions. In the latter case, my empirical results indicate that the most attractive competitions are those in which the actor has the best chance of winning. This is because being the winner can bring positive spillover effects and might improve the actor's chances of survival (in the case under examination, by compensating for liabilities of newness and smallness). Hence, it is the strongest contenders who show the greatest desire for rank-driven competition, and these responses are crucial if the ranks involved are to function drivers of competition, as described in the literature (Brankovic et al. 2018; deRijcke et al. 2015; Hasse and Krücken 2013; Kornberger and Carter 2010). Due to the multiplicity of competitions for which actors channel their desires, we must consider that one desire could exclude another, purely because of limited attention and resources. These linkages and trade-offs between competitions across fields need to be better understood in order to explain why actors develop a desire for certain goods, and thus enter a particular competition, or remain indifferent and choose to sit out of the game.

The possible avoidance of competition brings us to the second implication of the multiplicity of competitions. While ranks are often created with the intention of raising standards—and, especially, motivating poor performers to improve (Bullock 2017)—my empirical results confirm that losers may actually ignore the ranks completely (Giffinger et al. 2010). Some losers can afford to accept their stigmatizing position because they can focus on other competitions where victory is within their grasp. When there is a multiplicity of competitions across fields, therefore, inciting competition seems unlikely to steer the bad performers into the desired form and direction. In view of this insight, we should interrogate whose interests and desires are actually served by ranks and competition, as well as the societal effects of creating them. In doing so, it would be naïve to assume that stigmatization through low ranks and competition automatically leads to an improvement in performance and an upward trend in society.

References

Ahrne, G., Aspers, P., and Brunsson, N. 2015. 'The organization of markets'. *Organization Studies* 36 (1): 7–27.

Aldrich, H. and Auster, E. R. 1986. 'Even dwarfs started small: liabilities of age and size and their strategic implications'. *Research in Organizational Behavior* 8: 165–98.

Arnold, N. and Hasse, R. 2016. 'The organization of value inscription: the role of third parties in signalling moral qualities in markets'. *Berliner Journal für Soziologie* 26 (3–4): 329–51.

Arora-Jonsson, S., Brunsson, N., and Hasse, R. 2020. 'Where does competition come from? The role of organization'. *Organization Theory* 1 (1): 1–24.

Berger, P. L. and Luckmann, T. 1991. *The Social Construction of Reality: A Treatise in the Sociology of Knowledge*. Harmondsworth/New York: Penguin Books.

Boudon, R. and Bourricaud, F. 1992. *Soziologische Stichworte: Ein Handbuch*. Wiesbaden: VS Verlag für Sozialwissenschaften.

Bourdieu, P. and Wacquant, L. J. D. 1992. 'The logic of fields'. In *An Invitation to Reflexive Sociology*, edited by P. Bourdieu and L. J. D. Wacquant. Chicago: University of Chicago Press: 94–115.

Brankovic, J., Ringel, L., and Werron, T. 2018. 'How rankings produce competition: the case of global university rankings'. *Zeitschrift für Soziologie* 47 (4): 270–88.

Bullock, G. 2017. *Green Grades: Can Information Save the Earth?* Cambridge, MA: MIT Press.

Busch, L. 2011. *Standards: Recipes for Reality*. Cambridge, MA: MIT Press.

deRijcke, S., Wallenburg, I., Wouters, P., and Bal, R. 2015. 'Comparing comparisons. On rankings and accounting in hospitals and universities'. In *Practising Comparison: Revitalising the Comparative Act*, edited by J. Deville, M. Guggenheim, and Z. Hrdlickova. Manchester: Mattering Press: 251–80.

Dorn, C. 2019. 'When reactivity fails: the limited effects of hospital rankings'. *Social Science Information* 58 (2): 327–53.

Eurostat 2020. 'Municipal waste statistics'. Available at: https://ec.europa.eu/eurostat/statistics-explained/index.php/Municipal_waste_statistics#Municipal_waste_generation (accessed 18 March 2020).

Evans, D., Campbell, H., and Murcott, A. 2012. 'A brief pre-history of food waste and the social sciences'. *Sociological Review*, 60 (2_suppl): 5–26.

Fligstein, N. and McAdam, D. 2012. *A Theory of Fields*. New York: Oxford University Press.

Foucault, M. 1984. *Überwachen und Strafen. Die Geburt des Gefängnisses* (5th ed.). Frankfurt a/M.: Suhrkamp Taschenbuch.

Giffinger, R., Haindlmaier, G., and Kramar, H. 2010. 'The role of rankings in growing city competition'. *Urban Research & Practice* 3 (3): 299–312.

Goffman, E. 1986. *Frame Analysis: An Essay on the Organization of Experience*. Boston: Northeastern University Press.

Gregson, N., Crang, M., Fuller, S., and Holmes, H. 2015. 'Interrogating the circular economy: the moral economy of resource recovery in the EU'. *Economy and Society* 44 (2): 218–43.

Hartmann, E. and Kjaer, P. F. 2015. 'Special issue: a sociology of competition'. *Distinktion: Journal of Social Theory* 16 (2): 141–5.

Hasse, R. and Krücken, G. 2013. 'Competition and actorhood: a further expansion of the neo-institutional agenda'. *Sociologia Internationalis* 51 (2): 181–205.

Heinich, N. 2017. *Des Valeurs. Une Approche Sociologique*. Paris: Editions Gallimard.

Hoffman, A. J. 1999. 'Institutional evolution and change: environmentalism and the U.S. chemical industry'. *Academy of Management Journal* 42 (4): 351–71.

Hultman, J. and Corvellec, H. 2012. 'The European waste hierarchy: from the sociomateriality of waste to a politics of consumption'. *Environment and Planning A: Economy and Space* 44 (10): 2413–27.

Kette, S. 2018. 'Prognostische Leistungsvergleiche'. In *Vergleich und Leistung in der funktional differenzierten Gesellschaft*, edited by C. Dorn and V. Tacke. Wiesbaden: Springer Fachmedien: 73–98.

Kornberger, M. and Carter, C. 2010. 'Manufacturing competition: how accounting practices shape strategy making in cities'. *Accounting, Auditing & Accountability Journal* 23 (3): 325–49.

Lampel, J. and Meyer, A. D. 2008. 'Guest editors' introduction'. *Journal of Management Studies* 45 (6): 1025–35.

Lounsbury, M., Ventresca, M., and Hirsch, P. M. 2003. 'Social movements, field frames and industry emergence: a cultural–political perspective on US recycling'. *Socio-Economic Review* 1: 71–104.

Luca, M. and Zervas, G. 2016. 'Fake it till you make it: reputation, competition, and Yelp review fraud'. *Management Science* 62 (12): 3412–27.

Meyer, J. W. and Jepperson, R. L. 2000. 'The "actors" of modern society: the cultural construction of social agency'. *Sociological Theory* 18 (1): 100–20.

Mourad, M. 2016. 'Recycling, recovering and preventing "food waste": competing solutions for food systems sustainability in the United States and France'. *Journal of Cleaner Production* 126: 461–77.

Papargyropoulou, E., Lozano, R., Steinberger, J., Wright, N., and bin Ujang, Z. 2014. 'The food waste hierarchy as a framework for the management of food surplus and food waste'. *Journal of Cleaner Production* 76: 106–15.

Podolny, J. M. 1993. 'A status-based model of market competition'. *American Journal of Sociology*, 98 (4): 829–72.

Podolny, J. M. 2005. *Status Signals: A Sociological Study of Market Competition*. Princeton: Princeton University Press.

Projektgruppe Food Waste 2015. *Food Waste. Bilanz Stakeholderdialog 2013-2014*. Bern: Schweizerische Eidgenossenschaft.

Sauder, M. 2006. 'Third parties and status position: how the characteristics of status systems matter'. *Theory & Society* 35 (3): 299–321.

Sauder, M. and Espeland, W. N. 2009. 'The discipline of rankings: tight coupling and organizational change'. *American Sociological Review* 74 (1): 63–82.

Sauder, M., Lynn, F., and Podolny, J. M. 2012. 'Status: insights from organizational sociology'. *Annual Review of Sociology* 38 (1): 267–83.

Schwab, K. 2018. *The Global Competitiveness Report*. Geneva: World Economic Forum (WEF).

Sharkey, A. 2014. 'Categories and organizational status: the role of industry status in the response to organizational deviance'. *American Journal of Sociology* 119 (5): 1380–433.

Simmel, G. 1895. 'The problem of sociology'. *The ANNALS of the American Academy of Political and Social Science* 6 (3): 52–63.

Sorrell, S. and Dimitropoulos, J. 2008. 'The rebound effect: microeconomic definitions, limitations and extensions'. *Ecological Economics* 65 (3): 636–49.

Smith, P. 1993. 'Outcome-related performance indicators and organizational control in the public sector'. *British Journal of Management* 4 (3): 135–51.

Stinchcombe, A. L. 1965. 'Social structure and organizations'. In *Handbook of Organizations*, edited by J. G. March. Chicago: Rand McNally & Co: 142–93.

United Nations 2018. 'Ensure sustainable consumption and production'. Available at: https://sdgs.un.org/goals/goal12 (accessed 10 February 2021).

UVEK 2019. *Künftige Rolle von Gas und Gasinfrastruktur in der Energieversorgung der Schweiz*. Bern: Eidgenössisches Departement für Umwelt, Verkehr, Energie und Kommunikation (UVEK).

Warren, D. E. and Laufer, W. S. 2009. 'Are corruption indices a self-fulfilling prophecy? A social labeling perspective of corruption'. *Journal of Business Ethics* 88 (4): 841–9.

Wedlin, L. 2011. 'Going global: rankings as rhetorical devices to construct an international field of management education'. *Management Learning* 42 (2): 199–218.

Werron, T. 2015. 'Why do we believe in competition? A historical-sociological view of competition as an institutionalized modern imaginary'. *Distinktion: Journal of Social Theory* 16 (2): 186–210.

Zehnder, A. 2020. 'Auto-Energieetikette'. Available at: https://www.srf.ch/news/schweiz/auto-energieetikette-viele-neuwagen-fahren-trotz-a-an-den-klimazielen-vorbei (accessed 17 March 2020).

8
Competition and auditing: esteemed but incompatible ideas

Karin Brunsson and Katharina Rahnert

In this chapter, we describe a situation where two socially esteemed ideas co-exist: the idea of competition and that of financial auditing. We start from the observation that the idea of competition forms a constitutive part of ideas prevalent in notions of liberalism (or neoliberalism), capitalism, and free trade (Granovetter 1985; Hayek 1945; Hirschman 1982; 1992). Lower prices, better quality, innovation, and a larger variety of products are the expected and desirable effects of market competition (e.g. EU 2020). The idea of competition is economically oriented, implying that the efficiency and effectiveness of firms and a customer focus are means of enhancing both a dynamic economy and social wealth (Konkurrensverket 2020). In Sweden, as in many other countries, the expected benefits of competitive behaviour have led to reorganization of significant parts of the public sector (Arora-Jonsson et al. 2018; Wisell 2019).

We describe how this idea of competition fared when combined with a similarly cherished idea: that of financial auditing. By reviewing client firms' accounts, financial auditors should further a community of law-abiding, reliable, and responsible firms (Jensen and Meckling 1976). Information provided by auditors should provide assurance to investors and other stakeholders, thereby promoting sound economic transactions.

The two ideas come with similar expectations: they shall serve the interests of various groups of stakeholders—not only the firms that produce goods and services but also customers, investors, or any other citizen. Both ideas shall benefit the overall development of the national economy. Yet, the two ideas do not necessarily concur. Inherent in the idea of competition is an expectation of efficiency and effectiveness, equally beneficial for both providers and recipients of goods and services. Competition is not only about price, but it should also promote high quality and innovation (Porter 2001; 2008). When related to financial auditing, however, expectations to the effect that audit firms compete with price, audit quality, and innovative audit methods are not necessarily valid.

Typically, firms to be audited are anxious to reduce their expenditure for audits and to keep any critical remarks from the auditors within the boundaries of the firm,

Karin Brunsson and Katharina Rahnert, *Competition and auditing: esteemed but incompatible ideas* In: *Competition: What It Is and Why It Happens*. Edited by: Stefan Arora-Jonsson, Nils Brunsson, Raimund Hasse, and Katarina Lagerström, whereas financial statement users, who do not themselves have in-depth access to firms' accounts, are rather indifferent to audit costs but interested in audit quality, in terms of informative and trustworthy auditors' reports. Audit firms thus face a dilemma; they may want to comply with requests from client firms but must also consider the interests of financial statement users. They have professional and economic incentives to argue for extensive (and expensive) auditing but little incentives to disseminate the outcome of their work. The symmetric win-win situation that the idea of competition suggests is absent in the idea of financial auditing when all three parties— auditors, their clients, and financial statement users—are taken into consideration.

Applying a historical perspective, we seek to clarify how the relationship between the two ideas emerged and developed. How did financial auditors reconcile the contradictory demands of being simultaneously efficient and thorough, inexpensive and informative, creative and trustworthy? Was it possible for them to compete for the appreciation of both client firms and the users of financial statements, while claiming to uphold professional values? In sum, how does the idea of competition relate to the idea of financial auditing?

We base our discussion of the idea of financial auditing mainly on Swedish data, but believe that the expectations pertaining to financial auditing in Sweden are not very different from those in other EU countries.

The chapter is structured into four sections: first, as a background, we describe the rationale for financial auditing, the concurrent legislative initiatives, and financial auditors' dilemma of serving stakeholders with conflicting interests. Second, we observe how tendencies towards uniformity led to impaired prerequisites for competition in important respects. Third, we clarify influential actors' approach to competition among auditors, observing a common focus on one of the stakeholder groups. Finally, in the last section, we conclude that the ideas of competition and auditing are incompatible though institutionalized. Their combinative effects are hardly ever questioned.

Financial auditing as a social interest

A typical representation of a business firm is that of a black box in which transformation processes take place and 'value' is created (e.g. Engwall 2007). This metaphor illustrates a situation where interested parties outside firm boundaries are left ignorant about the fairness of the financial accounts, despite legitimate interests of being informed.

With the proliferation of large-scale organizations, complex production processes, and equally complex accounting systems, auditing has become a means of simplification and economizing. Those with little or no insight into the firms should be spared the trouble of assessing the firms' accounts or management—auditors should function as an independent and trustworthy link between the firms' responsible management team and financial statement users (Jensen and Meckling 1976; Wallace 1980/1985).

Financial auditing is based on presumptions of the simultaneous existence of distrust and trust, the idea being that those who are not themselves engaged within a specific firm have reasons to distrust firms that are likely to be partial to their own activities and non-informative. Instead, financial statement users should trust reports from auditors, who were allowed inside the 'black box' and permitted to scrutinize the preparation and compilation of firms' accounts. Firms benefit from being seen as rule abiding, honest, and well-managed, and auditing contributes to a positive view of a firm (cf. Power 2004; 2007).

Thus, both firms and financial statement users should benefit from financial auditing. In many countries, including Sweden, the legislator considered auditing to be so important to society that legislation was deemed necessary.

Legislative initiatives

In Sweden, embezzlements within firms, fraud, and misstated financial reports became a growing problem in the second half of the nineteenth century (SRS 1908; Wallerstedt 2009). This situation led to a debate in the Swedish Parliament about the need for an auditing profession. Accordingly, in 1895, the first Companies Act of 1848 (SFS[1] 1848: 43) was modified, and it became mandatory for all Swedish limited companies to have financial auditing, including reviews of firms' accounts and their management (SFS 1895: 65).

Over time, the Swedish Parliament reviewed and elaborated on the legislative requirements. The Companies Act was amended in 1910 (SFS 1910: 88). In the aftermath of the Kreuger Crash in 1932, a major reform with detailed regulations followed, namely the Companies Act of 1944 (SFS 1944: 705). In 1975, the Companies Act was reorganized into a principle-based law, which left room for interpretation of the details of auditing (SFS 1975: 1385). The auditors' professional organization, FAR[2], was to clarify the contents of the law by providing detailed recommendations.

After the Swedish EU membership, Swedish legislation was harmonized with EU regulations. From 2011 on, this meant an adoption of the International Standards on Auditing (ISA), issued by the International Federation of Accountants, IFAC, an organization founded in 1977 (FAR Akademi 2011).

These legislative initiatives mean that, as a collective, Swedish auditors have been guaranteed a minimum number of firm contracts. Though, naturally, the number of firms to be subject to mandatory auditing varies over time, audit firms can count on a certain number of clients to be annually contracted and for which to compete. But how auditors are to compete for appreciation from financial statement users has not been a matter of debate.

---

[1] SFS stands for Svensk författningssamling, Swedish Code of Statutes.
[2] FAR was previously an acronym for Föreningen Auktoriserade Revisorer, the Swedish Institute of Authorized Public Accountants. The professional organization's current name is FAR, understood as Institute for the Accountancy Profession in Sweden'.

Stakeholders with conflicting interests

Financial auditors have been left with the dilemma of serving two groups of stakeholders whose interests are in conflict. One group—the client firms—may expect to profit from the advice given by the auditors and from demonstrating that they are law-abiding and hire auditors with a good reputation. Typically, however, their interests are best served when auditors comply with their obligation to secrecy as stated in the Companies Act and the Law for Auditors (SFS 2001: 883; SFS 2005: 551), and any critical information detected during audit work stays within the firms' boundaries.

The other group, financial statement users, are heterogeneous and consist of owners with limited access to firms' accounts, potential investors, or any other interested citizen, as well as government authorities, including the tax authority. Because different groups or individuals probably look for different types of information, they should best be served by detailed information about auditors' findings and judgement, especially if the auditors make critical remarks or express scepticism about future earnings. The users of financial statements are in a different position compared to the firms that are audited, because they depend on the information that auditors make public when their work is completed. Only rarely do they have an opportunity to evaluate the accounting expertise, or any personality or behavioural traits of individual auditors; to them, auditing is an anonymous function. Whether or not they appreciate it becomes evident only by their tolerance (cf. Luhmann 1968).

Besides considering conflicting interests concerning the publication of critical audit information, auditors must take diverse economic relationships into account. Client firms hire and pay for auditors and provide the economic means necessary for auditors' survival. Like other customers, they are likely to take price into account when contracting auditors—the cheaper the audit services, the better, at least as long as the audit firms are seen as competent and serious. Financial statement users are of little economic interest to the auditors; only few are engaged in the selection of specific auditors, for example in a shareholder capacity. Moreover, users receive audit information for free. Yet, the users of financial statements remain the very rationale for auditors' existence. If there were no idea of organizational boundaries, and no distrust in accounting behaviour within such boundaries, the very idea of financial auditing would lose its meaning.

The precarious situation of auditors was observed already in the first half of the twentieth century, when Jackson (1926: 63), for one, noted that 'the professional auditor should bear in mind that he has a double responsibility—his responsibility to the public requiring an even finer sense of candor and justice than that to his client'.

In sum, auditors must be tolerated, preferably appreciated, by both client firms and financial statement users. Firms that enter a contract with an audit firm may seek to lower their auditing costs. Financial statement users, on the other hand, should be interested in safeguarding auditors' expertise, independence, and the resources necessary for thorough audit work. The conflicting interests of the two groups leave auditors with the dilemma of accommodating to this 'double responsibility'.

Impaired prerequisites for auditor competition

The Swedish auditing profession evolved due to observed deficiencies within firms' accounts (Sjöström 1994; Wallerstedt 2009). Professional—independent—auditors became a social interest, motivated by an ambition to stimulate a sound business environment. In this process, there was little discussion about competition among auditors. Rather, making auditing a professional undertaking stimulated a development towards uniformity. Various influential individuals and organizations were involved: the government cooperated with representatives of the business community, academia, individual auditors, and auditors' professional organizations, all sharing a vision of a strong profession. With time, uniform requirements for auditors, their work, conduct, and reporting were developed. Consequently, auditors' scope for attracting clients by highlighting their unique competence was reduced.

Uniform auditors

At the end of the nineteenth century, when auditing of all Swedish limited companies was made mandatory (SFS 1895: 65), auditors established their first professional organization, the Swedish auditors' association (SRS, Svenska Revisorsamfundet). The objective of SRS was to create an arena for professional exchange and guarantee 'a body of competent and trustworthy auditors and accountants, who independently, professionally, and fully might execute assigned audit engagements' (Eurenius 1912: 3; our translation from Swedish).

In the first half of the twentieth century, in connection with the founding of the Stockholm School of Economics in 1909, academics, together with representatives of the Stockholm Chamber of Commerce, installed uniform training and authorization of auditors (Wallerstedt 2009). Auditors' professional training should assure a minimum level of accounting knowledge and practical audit competence, implying not only uniform accounting competence but also a uniform comprehension of the fundamentals of auditing.

In 1923, some of the first authorized auditors founded a second professional organization, FAR. Like SRS, FAR created an atmosphere of fellowship, where shared values and cooperation played an important role (Wallerstedt 2009). The objective of forming professional organizations was thus to instil a uniform mindset among auditors. With the introduction of the Companies Act of 1944 (SFS 1944: 705), auditors received legislative protection for their professional title, an initiative that further strengthened the constitution of auditors as a coherent professional group. This idea of a coherent group has proved stable over time. In the twenty-first century, auditors are still renowned for belonging to a 'gilded elite' (Brooks 2018).

Uniform requirements

In 1902, SRS published its first guidelines for auditors' work (SRS 1902). Successively, guidelines for different aspects of the audit process were published in pamphlets and in connection with membership registers (Wallerstedt 2009). Also, auditors discussed guidelines for proper audit performance in national and international conferences and in the professional journal *Revisorn* (The Auditor). Moreover, FAR members promoted uniform requirements of auditors' work, allegedly to safeguard audit quality. Their engagement resulted in a decisive influence on the details of the Companies Act of 1944 (SFS 1944: 705).

In the 1960s, internationalization and an increasingly complex business environment incited FAR to appoint an audit committee, whose task it was to suggest recommendations for uniform audit work (Wallerstedt 2009). As mentioned, the Swedish government recognized FAR's authority to independently develop the details of audit work. FAR engaged in the interpretation of the principle-based Companies Act of 1975 (SFS 1975: 1385) and published even more specific, uniform recommendations. Later, international standards on auditing were to guarantee uniformity of audit work across nations (FAR Akademi 2011).

Uniform auditor conduct

FAR members discussed issues related to ethics at an early stage of the organization's existence, and in 1933, FAR published its first code of ethics (Wallerstedt 2009). The objective was to protect solidarity and a non-competitive behaviour among auditors. Officially, the code was made invalid in 1965, though it seems to have remained a vital document for auditor practice (FAR 1998). An interest in ethical issues revived in 1974, when European ethical rules were translated and disseminated. These rules largely overlapped with those of AICPA (the American Institute of Certified Public Accountants).

Some years later, IFAC issued codes of ethics, which have been subject to gradual refinement with ever-more detailed principles and clarifying instructions to be applied by auditors internationally (IFAC 2018). The 2018 edition starts with an explicit emphasis on financial statement users ('the public interest'): 'A distinguishing mark of the accountancy profession is its acceptance of the responsibility to act in the public interest. A professional accountant's responsibility is not exclusively to satisfy the needs of an individual client or employing organization' (IFAC 2018: 16).

In sum, national and international professional organizations have sought to regulate auditor behaviour, expecting high ethical standards with regard to both groups of stakeholders.

Uniform auditors' reports

In parallel with the professionalization of auditors, auditor reporting developed into a uniform activity. Having once provided firm-specific information, at times with critical remarks—concerning, for example, the level of depreciations, or expectations and hopes for the future—the auditors' reports gradually became uniform, later even standardized, internationally harmonized, and with a minimum of firm-specific information (Rahnert 2017). The absence of firm-specific information even led the so-called Cohen Commission in the USA to suggest that the function of the reports was primarily symbolic, as their standardized language made the reports uninteresting and inaccessible (AICPA 1978). In the late 2010s, due to recurrent criticism, standards were issued to reintroduce certain firm-specific information in a so-called key audit matter section for firms of public interest (IFAC 2015a; 2015b). Basically, however, to a large extent, the texts provided in the reports remained uniform, with little firm-specific information.

Uniformity and impaired prerequisites for competition

The development of the auditing profession entailed a pursuit for uniformity. Important aspects of auditing became irrelevant for competition as auditors had little reason to seek to attract clients, or please financial statement users, by highlighting their competence, their audit work, their professional conduct, or their reports. Those who collaborated to create an audit profession did not refer to competition as a means of organizing for effective work, nor did they include competition as an advantageous component within the idea of financial auditing.

The irresistible idea of auditor competition

Given the insistence on uniformity among auditors and their work, behaviours, and reporting, one would expect the auditing profession to be indifferent, even opposed, to any idea of competition. Arguably, the benevolence of regulators and high professional status should suffice to make financial auditing an attractive profession.

Nonetheless, as noted, the idea of competition, with its connotations of efficiency and effectiveness, is a highly esteemed idea, which has become ingrained within the dominant social ideology and has proved irresistible to ever-larger parts of society. The idea that auditors should compete evolved in tandem with a concentration of auditors in large audit firms. When audit firms appear to be little different from other service providers, and, besides, sell non-audit services as a complement to auditing, the idea that these firms should compete is not very surprising. But for whose appreciation should auditors compete? As it turns out, different groups—the auditors, regulators, and academics—have all referred the idea of competition exclusively to auditors' relationship with client firms, ignoring that with financial statement users. In the next section, we provide details on the positions of each group.

Auditors' approach to auditor competition

Following on a concentration of auditors in a few dominant audit firms, auditors changed their attitudes towards competitive audit behaviour, as evident by gradually changed rules for marketing. Earlier, auditors typically operated in sole practice, understanding their work as a calling and competing only subtly by means of their reputation (cf. Freidson 2001; Jönsson 2004). From the 1960s onwards, Swedish audit firms started to cooperate with international audit firms. Some grew by means of mergers and acquisitions and from the 1970s formed what came to be known as the 'Big 4' (Wallerstedt 2001; 2009). From the 1970s and 1980s, auditors also provided a variety of non-audit services, such as risk management, taxation, and later even sustainability and cybersecurity (EY 2019a; 2019b; Zeff 2003a; 2003b). Arguably, these services played an important role when audit firms came to be regarded as actors who competed for market shares and income (Jönsson 2004; Wallerstedt 2009).

In connection with these changes, auditors modified their marketing rules and marketing behaviour. The extent to which audit firms should be allowed to increase their visibility through marketing activities became a controversial issue, extensively discussed (Picard 2016; Rahnert and Brunsson 2019; Wyatt 2004; Zeff 1987). Auditors who argued against liberal marketing rules lamented that the spirit of a professional egalitarian audit community had disappeared and that 'competitor' replaced the term 'colleague'. They found that auditors substituted the importance of doing business for their professional values including objectivity, integrity, rigor, and independence (Malsch and Gendron 2013). The emphasis on being an egalitarian community of individual professionals was abandoned in favour of a stance where audit firms should engage in competition, like most other firms.

In Sweden, from the early 1980s, when only restrained, informative marketing was permitted, to the early 1990s, a radical change took place, leading to a general acceptance of competitive marketing (Rahnert and Brunsson 2019). Allegedly, auditors at that time were at the height of their reputation and influence (Jönsson 2004; Wallerstedt 2009). Yet, the professional organization of auditors, FAR, adapted to the prevalent behaviour of most firms and changed its marketing rules, thereby acknowledging that many auditors now worked for audit firms, which were subject to the same conditions as other firms. Intensified marketing activities in the USA functioned as additional arguments for accepting competitive behaviour, as did a general reference to 'modernity' (Rahnert and Brunsson 2019).

From being devoted to professionalism and a view on competition as unethical and incompatible with professional behaviour, FAR gradually relented to the behaviour that large audit firms had already introduced. Perhaps, these firms believed that competition would serve the interests of their own organizations; perhaps, they subscribed to vague notions of the benefits of competition generally; or perhaps, they just imitated the behaviour of other audit firms. Whichever the case, it was evident that competition concerned contracts with firms to be audited. We have found no suggestions to the effect that audit firms might compete for the appreciation of financial statement users.

Regulators' approach to auditor competition

Regulators have been concerned about the concentration of audit firms over the past four decades (Willekens et al. 2019). Some feared that a situation with a few dominant audit firms ('Big 4' instead of 'Big 8') would affect the degree of price competition, audit quality, and the possibility for potential clients to choose among auditors. However, studies by several international governmental bodies indicated that although a concentration trend was observable, there was no need to address it because no adverse effects on competition were evident (e.g. FRC 2006; US Chamber of Commerce 2006).

Regulators' concern with competition among audit firms intensified with the financial crisis in 2008 and led to the EU Statutory Audit Reform in 2014 (EC 2010; EU 2014a; 2014b), including, for example, mandatory audit firm rotation (i.e. mandatory change of audit firm at regular intervals), restrictions on income from non-audit services, and the prohibition of certain non-audit services. After the reform, the concentration of audit firms decreased in almost half of the EU Member States, and there were indications of intensified competition among audit firms (Willekens et al. 2019). Nonetheless, the overall concentration of audit firms in the EU remained high.

A concern with the number of large audit firms indicates that regulators have considered the increased concentration of audit firms as a threat to the benefits of auditor competition. Auditor competition must be monitored, the understanding being that competition among audit firms is worth stimulating by interference through regulatory means. Again, competition concerned contracts with client firms only. No regulator expected audit firms to compete for the appreciation of financial statement users.

Academics' approach to auditor competition

Academics, who studied auditor competition, focused on competition as a social structure and used the reduced number of dominant audit firms as a proxy for competition. In this research, the number of audit firms was used as the independent variable and related to audit pricing and audit quality (e.g. Bandyopadhyay and Kao 2004; Casterella et al. 2004). Some used alternative measures for auditor competition, such as the geographical distance of an auditor from its closest competitor (Bills and Stephens 2015; Numan and Willekens 2012). Others sought to explain variations in the level of competition across different industries (e.g. Chang et al. 2009; Dekeyser et al. 2017). They saw competition as the dependent variable, to be correlated with, for example, market share mobility (i.e. the sum of market share changes of all audit firms in a market segment) and audit 'leader dethronement' (i.e. whether the dominant audit firm is replaced by a rival in a certain industry).

A review of the literature on audit market concentration showed that the size of audit firms and their professed use of structured audit methodologies brought competitive advantages in terms of price (Toscano et al. 2017). However, research results were inconclusive. Some found mandatory audit services to be so regulated as to leave room only for differentiation of price, others found that the audit firms compete also by the auditor chosen and the reputation and image of the audit firm.

As these studies showed, a substantial amount of research concentrated on competition for contracts with client firms, but there are also studies concerned with the interests of financial statement users. A recurrent observation has been that auditors do not meet the expectations of these users. A number of 'expectations gaps' were identified, and more informative auditors' reports asked for (Humphrey et al. 1992; Porter 1993; Vanstraelen et al. 2012). There were even suggestions to the effect that auditors' reports be differentiated, depending on various stakeholders' interests and willingness to pay (Boyd et al. 2000; Öhman 2007). Studies concerned with the interests of financial statement users did not refer to competition, however.

In sum, academics accepted the view of auditors and regulators, namely that competition concerns only the relationship between audit firms and client firms.

Competition as a business-to-business relationship

A high degree of consensus has characterized the understanding of competition among audit firms. Auditors, regulators, and academics have all applied the idea of competition to the relationship between audit firms and the firms to be audited, oftentimes deploying the number of audit firms as an approximate measurement of the existence and strength of competition.

The counterproductive effects of auditor competition

Can financial auditors simultaneously satisfy the expectations of two stakeholder groups with conflicting interests? Our discussion so far indicates that this dilemma did not appear overnight, nor was it immediately solved. Instead, the establishment of professional financial auditing was an instance of a long-term development, whereby certain assumptions and behaviours were accepted and became institutionalized.

We observed how the idea of professional financial auditing implied a predilection for uniformity. Not only should auditors be uniform, in the sense that they have a similar academic education and an exclusive right to call themselves authorized, but they should also follow rules set up to guarantee uniform audit work. In addition, the auditors' professional organizations formulated rules to regulate auditor behaviour generally and rules on how to design an auditor's report.

The professionalization of auditors did not come about with any idea of competition. This idea emerged later, in parallel with the establishment of large audit firms and the gradual reorganization of financial auditing. When audit firms found non-audit services to be a profitable source of income, the idea of competition followed. Audit firms were seen as little different from other profit-seeking firms. As a result, the monetary exchange between audit firms and client firms became a dominant feature of auditing (Brooks 2018; Brunsson and Rahnert 2019). Firms are clearly defined customers, or 'actors', with whom audit firms can negotiate and to whom they can make themselves appear special by means of marketing and price. Financial statement users, in contrast, constitute a heterogeneous, largely anonymous, group. Auditors have little or no incentives to make themselves appear unique with relation to this group.

The view that auditor competition concerns primarily economic relations among firms coincides with the conventional mode of describing the idea of competition (cf. EU 2020). Auditors, regulators, and academics relate the idea of competition to client firms, disregarding the interests of financial statement users and the consequences of this stance as a matter of course.

We conclude that in a situation where stakeholder groups have conflicting interests, the idea of competition relates first of all to economic relationships with clearly defined customers. Relationships with no monetary consequences may be ignored, irrespective of the legitimacy of the interests involved.

As noted, the users of financial statements may be all sorts of interested groups or individuals. Most likely, they have highly diverging interests. Yet, uniform reports seem to be based on the notion that these users are all similar and can be treated in a uniform way. This makes one-directional, perfunctory information appear natural; auditors see no need for personal contacts or other means of communication.

Rather than regarding the appreciation of financial statement users as worthy of competition, audit firms left it to their professional organizations to emphasize time and again the importance of this stakeholder group. By separating the attention to the two groups by organizational means, a type of division of labour was established—audit firms concentrating on client firms, and their professional organizations on financial statement users (cf. Meyer and Rowan 1977; Rahnert and Brunsson 2019). Although controlled by audit firms, IFAC, like national professional organizations, has been loosely coupled to audit practice; it has been free to make ambitious pronouncements concerning the importance of 'the public interest' (cf. Crozier 1964/2010). Despite the fact that the very rationale for financial auditing rests on an assumption that financial statement users have legitimate interests in being informed about firms' accounts, they may then be treated as an abstract, even hypothetical, entity. The situation is similar to that of the fictitious users of financial accounting or social science research (Shove and Rip 2000; Stenka and Jaworska 2019; Young 2006).

We conclude that in a situation where stakeholder groups have conflicting interests, loose coupling by means of organizational specialization can be a way of handling the interests of the different groups. Competitive efforts can then be directed towards one of the groups, while another is recognized rhetorically.

If it is true that competition serves the interests of customers and society at large by stimulating efficiency and effectiveness, competition among audit firms for contracts with client firms may contribute to lower prices and an audit process that is reduced to a minimum. Any interest that financial statement users might have in thorough, informative, and trustworthy auditing is then subdued. In this respect, the idea of competition has proved to be counterproductive.

Should professional auditors, however, seek to sell thorough and critical auditing to their clients, the interests of financial statement users may help them argue for voluminous and expensive audits. When that is the case, the interests of audit firms are satisfied, but their clients pay for excessive auditing that they did not ask for. The expectations that competition should benefit client firm efficiency and effectiveness are not fulfilled.

We conclude that in a situation where stakeholder groups have conflicting interests, combining the idea of competition with another socially esteemed idea, such as that of financial auditing, does not necessarily elicit the expected benefits of any of the ideas.

Situations with incompatible ideas have been found to trigger institutional change, if not immediately, then in the long run (Seo and Creed 2002). Yet, the co-existence of the idea of competition and the idea of financial auditing has proved stable over the decades. Each on its own merits, these socially esteemed ideas have become institutionalized. It does not matter, then, whether or not they in fact promote the national economy.

We conclude that in a situation where socially esteemed ideas have become institutionalized, their compatibility can be ignored, even when this goes contrary to the expected benefits of these ideas.

The idea of competition and the idea of financial auditing were both motivated by another attractive idea—that of efficiency and effectiveness. When used as an argument for the organization of society, this idea appears irrefutable—who can argue in favour of ineffective social organization? Numerous ideas may subsume under the idea of efficiency and effectiveness (cf. Searle 1995), making a closer scrutiny of the compatibility of various subordinated ideas appear superfluous. Perhaps, the overarching idea of efficiency and effectiveness serves to camouflage the incompatibility of the idea of competition and that of financial auditing. Or perhaps, these ideas have become so well established that they take on ideological overtones and remain unaffected by arguments as to their combinative effects. Whichever the case, it seems evident that when related to other socially esteemed ideas, the understanding of competition as always advantageous must be reconsidered.

References

American Institute of Certified Public Accountants [AICPA] 1978. *Report, Conclusions and Recommendations of the Commission on Auditor's Responsibilities.* New York: American Institute of Certified Public Accountants.

Arora-Jonsson, S., Blomgren, M., Forssell, A., and Waks, C. 2018. *Att styra organisationer med konkurrens.* Lund: Studentlitteratur.

Bandyopadhyay, S. P. and Kao, J. L. 2004. 'Market structure and audit fees: a local analysis'. *Contemporary Accounting Research* 21 (3): 529–61.

Bills, K. L. and Stephens, N. M. 2015. 'Spatial competition at the intersection of the large and small audit firm markets'. *Auditing: A Journal of Practice & Theory* 35 (1): 23–45.

Boyd, D. T., Boyd, S. C., and Boyd, W. L. 2000. 'The audit report: a misunderstanding gap between users and preparers'. *National Public Accountant* 45 (10): 56–60.

Brooks, R. 2018. *Bean Counters. The Triumph of Accountants and How They Broke Capitalism*. London: Atlantic Books.

Brunsson, K. and Rahnert, K. 2019. 'Everything you can imagine is real: a Luhmannian understanding of financial auditing'. Conference paper presented at the 10th EARNet Symposium. Parma, Italy. 6–7 September 2019.

Casterella, J. R., Francis, J. R., and Lewis, B. L. 2004. 'Auditor industry specialization, client bargaining power, and audit pricing'. *Auditing: A Journal of Practice & Theory* 23 (1): 123–40.

Chang, W. J., Chen, Y. S., and Chan, M. P. 2009. 'Impact of audit fee deregulation on audit-market competition'. *Asia-Pacific Journal of Accounting & Economics* 16 (1): 69–94.

Crozier, M. 1964/2010. *The Bureaucratic Phenomenon*. New Brunswick: Transaction Publishers.

Dekeyser, S., Gaeremynck, A., Knechel, R., and Willekens, M. 2017. 'Strategic competition by audit firms'. Available at: http://wp.unil.ch/earnet2015/files/2014/10/Strategic-Competition-by-Audit-Firms.pdf (accessed 21 August 2020).

Engwall, L. 2007. 'The anatomy of management education'. *Scandinavian Journal of Management* 23: 4–35.

European Commission [EC] 2010. *Green Paper. Audit Policy: Lessons from the Crisis*. Brussels: European Commission.

European Union [EU] 2014a. 'Directive 2014/56/EU of the European Parliament and the Council of 16 April 2014'. *Official Journal of the European Union*, I. 158/196.

European Union [EU] 2014b. 'Regulation (EU) No. 537/2014 of the European Parliament and the Council of 16 April 2014 on specific requirements regarding statutory audit of public-interest entities and repealing Commission Decision 2005/909/EC'. *Official Journal of the European Union*, L 158/77.

European Union [EU] 2020. 'Why is competition policy important for consumers?'. Available at: https://ec.europa.eu/competition/consumers/why_en.html (accessed 21 August 2020).

Eurenius, A. G. J. 1912. *Svenska Revisor Samfundet 1899–1919: Minnesskrift*. Nyköping: Södermanlands läns tidnings tryckeri.

EY 2019a. 'Sustainability and supply chain advisory'. Available at: https://www.ey.com/en_gl/sustainable-impact-hub (accessed 21 August 2020).

EY 2019b. 'Cybersecurity'. Available at https://www.ey.com/se/sv/services/advisory/cybersecurity (accessed 21 August 2020).

FAR Akademi 2011. *Fars samlingsvolym Revision 2011*. Stockholm: FAR Akademi.

FAR 1998. *FAR 75 år—en rapsodisk skildring av utvecklingen 1923–98*. Stockholm: FAR Förlag.

FRC 2006. 'Promotion audit quality: discussion paper'. Available at: www.frcpublications.com (accessed 21 August 2020).

Freidson, E. 2001. *Professionalism: The Third Logic*. Cambridge: Polity Press.

Granovetter, M. 1985. 'Economic action and social structure: the problem of embeddedness'. *American Journal of Sociology* 91 (3): 481–510.

Hayek, F. A. 1945. 'The use of knowledge in society'. *American Economic Review* 35 (4): 519–30.

Hirschman, A. O. 1982. 'Rival interpretations of market society: civilizing, destructive, or feeble?'. *Journal of Economic Literature* 20 (4): 1463–84.

Hirschman, A. O. 1992. *Rival Views of Market Society and Other Essays.* Cambridge, MA: Harvard University Press.

Humphrey, C., Moizer, P., and Turley, S. 1992. 'The audit expectations gap—Plus ça change, plus c'est même chose?'. *Critical Perspectives on Accounting* 3: 137–61.

International Federation of Accountants [IFAC] 2015a. *International Standards on Auditing 701: Communicating Key Audit Matters in the Independent Auditor's Report.* New York: International Federation of Accountants. Available at: https://www.ifac.org/system/files/publications/files/ISA-701_2.pdf (accessed 21 August 2020).

International Federation of Accountants [IFAC] 2015b. *International Standards on Auditing 705 (Revised): Modifications to the Opinion in the Independent Auditor's Report.* New York: International Federation of Accountants. Available at: https://www.ifac.org/system/files/publications/files/ISA-705-Revised_0.pdf (accessed 21 August 2020).

International Federation of Accountants [IFAC] 2018. *Handbook of the Code of Ethics for Professional Accountants, 2018 Edition.* New York: IFAC.

Jackson, J. H. 1926. 'Audit certificates and reports'. *Accounting Review* 1 (3): 45–63.

Jensen, M. C. and Meckling, W. H. 1976. 'Theory of the firm: managerial behavior, agency costs and ownership structure'. *Journal of Financial Economics* 3 (4): 305–60.

Jönsson, S. 2004. *Revisorrollens nedgång och fall. GRI-rapport 2004:7.* Gothenburg: Gothenburg Research Institute.

Konkurrensverket 2020. 'Welcome to the Swedish Competition Authority'. Available at: http://www.konkurrensverket.se/en (accessed 21 August 2020).

Luhmann, N. 1968. *Vertrauen, Ein Mechanismus der Reduktion Sozialer Komplexität.* Stuttgart: Ferdinand Enke Verlag.

Malsch, B. and Gendron, Y. 2013. 'Re-theorizing change: institutional experimentation and the struggle for domination in the field of public accounting'. *Journal of Management Studies* 50 (5): 870–99.

Meyer, J. W. and Rowan, B. 1977. 'Institutionalized organizations: formal structure as myth and ceremony'. *American Journal of Sociology* 83 (2): 340–63.

Numan, W. and Willekens, M. 2012. 'An empirical test of spatial competition in the audit market'. *Journal of Accounting and Economics* 53: 450–65.

Öhman, P. 2007. *Perspektiv på Revision: Tankemönster, Förväntningsgap och Dilemman.* Dissertation. Mittuniversitetet: Sundsvall.

Picard, C. F. 2016. 'The marketization of accountancy'. *Critical Perspectives on Accounting* 34: 79–97.

Porter, B. 1993. 'An empirical study of the audit expectation-performance gap'. *Accounting and Business Research* 24 (93): 49–68.

Porter, M. E. 2001. 'The value chain and competitive advantage'. In *Understanding Business: Processes,* edited by D. Barnes. London: Routledge: 50–66.

Porter, M. E. 2008. *On Competition.* Boston: Harvard Business Review.

Power, M. 2004. *The Risk Management of Everything: Rethinking the Politics of Uncertainty.* London: Demos.

Power, M. 2007. *Organized Uncertainty: Designing a World of Risk Management.* Oxford: Oxford University Press.

Rahnert, K. 2017. *The Evolution of the Swedish Auditor's Report.* Dissertation. Karlstad: Karlstad University Studies.

Rahnert, K. and Brunsson, K. 2019. 'Från kollega till konkurrent'. *Organisation & samhälle* 1: 58–63.

Seo, M. and Creed, W. E. D. 2002. 'Institutional contradictions, praxis, and institutional change: a dialectical perspective'. *Academy of Management Review* 27 (2): 222–47.

Searle, J. R. 1995. *The Construction of Social Reality.* London: Penguin Books.

SFS 1848: 43. *Kongl. Maj:ts Nådiga Förordning angående Aktiebolag.*

SFS 1895: 65. *Lag om aktiebolag.* Stockholm: Justitiedepartementet.

SFS 1910: 88. *Lag om aktiebolag.* Stockholm: Justitiedepartementet.

SFS 1944: 705. *Lag om aktiebolag.* Stockholm: Justitiedepartementet.

SFS 1975: 1385. *Aktiebolagslag.* Stockholm: Justitiedepartementet.

SFS 2001: 883. *Revisorslag.* Stockholm: Justitiedepartementet.

SFS 2005: 551. *Aktiebolagslag.* Stockholm: Justitiedepartementet.

Shove, E. and Rip, A. 2000. 'Symbolic users. Users and unicorns: a discussion of mythical beasts in interactive science'. *Science and Public Policy* 27 (3): 175–82.

Sjöström, C. 1994. *Revision och Lagreglering—Ett Historiskt Perspektiv.* Lic. Linköping: Department of Computer and Information Science, Linköping University.

Svenska Revisorsamfundet [SRS] 1902. *Vägledning för Revisorer.* Stockholm: Wilhelmssons Boktryckeri.

Svenska Revisorsamfundet [SRS] 1908. *Utredning angående behofvet af offentliga revisorer verkställd af Svenska Revisor Samfundets Revisionskommitté.* Stockholm: Aktiebolaget Nordiska boktryckeriet.

Stenka, R. and Jaworska, S. 2019. 'The use of made-up users'. *Accounting, Organizations and Society* 78 (7): 1–7.

Toscano Moctezuma, J. A. and García Benau, M. A. 2017. 'Why the Big 4 are leaders in the audit market? A literature review'. *Archives of Business Research* 5 (12): 227–44.

US Chamber of Commerce 2006. *Auditing: A Profession at Risk.* Washington, DC: US Chamber of Commerce. Available at: https://www.uschamber.com/sites/default/files/legacy/reports/0601auditing.pdf (accessed 21 August 2020).

Vanstraelen, A., Schelleman, C., Meuwissen, R., and Hofmann, I. 2012. 'The audit reporting debate: seemingly intractable problems and feasible solutions'. *European Accounting Review* 21 (2): 193–215.

Wallace, W. 1980/1985. 'The economic role of the audit in free and regulated markets'. The Touche Ross and Co. aid to education program. Reprinted in *Auditing Monographs.* University of Rochester, New York: Macmillan.

Wallerstedt, E. 2001. 'The emergence of the Big Five in Sweden'. *European Accounting Review* 10 (4): 843–67.

Wallerstedt, E. 2009. *Revisorsbranschen i Sverige under hundra år.* Stockholm: SNS förlag.

Willekens, M., Dekeyser, S., and Simac, I. 2019. 'EU statutory audit reform—Impact on costs, concentration and competition'. Available at: http://www.europarl.europa.eu/supporting-analyses (accessed 21 August 2020).

Wisell, K. 2019. *The Liberalization Experiment: Understanding the Political Rationales Leading to Change in Pharmacy Policy*. Uppsala: Acta Universitatis Upsaliensis.

Wyatt, A. R. 2004. 'Accounting professionalism—They just don't get it!'. *Accounting Horizons* 18 (1): 45–53.

Young, J. J. 2006. 'Making up users'. *Accounting, Organizations and Society* 31 (6): 579–600.

Zeff, S. A. 1987. 'Does the CPA belong to a profession?'. *Accounting Horizons* 1 (2): 65–8.

Zeff, S. A. 2003a. 'How the U.S. accounting profession got where it is today: part I'. *Accounting Horizons* 17 (3): 189–205.

Zeff, S. A. 2003b. 'How the U.S. accounting profession got where it is today: part II'. *Accounting Horizons* 17 (4): 267–86.

9

The allure of prizes: how contests trap us in competitive relationships

Michael Scroggins and Daniel Souleles

> *It is a truth universally acknowledged, if not a quantified fact, that an organization with capital to spare must be in need of a prize to offer.*[1]

Implicit in our reworking of Jane Austen's line is the dimmer, yet still universal, truth that individuals and organizations whose capital and media profile are lacking must be in need of a contest to win.* For Austen, the allure of fortune, and its unspoken but significant charms, sets a contest of the heart in motion, drawing the participants deeper into a relationship whose boundaries and possibilities draw tighter as a potential fortune draws near. Like all human activities, contests of the heart are both naturally occurring and highly cultured. Everywhere humans seek mates, but not necessarily with the stakes, or in the style, of early nineteenth-century England. In theorizing contests of the heart as a social drama and, less famously, as 'a manoeuvring business', Austen captured the flirting, flattering, and luring inherent in contests that were lost as analysts like Simmel and Marx took up competition and contests and gave them a scientific sheen.

Our starting point for recapturing the luring and manoeuvring inherent in contests, whether they are motivated by the heart, the head, or monetary gain, is Simmel's pioneering work on competition and the elaboration on his work in Chapter 1. In Simmel's (1950: 135–7) formulation, competitions are naturally occurring phenomena, the result of two, or presumably more, parties competing for material or symbolic gain. His contribution lies in theorizing these naturally occurring competitions as benefitting a third party. As Simmel notes, '[the Tertius Gaudens] has an equal, and equally independent, and for this very reason, decisive, relation to the two others' (1950: 159). While he conceptualizes competition in the abstract, our concern is with a concrete form of competition, the contest. We join Chapter 1 in the elaboration on Simmel's triad by conceptualizing contests as the result of a 'fourth party' who, rather

---

* Souleles's project has received funding from the European Research Council (ERC) under the European Union's Horizon 2020 research and innovation programme (Grant Agreement No 725706).

[1] We have taken liberty with the opening line of Jane Austen's *Pride and Prejudice* in which she suggests that assumed truths contain hidden complexities. Following Austen, we argue that prize giving and seeking are more complex than commonly assumed.

Michael Scroggins and Daniel Souleles, *The allure of prizes: how contests trap us in competitive relationships* In: *Competition: What It Is and Why It Happens*. Edited by: Stefan Arora-Jonsson, Nils Brunsson, Raimund Hasse, and Katarina Lagerström, Oxford University Press. © Michael Scroggins and Daniel Souleles 2021. DOI: 10.1093/oso/9780192898012.003.0009

than extracting value from naturally occurring contests, intentionally creates the form and sets the stakes of contests through clever design. In this conceptualization, competition is not a necessary feature of human life but rather is brought into being, and is mediated through, the contours of human relationships.

In what follows, we join Austen's observations and Simmel's theorizing to the anthropological literature on traps and trapping, with the aim of recapturing the social drama inherent in contests and understanding how contests organize competitive relationships in late capitalism. Our argument is simple: contests are traps, funnelling both the wary and unsuspecting into competitive relationships through the lure of material and symbolic rewards. Anthropologists have conceptualized traps as sites of unfolding social dramas (Gell 1996)—social dramas initiated by a lure, designed to imitate a naturally occurring object or process, and brought to fruition or thwarted by the designs of the trapper or trapped, respectively. We join it to our earlier work (Souleles and Scroggins 2017) on the stakes of games that disruptive innovators can compel others to play and the theory developed in this volume towards a straightforward goal: examining how contests create, mediate, and enforce the contours of competitive relationships.

Traps and trapping have been part of anthropological discourse since Otis Mason, a contemporary of Simmel, wrote of their design and implementation: 'a trap is an invention for inducing animals to commit incarceration, self-arrest, or suicide' (1900: 657). Mason went on to form a typology of traps, considering them of prime importance to ongoing debates over the culture concept. However, it was Gell (1996), in forming an anthropological theory of artwork, who first compared the pull of cultural productions to traps by analogizing an animal encountering a trap with a visit to an art gallery; each becomes captivated by the trap and artwork, respectively, pulled in by the promise of an alluring experience.

From the form of the trap, the dispositions of the intended victim could be deduced. In this sense, traps can be regarded as texts on animal behaviour. The trap is therefore both a model of its creator, the hunter, and a model of its victim, the prey animal. But more than this, the trap embodies a scenario, which is the dramatic nexus that binds these two protagonists together and which aligns them in time and space (Gell 1996: 27).

In a context closer to our own, Seaver (2018) argues that the drama of trapping plays out in the digital landscapes through engagement with algorithms that recommend and serve content across the internet. Seaver notes that recommender systems work by promising potential consumers' alluring and personalized experiences as they travel down a 'product funnel' where they are trapped, sorted, and served up matching product recommendations.

Like the lures used to attract and trap animals, prizes come in a dizzying variety of styles and employ a dizzying number of techniques in use, each tailored to specific social situations, made attractive to specific individuals, and intended to create specific outcomes. As we argue further on, prizes are such powerful lures and attractants, at times luring us into social action and at times simply holding our attention, that they need not be explicitly offered to be effective. Like a trap, a contest embodies a scenario that binds the prize creator and prize seeker together and aligns them in time and space. We might notice one additional and telling feature of traps. Traps crisscross the boundary between the natural and the cultured in complex ways, intertwining, intercutting, and interweaving, rather than separating the two.

The consulting firm McKinsey (see Figure 9.1) has categorized prizes (which they assume are natural features of their own material epoch, what we are calling late capitalism, although they do not call it that) by the kind of change they intend to bring and how that change is to be achieved, providing a good enough start.

Beyond butterfly collecting, McKinsey's chart is useful in its explicit reference to social manipulation. Prize by prize, they explain how specific kinds of contests call for specific kinds of competitors and manipulate the competitor's social world in specific ways, all to benefit the contest creator. Take one example, 'The Exemplar'. The Exemplar is designed to set standards and personify excellence, shaping the commonly held perception of a field. If we take any of the various Nobel prizes, we can see the way they valorize a particular approach to a discipline or endeavour and grant worldwide fame and no small amount of money to those who win.

It is worth noting, too, that all this is achieved by a small group of Swedes and Norwegians acting at the behest of a long-dead dynamite tycoon, and the whole world pays attention. Dead or alive, corporate or individual, in the continuation of the Nobel prize, the power of the contest creator in the fourth position is made visible. The persistence of the Nobel prize beyond the temporal bounds of Alfred Nobel's life illustrates a point of confluence between prizes, traps, and the formulation of the fourth position in Chapter 4: the power of the fourth position to design the terms of social action that persists through the interaction of the design, in this case a prize, and those caught in the design's allure.

A funnel trap works by degree; as an animal progresses deeper into the trap, the animal's ability to manoeuvre, and therefore leave the trap, is slowly taken away. Animals are left alive, but their ability for independent action is slowly curtailed. From the trapper's point of view, the advantage of a funnel trap is its ability to discriminate between animals worth keeping and animals to be discarded. It allows the trap maker to decide, at the trapper's leisure, the value of the animals in the trap. This design feature in itself is a decision ladder. Built into the trap is a type of logic that denies entrance to undesirable and oversized animals.

Figure 9.2 shows a diagram of a lobster cage, a simple type of funnel trap designed to trap only lobsters of a certain size. A lure is placed in the more open area beyond the narrow end of the funnel, drawing the lobster into the funnel. Note that the size of the chambers slowly decreases as the animal reaches the end of the funnel. Once entered into the funnel, the lobster cannot decide to leave. The funnel trap is a one-way valve. When the trap is pulled off the sea floor, the trapper judges the lobsters in the trap, keeping those deemed legal catch and letting the rest return to the sea floor, their brief trip over.

As Gell (1996) and Seaver (2018) have argued, traps intended to lure and capture the humans of late capitalism work through a similar process, if through differing forms. Like Mason's typology of traps, McKinsey's typology of prizes exemplifies the

Exhibit 12: Six prize archetypes

	Archetype	Goal of prize	Primary change levers	Some Examples
	Exemplar	• Focus attention on, set standards in, and/or influence perception of a particular field or issue	• Identifying excellence • Influencing perception	Man Booker Prize (Literature), World Food Prize (environment)
	Exposition	• Highlight a range of best practices, ideas, or opportunities within a field	• Identifying excellence • Mobilizing capital	PICNIC Green Challenge (environmental)
	Network	• Celebrate and strengthen a particular community	• Identifying excellence • Strengthening community • Mobilizing capital	EI Pomar, X PRIZEs
	Participation	• Educate and change behavior of participants through the prize process	• Strengthening community • Educating/improving skills	FIRST Robotics Competition
	Market stimulation	• Emulate market incentives, driving costs down through competition and exposing latent demand	• Identifying excellence • Mobilizing talent, capital • Focusing a community • Influencing perception	X PRIZEs
	Point solution	• Solve a challenging, well-defined problem requiring innovation	• Focusing a community • Mobilizing talent	NetFlix Prize, X PRIZES

Figure 9.1 McKinsey's six prize archetypes (McKinsey & Company 2009: 48).

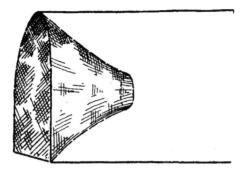

Figure 9.2 A funnel trap.

varieties and valences of the forms, lures, and social dramas envisioned by the designers of both traps and contests. In the next section, we examine the metaphoric netting and lures used by contest designers to create competitive relationships. Our twinned cases demonstrate how prizes work to lure both the wary and the unsuspecting into a particular kind of social drama—the contest. Borrowing a term from film criticism, we conceptualize the prize as a MacGuffin, a device commonly used in theatre and film to lure an audience into the drama of plot and character, but otherwise immaterial and unimportant to the larger exercise of power prize-setting and the 'fourth position' entailed. A MacGuffin, in other words, is an excuse or conceit for luring an audience in the unfolding of a social drama; they work in the same manner as a lure in a trap or a prize at the end of a contest. Put in more academically familiar language—one could think of it as a fetish that hides agency and a larger structure.

We will illustrate this definition of contests in a pair of case studies. Like our opening vignette, each case study addresses the interaction between those who create prizes and those who seek to win prizes. Further, we argue that this is the case even when the prize on offer is little more than a MacGuffin. Like the MacGuffins familiar from Alfred Hitchcock's work, a spare key in *Dial M for Murder* or a piece of microfilm in *North by Northwest*, the imagined reward from winning a prize heightens the social drama of competition, raising the stakes of competition and resolving ambiguous relationships into competitive relationships.

Scroggins' case study examines his participation in the Bioluminescent community project at the Silicon Valley Do-it-Yourself Biology laboratory BioCurious. What started out as a straightforward (if technically daunting) educational project designed to teach newcomers the basics of wet lab techniques by creating a bioluminescent sign to hang in BioCurious' front window quickly transformed into a potential commercial enterprise dominated by Silicon Valley entrepreneurs, as the lure of an international competition, a Participation Prize in the McKinsey parlance, was dangled in front. In short order, the local ends of the small-scale project were bent to the large-scale and global ends of International Genetic Engineering Machine (iGEM) competition—'tackling everyday issues facing the world'.

Souleles' case study examines how people spontaneously organize and compete with each other around the promise of an amorphous and fictitious prize. For the last three years, he has been working on a large project studying changes in financial markets due to the rise of algorithmic, automated, and high-frequency trading. Most scholarly and journalistic accounts have framed the development of this new market as a 'high-frequency arms race', in which competitors vie for the fastest data feeds and exchange connections. This assumed prize, in turn, hides other market activities within financial markets that are equally as consequential as the rise of high-frequency algorithmic trading.

Lured into a contest

The lure of the iGEM competition

Almost a decade ago, a new type of science and a new type of scientist emerged from the private spaces of garages and kitchens into public view as the first Do-it-Yourself Biology (hereinafter DIYbio) laboratories opened. At the DIYbio laboratory BioCurious, where Scroggins conducted two years of fieldwork, several months after opening to fanfare and media coverage, only a handful of people were using the wet lab to do biological experiments (Scroggins 2017; Scroggins and Varenne 2019). While the space quickly became a mecca for Silicon Valley tourists, laboratory work remained the province of a handful of professional scientists who worked at BioCurious due to lack of university affiliation or funding. To rectify this problem, the BioCurious board of directors decided to host a competition to develop 'community projects' that would create a structured apprenticeship programme, turning members from biological novices to skilled experimenters.

To select the 'community projects', a contest was held at BioCurious. Entries would be submitted to a panel of BioCurious board members, who would then select the most suitable projects. Per the contest announcement, the prize for winning entries was support from BioCurious in the form of free publicity and laboratory space. Potential projects were to engage the public, offer an easy path into laboratory work for new members, and offer media audiences a compelling example of DIYbio's potential. Out of nearly a dozen entrants, two projects were selected. One of the two winning projects was the Bioluminescent community project, aimed at creating a household lamp that would operate via the metabolism of bioluminescent bacteria rather than electricity. The Bioluminescent community project was led by a local artist illegally living in an attic space above his studio, without electricity. As he informed us at the inaugural project meeting, he was inspired by the Philips Microbial House design probe, which had recently won an award at a design competition in the Netherlands, to create an electricity-free form of lighting so he could read in bed without attracting the kind of attention that might see him evicted from his living space. The initial meetings were attended by several local graduate students, one professional scientist, a couple of software engineers, and several serial entrepreneurs who were attracted to DIYbio for the technical challenges and the possibility of working on, as one entrepreneur opined, 'the next big thing'.

In the course of our amateur research into bacterial plasmids, several members of the project discovered the iGEM competition. The competition was founded by the synthetic biologist Drew Endy to spur innovation and interest in the field of synthetic biology. For the last fifteen years, teams of collegiate synthetic biologists from around the world have converged in Boston for the annual iGEM competition, or, as it is colloquially referred to among those who judge and compete, the Giant Jamboree. Entering the iGEM competition requires a yearlong commitment. Teams must be organized a year in advance, faculty advisors must be secured, registration of intent is required on the iGEM website, and once these preliminaries are satisfied, a longer list of requirements must be satisfied. In exchange for registering and formally entering the competition, teams receive a distribution of standardized biological parts that can be used in the construction of their entries. The rub that lends iGEM the air of a MacGuffin is that there was no mechanism for a 'community laboratory' like BioCurious to enter the iGEM competition. At the start of our project, our initial steps down the funnel, we did not consider our unsuitability a problem but, as another serial entrepreneur put it, 'a minor hurdle' to be negotiated with the iGEM organizers. As will be made clear later, this minor hurdle would grow into an impasse.

The goal of the iGEM competition was the creation of a library of interchangeable biological parts, cleverly named BioBricks, to be used in the construction of novel biological organisms. In exchange for sharing engineering diagrams and schematics describing their entry in the iGEM competition, participants would receive access to all previous applicants' schematics, engineering diagrams, and, most importantly, the full library of synthesized biological parts ready to be used in the construction of novel bacterial plasmids. Fuelled by the unwarranted assumption that a library of synthesized biological parts is equivalent to a library of software modules, we decided at an early meeting that access to this library was the real prize for entering the iGEM competition. As the iGEM website explains:

> iGEM's main program is the iGEM Competition. The iGEM competition gives students the opportunity to push the boundaries of synthetic biology by tackling everyday issues facing the world. Made up of primarily university students, multidisciplinary teams work together to design, build, test, and measure a system of their own design using interchangeable biological parts and standard molecular biology techniques. Every year nearly 6,000 people dedicate their summer to iGEM and then come together in the fall to present their work and compete at the annual Jamboree.   (igem.org n.d.)

What our enthusiasm elided was that in entering the iGEM competition (with the promise of attending the Jamboree, a literal party), a team must slowly, over a period of time, bend its purpose and attention to match those of the competition organizers. Rather than a project designed to further the laboratory skills of BioCurious members, ostensibly what the winner of the community project competition was supposed to pursue, every step down the funnel drew us closer to the iGEM's preferred ends and preferred social drama of finding a solution to 'everyday problems' using synthetic biology—though, as we were soon made to realize, illicitly reading in bed was not the kind of 'everyday problem' the iGEM organizers wanted to see solved through synthetic biology. We might put the point spatially and temporally: the closer the Jamboree comes, the more intense the pull of the competition on the participants.

This was the case for the 'community laboratory' team in which Scroggins participated during the spring and summer of 2012 at BioCurious. First, the artist's idea to create a lamp that did not need electricity morphed into creating a BioCurious sign to be hung in the office window, powered by bioluminescent action. In time, the project would morph yet again into creating a generalized platform for plasmid engineering. With the iGEM fame and possible fortune in the form of a new market for direct-to-consumer bioengineered products, the original plans and the preparatory technical work that had been done were discarded in favour of using iGEM's library of BioBricks. Each iteration pulled the team further from the vision of using the 'community project' to create new DIYbiologists, motivated by artistic or critical concerns and pushed towards the iGEM vision of engineered solutions for 'everyday problems'.

The lure of high-speed trading

Prizes and games are transparent in a way because they are explicitly tagged as competitions and we can respond accordingly. In the wider world, however, what may not be explicitly defined and governed as competitions for prizes are often treated as such, due to our assumption that this is just how the world works, conditioned as we are to expect competitions and prizes in all aspects of our daily lives. We suggest that this second possibility may be a bleeding out of prize logics across the particular moment in capitalism that we are gesturing to as late capitalism. Many things, other than explicit prizes and specific competitions, seem to be perceived and treated as such.

Over the last thirty years, the way in which one buys publicly listed financial instruments (stocks, futures, options, etc.) in the USA has shifted dramatically. It used to be the case that you could call a broker in New York and commission an order. Then, your broker would send it to the floor of a stock exchange where a runner would sprint the order to a trader milling in some pit or another. Then, the trader would yell his/her order to his/her colleagues and find a buyer/seller for your order. Often this buyer or seller would be a market-making trader (or a specialist), a representative of a proprietary trading firm who made money ensuring that there would always be a liquid market in the pit. This market-maker would both buy and sell, and then collect the spread between as profit. Endless repetitions of this sort of market-making would make for a living. You, in turn, would pay a commission to your broker and that would be that.

However, in the last few decades, the US Securities and Exchange Commission (SEC) has interpreted its authority to create a national securities market to mean that trading should be electronic via networked limit order books, and buyers and sellers should be aware of the best prices as near instantaneously as possible (MacKenzie et al. 2012: 281–3). As a consequence, trading has fragmented across more than a dozen exchanges in the USA, in addition to 55 'Dark Pool' or 'Alternative Trading Systems', managed by financial service firms according to their own rules of order prioritization and fulfilment ('SEC.Gov|Alternative Trading System ("ATS") List' n.d.). This, coupled with derivatives trading, primarily happening in servers in Chicago suburbs and equities trading primarily happening in servers outside of New York, has created a total technological transformation of the securities industry (MacKenzie and Pardo-Guerra 2014). Electrification has led to demands for up-to-the-nanosecond information on markets across the country, as well as automation and algorithmization to allow trading to happen at the speed of information, far beyond what humans can handle.

One remarkable encapsulation of this is the 'flash crash' in which, on 6 May 2010, for over four minutes or so, the Dow Jones Industrial Average lost '998.5 points (or more than 9 per cent), equivalent to around one trillion dollars' (Borch 2016: 351). Though the exact cause of the 'flash crash' is hard to parse, it appeared to be due to some combination of mechanical trading algorithms getting stuck in a positive feedback loop and automated and linked trading strategies responding to that loop far more quickly than any human could cope.

The exact cause of events like the 'flash crash' is not our concern here. Rather, our concern is with the way in which reporters and journalists seize on the possibility of events like the 'flash crash' and the algorithmic and informational speed they entail to typify new forms of markets and focus on academic and journalistic scrutiny (as in Borch 2016). We are curious why 'Flash Boys' (Lewis 2014) and the 'high speed arms race' become *the* agenda, the MacGuffin for imagining markets, and why high-frequency algorithmic trading fills up whole journal special issues (*Economy and Society* 45(2)), when there seems to be no equivalent blockbuster literary events or extended sociological scrutiny for the rise of passive investing (e.g. Wigglesworth 2018) or why trading volatility seems to stabilize at comparatively low levels for long periods of time ('Why is volatility so low?' Bloomberg 19 January 2018).

In short, we are curious about the effects in knowledge production and what is included and occluded by focusing on the imagined prize to the exclusion of other stories about markets or the larger story of how people structure markets via regulations and laws. Here, it is not so much that anyone explicitly designed a prize for the best story about the fastest order router. Rather, it is as though the representational community responsible for understanding finance and transmitting that understanding to the rest of society, without any formal deliberation or explicit consideration, nevertheless, decided as a group that 1) there was (and is) basically a single prize at stake among market actors, 2) the representational community themselves would *also* compete to describe that prize (as in the financial journalist and academics cited earlier), and 3) the competition would basically be a contest. It is not so much that there was not a prize for a subset of traders who *needed* to be the fastest to make their trades (they exist and act exactly like that). And it is not so much that other traders do not have to deal with them (directly or indirectly, everyone on the market spends a little bit of time doing just that). It is that the whole rest of the financial universe is left out of the sprint against the speed of light, both materially and representationally. We suggest that a focus on the high-speed arms race and all its flashy material appurtenances may have hidden other market dynamics, subject to less overt forms of competition but equally consequential for market behaviour, because representational specialists acted as though there was a singular competition with a singular prize. Reporters and academics, in other words, followed the MacGuffin, which worked, as all MacGuffins do, to organize their attention.

The contest as social drama

Laboratory drama

As the Bioluminescent community project progressed throughout the spring, Scroggins and his colleagues spent several meetings watching videos made by winning iGEM teams. The videos had fantastic production values and made for compelling viewing. Each demonstrated the possibilities inherent in the creation of the standardized library of biological parts and assemblies the iGEM competition sought to create. There were sensors built from bacterial plasmids that lit up in a rainbow of colours as differing toxins and pollutants were detected, and bacterial plasmids were used as tiny automata in the service of manufacturing precious molecules. The videos were a cunning element of the contest as a trap. We had set out with a straightforward project, a lamp that works via bioluminescent action rather than electricity, designed as an apprenticeship into lab work. Yet, within a few weeks, the allure of the iGEM videos and the promise of access to BioBricks and recognition at the Jamboree had transformed the goal of the project into creating a platform for engineering bacterial plasmids. No doubt our direct move to build an engineering platform, a Google or Facebook for plasmid engineering, was a direct result of the entrepreneurial savvy at BioCurious. The half dozen veteran entrepreneurs immediately recognized that the ultimate prize of late capitalism, a platform that others are compelled to use, was there to be seized. And with that, we transitioned from making DIYbiologists for BioCurious to entering and winning the iGEM competition.

Our decision to change course revealed the iGEM competition to be, for our purposes at least, little more than a MacGuffin. Today, iGEM accepts teams composed of high school students, university undergraduates and graduate students, and community laboratories, but in 2012, iGEM only accepted university teams. However, being in Silicon Valley and with a cadre of formerly successful entrepreneurs at the helm, we considered the question of whether or not a 'community lab', as opposed to an academic lab, could enter the competition to be an open question, so we emailed the iGEM committee, assumed we would receive a positive response, and waited for our allotment of BioBricks to arrive in the mail. The iGEM organizers, though, were cagey, initially signalling that they would allow our entry but eventually backing out on the grounds that community labs were just too much of an unknown, leaving us without plot or purpose. The library of iGEM parts could not, for reasons of liability, be made available to laboratories unaffiliated with an academic laboratory.

Following the evaporation of our chance to enter the iGEM competition, a decision was made by one of the serial entrepreneurs in the project to befriend a postdoctoral researcher at a local university whose laboratory contained the full iGEM library. Though we were banned from entering the iGEM competition, we rationalized that we could still enjoy the fruits of victory by bending the rules of the competition. Through a bit of what is often called 'social hacking', the entrepreneur convinced the postdoctoral researcher to duplicate his laboratory's library of iGEM parts and smuggle them, without the legally mandated Material Transfer Agreement, to BioCurious. This exercise in piracy was justified by appealing to the intertwined spirits of competition and capitalism and specifically to the long history of rule breaking in the formation of Silicon Valley. The future is here, we argued; better to seek forgiveness tomorrow than to ask permission today.

Unfortunately, having laid hands, or rather petri dishes, on the BioBricks we coveted but were denied, we discovered to our surprise that none of them worked as described. Our time, our trouble, our organization, and our work were all pulled in a particular direction by the promise of a competition that we not only failed to win but failed to enter! And yet, the pull of the prize, both the library of standardized parts and the promise of a direct-to-consumer market for genetically modified organisms, continued to work within BioCurious. The year after the Bioluminescent community project failed to enter the iGEM competition, three BioCurious members, who were veterans of the Bioluminescent community project, raised a half million dollars via a Kickstarter campaign to launch a start-up company with the aim of engineering a houseplant to glow like a lamp at night.

Lost as we slid down the funnel of the iGEM competition was any focus on bioart, as discussed in the initial Bioluminescent meetings or critical interventions into the social and environmental conditions in Silicon Valley—air and water sensors or DNA barcoding that investigated food safety—that we had initially thought to pursue. Also eclipsed was the very notion of DIYbio as a biological science directed by amateur biologists and informed by their interests and concerns. Eighteen months after the start of the Bioluminescent community project, as Scroggins' fieldwork was ending, BioCurious still had not worked out how to make enough DIYbiologists to support the laboratory on membership dues. Instead, the BioCurious board of directors was forced to rely even more heavily on corporate donations to keep the lab afloat, slowly abandoning the idea of making DIYbiologists in favour of viewing the laboratory space as an informal venue for corporate sponsors to recruit unemployed or unaffiliated professional scientists and for serial entrepreneurs to test proof of concept ideas.

What has been gained by iGEM? What interesting ideas have made their way down their funnel? For one, teams entering the iGEM competition no longer have to submit fabricated assemblies, only information written as a standard protocol that describes the biological parts developed during the project. The cost of DNA synthesis, partly due to economies of scale generated by iGEM, has fallen far enough in the ensuing decade to make information the commodity of circulation for iGEM. And information is the commodity of record for iGEM, with more than three hundred teams from over forty countries entering the competition each year. The upshot for iGEM has been the creation of a database of talent and a library of parts, all of which can be, at some future date, monetized. More important, perhaps, is the iGEM competition's ability to set the terms of a social drama over the ends of synthetic biology by trapping the excitement and attention of aspiring synthetic biologists.

Market drama

Souleles became familiar with the high-speed arms race in the course of three years of fieldwork he has been conducting in New York, Chicago, Washington DC, and San Francisco, studying algorithmic trading as part of a team research project based at the Copenhagen Business School. Souleles and his colleagues were trying to understand how market behaviour, trading, and the allocation of wealth via financial channels have changed due to electrification, automation, and the creation of a nationwide network of financial exchanges. Again, high-frequency trading is only a subset of these changes. So, from 2017 onward, he has been conducting interviews with traders, regulators, exchange workers, and portfolio investors to understand how markets work and how money is moving around. Souleles would interview and observe and take the findings back to his team who would then integrate them with their fieldwork and use them to build up an agent-based modelling platform to simulate various market conditions.

As is often the case in ethnographic work, Souleles heard about whatever was on the mind of his informants: other financial dynamics and concerns in dribs and drabs through the course of his interviews and observations. One financial analyst starting an app-based retirement planning company noted that the rise of passive investing is what is shaping markets in his estimation. He felt that there was so much trading volume in electronically traded funds and index funds, set automatically in the service of portfolio balancing, that natural investors making informed decisions—speculators, value investors, hedge funds, and so on—were losing their ability to move markets. This, in turn, pushed prices up and volatility down, leading to an inscrutable market environment. His response to this was to make all this passive investing more accessible to people in their retirement saving, likely expanding the proportion of the market moving automatically and in lock step.

Speed here is secondary and becomes irrelevant as everyone trades automatically and quickly.

Another dynamic Souleles saw was the creation of alternative trading venues, or dark pools. Initially, financial services firms created these trading venues in order to give mostly large institutional investors shelter from high-frequency predations on open markets. As dark pools have expanded, however, they have introduced trading dynamics of their own. Often, large retail trading platforms like E-Trade would sell their order flow to large equity market-makers, who, in turn, would internally fill those orders, never sending them to public markets. Moreover, these trades could be filled by logics other than time priority, neutering the advantage high-speed transmission and information technology might grant.

What Souleles also saw was the commodification of high-speed trading technology. Any advantage accrued by being the fastest seems to have a fairly limited half-life. Access to microwave towers for the transmission and reception of market data was no longer the province of technological specialists; an old firm can simply purchase this sort of data access now. Ditto for server colocation in exchanges, as well as access to intelligent execution algorithms to avoid being taken advantage of by high-frequency traders. This sort of commodification led one partner in a proprietary trading firm to observe that the technological part of their job has perhaps been expensive, but they have always managed to stay ahead of it. All told, Souleles' informants could readily point to all sorts of things aside from the high-speed arms race that was affecting markets due to the rise of computerization and algorithms. This, however, would not be apparent from most journalistic or academic accounts. They only seem to have their eyes on the prize.

The universality of contests in late capitalism

> The main thing I've learned over the years is that the MacGuffin is nothing.
> I'm convinced of this, but I find it very difficult to prove it to others.
>
> – **Alfred Hitchcock**

We have focused our attention on how contests, using lures both material and symbolic, organize competitive relationships. We have drawn on the elaboration of Simmel in Chapter 1 to argue that these relationships are not spontaneous or naturally occurring. Rather, the contests that organize competitive relationships are both partially designed and partially natural. As denizens of late capitalism, our common sense and everyday experience of navigating markets and contests tell us that competitive relationships are a natural state, that we spontaneously organize ourselves into winners and losers mediated by the terms of contests, implicit and explicit (see also Varenne and McDermott 2018). While competition is one state of human relationships, it is by no means the only, or the most compelling, state of human relationships. We have taken small, but important steps, in this chapter to demonstrate how competitive relationships are naturalized through the design and ubiquitous deployment of contests, implicit and explicit, in late capitalism.

Designing contests and luring both the unsuspecting and wary into them, as Austen notes of nineteenth-century contests of the heart, is 'a manoeuvring business'. Moreover, in our late capitalist moment, the business of organizing social action through prizes is booming. Social dramas must be fully imagined and carefully materialized, lures must be carefully placed, and their funnels made as invisible as possible. Throughout, we have emphasized the stakes of these contests, from marriage to the Nobel prize and onto to the smaller, but no less dramatic, stakes of the purpose and direction of a DIYbio project, and the imagined winner of a high-speed trading contest. Scroggins has shown how a prize seeker can be trapped by a savvy prize creator and that the ends of the prize creator can come to replace those of the prize seeker, even when the competitive relationship is only imagined. This is one type of social drama. Souleles has shown how attention can be trapped. High-speed trading is a MacGuffin, a plot device that directs attention towards particular events and elides others, which may be more important and relevant to market formation but lacks the dramatic element of competition between rivals.

Our lens for understanding how contests organize competitive relationships has been the anthropological literature on traps and trapping (Gell 1996; Mason 1900; Seaver 2018). Traps are a useful lens because they, as we have argued of contests, are both partly natural and partly design, inhabiting the liminal space between natural and artificial. Following Mason's (1900) lead, we have emphasized the social drama unfolding between the trapper and the trapped, using the work of the consulting firm McKenzie as an exemplar of a contemporary trapper who deploys a wide range of lures (prizes), to attract specific kinds of individuals and organizations into particular kinds of competitive relationships. Further, we have argued that an effect of organizing these contests, made explicit by consultants like McKenzie, is the replacement of the contestants' purposes and means with those of the contest organizers.

Though explicit and implicit commercial contests are a powerful mechanism for the naturalizing competitive relationships, they do not exhaust the range of traps, contests, lures, and prizes we must confront in commercial, academic, and personal spheres. All of us, in even the most sentimental and private spheres of life, whether taking the field intending to seize the prize or not, are caught in the netting of competition and the stark social drama of success and failure.

References

Bloomberg.com 2018. 'Why is market volatility so low?' 19 January 2018. Available at: https://www.bloomberg.com/news/articles/2018-01-19/why-is-volatility-so-low-some-see-crowded-trades-minsky-moment (accessed 25 August 2020).

Borch, C. 2016. 'High-frequency trading, algorithmic finance and the Flash Crash: reflections on eventalization'. *Economy and Society* 45 (3–4): 350–78.

Gell, A. 1996. 'Vogel's net: traps as artworks and artworks as traps'. *Journal of Material Culture* 1 (1): 15–38.

igem.org (n.d.). Available at: https://igem.org/Main_Page (accessed 25 August 2020).

Lewis, M. 2014 *Flash Boys: A Wall Street Revolt*. New York: W. W. Norton.

MacKenzie, D., Beunza, D., Millo, Y., and Pardo-Guerra, J. P. 2012. 'Drilling through the Allegheny Mountains'. *Journal of Cultural Economy* 5 (3): 279–96.

MacKenzie, D. and Pardo-Guerra, J. P. 2014. 'Insurgent capitalism: island, bricolage and the re-making of finance'. *Economy and Society* 43 (2): 153–82.

McKinsey & Company 2009. *'And the Winner Is…' Philanthropists and governments make prizes count*. Sydney, Australia: McKinsey & Company. Available at: https://www.mckinsey.com/industries/social-sector/our-insights/and-the-winner-is-philanthropists-and-governments-make-prizes-count (accessed 10 August 2019).

Mason, O. T. 1900. 'Traps of the Amerinds—A study in psychology and invention'. *American Anthropologist* 2 (4): 657–75.

Scroggins, M. 2017. *This Is a New Thing in the World: Design and Discontent in the Making of a 'Garage Lab'*. Teachers College. Available at: https://doi.org/10.7916/D8GM8CZQ (accessed 25 January 2019).

Scroggins, M. and Varenne, H. 2019. 'Designing, animating, and repairing a suitable do-it-yourself biology lab'. In *Educating in Life: Educational Theory and the Emergence of New Normals*, edited by H. Varenne. New York: Routledge: 49–62.

Seaver, N. 2018. 'Captivating algorithms: recommender systems as traps'. *Journal of Material Culture* 24 (4): 421–36.

'SEC.Gov|Alternative Trading System ("ATS") List' no date. Available at: https://www.sec.gov/foia/docs/atslist.htm (accessed 3 May 2019).

Simmel, G. 1950. *The Sociology of Georg Simmel*. New York: Simon & Schuster.

Souleles, D. and Scroggins, M. 2017. 'The meanings of production(s): showbiz and deep plays in finance and DIYbiology'. *Economy and Society* 46 (1): 82–102.

Varenne, H. and McDermott, R. 2018. *Successful Failure: The School America Builds*. New York: Routledge.

Wigglesworth, R. 2018. 'Passive attack: the story of a Wall Street revolution'. *Financial Times*, 20 December 2018. Available at: https://www.ft.com/content/807909e2-0322-11e9-9d01-cd4d49afbbe3 (accessed 25 August 2020).

10
The organization of competition and non-competition in schools

Søren Christensen and Hanne Knudsen

This chapter explores competition in the context of education. We invite the reader into a Danish school filled with stars, trophies, and triumphant sounds. We point to the hard work done by the teacher to organize a sense of competition—but also to control and to reduce competition. We also suggest that this leaves students with the responsibility for assessing whether they are best motivated by comparing and competing with classmates or by focusing on their own learning paths. Ambivalence, volatility, and unpredictability are key words in understanding what is going on when it comes to competition in the classroom.

Now we are jumping to conclusions. Let us slow down a little and first dwell on the historical changes that have occurred with regard to the way competition is practised and understood in education. Subsequently, we will set out our understanding of competition as an analytical concept, which we will then use for our empirical analysis of a Danish school setting. We conclude with a discussion of ways in which competition is currently used in education, as well as the ambivalent attitudes that remain associated with it.

Educational ambivalences towards competition

In 2017, the Danish Ministry of Education issued guidelines for teachers on how to administer national tests for students in the most appropriate way. The ministry recommended that 'in order to reduce a potential atmosphere of competition' no student should be allowed to leave before the testing period expired. 'Some students simply believe that the best students are those who finish up first' (Undervisningsministeriet 2018: 11). This concern turns out to be relevant if children are asked about their perspective on assessment—and the similarities to computer gaming strategies (Kousholt 2016). A few paragraphs later, teachers are admonished that 'it is important that students are seated in such a way that they will not be able to see your test page. If students are able to track how many questions their classmates have answered, this may create the basis for competition and discomfort for some students.' (Undervisningsministeriet 2018: 11).

Søren Christensen and Hanne Knudsen, *The organization of competition and non-competition in schools* In: *Competition: What It Is and Why It Happens*. Edited by: Stefan Arora-Jonsson, Nils Brunsson, Raimund Hasse, and Katarina Lagerström, Oxford University Press. © Søren Christensen and Hanne Knudsen 2021. DOI: 10.1093/oso/9780192898012.003.0010

The association made here between competition and discomfort is not fortuitous; and the sense of discomfort applies not only to the students but also to the education system itself. In these guidelines, the ministry suggests how national testing can be organized so as to reduce or even eliminate competition. In the context of national testing, competition seems to be a spontaneous (and irrational) product of the way in which students observe each other—something against which the education system must organize itself.

This sense of discomfort with regard to the idea of competition has not always been equally pronounced in the history of education. In fact, competition is one of the oldest and most common techniques for strengthening discipline and motivation for learning in the classroom. To our knowledge, the first educational thinker to discuss student competition in such terms was the Roman rhetorician and schoolmaster Quintilian. The potential for student competition was one of Quintilian's main arguments for the educational superiority of the school as compared to the domestic teacher. According to Quintilian, competition (properly organized) could be used to intensify the motivation for learning in a manner unparalleled by any other pedagogical device:

> I remember that my own masters had a practice which was not without advantages. Having distributed the boys in classes, they made the order in which they were to speak depend on their ability, so that the boy who had made most progress in his studies had the privilege of declaiming first. The performances on these occasions were criticized. To win commendation was a tremendous honour, but the prize most eagerly coveted was to be the leader of the class. [...] I will venture to assert that to the best of my memory this practice did more to kindle our oratorical ambitions than all the exhortations of our instructors, the watchfulness of our *paedagogi* and the prayers of our parents.   (Quintilian 1980: I.2.25)

Quintilian's masters organized competition by offering themselves as the third party for whose recognition students were invited to compete. They thereby exploited the natural limitations of teacher attention in a classroom setting with many students and one teacher in a way that turned teacher attention (or recognition) into the scarce object of their common desire.

According to Quintilian, this also profoundly changed the relationship between teacher and students, as compared to the domestic teacher. In the school, with its many students and a single master, the master appeared not so much as the one *from* whom students learned but as the one *for* whom they learned. To the extent that students learned, this was not primarily because the master taught them. It was because, through the organization of contests, learning was constituted as the object of the master's recognition: it was by being 'number one', by displaying signs of superior learning as compared to their peers that students would gain the recognition of their teachers.

In different versions, this use of student competition as a motivational technology has played a huge role throughout the entire history of (Western) education, and not least the Christian tradition. In the sixteenth and seventeenth centuries, the Jesuit system of education, which was based to an unprecedented degree on student competition (*aemulatio*), was the most successful educational system in Europe (Durkheim 1938). To emulate means to imitate someone with a view to exceeding them. Here competition is embedded in a learning relationship: you can only surpass other people if you learn from them. However, Christianity charged competition with moral ambivalence, highlighting the dark sides of competition in a wholly new way. So even as the Jesuit system of education triumphed across Europe, its detractors, ranging from the Jansenists to Rousseau, were numerous and passionate. In their view, student competition was fundamentally a recipe for vice. For Quintilian and his contemporaries, student competition was not morally problematic. It served to develop the confident and agonistic spirit, which befitted the Roman (male) citizen and public speaker. In a Christian perspective, on the other hand, it could easily be viewed as fostering pride and vanity on the part of winners and envy and anger on the part of losers—thereby running counter to the very purpose of education, that of fostering virtuous Christian subjects.

While the hold of Christian morality on education gradually weakened in the nineteenth and twentieth centuries, the critique of competition did not. Instead, it took a new turn. In the Nordic countries, especially, the purpose of schooling was re-conceived in the light of the catastrophic experiences with Fascism before and during World War II. From this perspective, the most important purpose of education was to educate students into democratic citizens capable of cooperation, dialogue, and mutual understanding. This ruled out any legitimate role for student competition in schooling. Competition was viewed as something which created conflicts and pitted students against each other—thus undermining the harmonious and democratic community that schooling was supposed to foster (Husén 1966). Educational psychology has treated competition almost solely in tandem with cooperation (Fulüp 2004). This sense of discomfort with regard to competition became even more pronounced as the expanding post-World War II welfare states sought to turn schools into engines of social equality under slogans like 'equality through education'. In this context, educational competition was vehemently criticized as the engine through which existing class structures were reproduced within the education system (Bjerregaard 1977). According to the most principled proponents of this view, grades and examinations would also have to in order to get rid of competition within the education system.

Today, it is clear that this did not happen. What did happen to competition, however, is less clear. Since the 1970s, the question of competition between students has played a very limited role in educational research and public debate (for analysis of discussions of downsides of competition in Singapore, see Christensen 2015). Policy makers and educationists are much more concerned with learning than with competition. The main concern of today's dominant educational paradigm is to *maximize learning* and to do so not only for students as a group but for each *individual* student (Hattie 2012; Knudsen 2017; Thompson and Cook 2017). Efforts are made to make students *want* to do what they *have to* do: to be motivated to learn more

(Staunæs 2018). In this context, competition is rarely mentioned. Various authors (Allen 2015; Thompson and Cook 2017) have suggested that this new educational paradigm may give rise to new modes of competition, but they have not developed this point in any kind of detail. We try to approach this problem by looking into the ways in which competition arises and is handled in a contemporary Danish classroom informed by the current educational paradigm. We ask if competition can be controlled and organized, and we point out the difficulties in doing this because competition is volatile and unpredictable and because of inherent paradoxes in the contemporary educational paradigm. As we shall see in our empirical analysis, both students and teacher work hard to get the best out of new modes of competition, handling the risks of comparison and forms of motivation which are deemed to be wrong. Before we turn to this, we need to develop competition as an analytical concept with a view to grasping what is going on in the classroom.

Competition, observation, and desire

In order to explain our approach to competition in education, we take our point of departure in a quotation from one of the lesser-known theorists of competition—the Danish-German sociologist Theodor Geiger. In his book on competition, originally published in Danish in 1941, Geiger (1941: 13) states that for competition to occur: '[t]he parties must subjectively experience each other in their competitive roles. A side-glance to the other constitutes the competitive relationship.' In this short statement, Geiger makes a number of points which we believe are important for an analysis of social competition in general and educational competition in particular.

First, Geiger claims that a sociological conception of competition cannot ignore the subjective experience of social actors. Whereas natural scientists speak of competition as an objective relationship between entities (animals, plants, and even genes) that are blissfully ignorant of competition, social competition cannot be conceived independently of the ways in which social actors define the situation in which they find themselves. In the same vein, Niklas Luhmann (1995: 382) states that competition is a special kind of social experience, the characteristic being that one system's goals can only be attained at the expense of another system's goals.

Second, Geiger suggests that the experience of social actors involved in competition can be conceived as a form of observation. He does this through the notion of a 'side-glance' through which competitors relate to each other. In other words, he conceives of competition as a specific gaze imposed by social actors upon each other. In his exposition of this idea, however, he seems to presuppose that this form of observation is reciprocal by nature. For competition to occur, the relevant social actors all have to observe each other as competitors. We want to argue, however, that reciprocity cannot simply be assumed if we conceptualize competition as a form of observation. For instance, it is possible to imagine a situation in which a younger sister wants to be the best in her class because her older sister was the best in her class. This younger sister competes both with her classmates to be number one in her class and with her older sister to be the best school performer. The older sister may not even know that her younger sister is competing with her, while (in the same vein) her classmates may not know that they are involved in a competition. Consequently, we want to keep open the possibility that the same situation can be construed differently by different social actors: some people may regard it as a competitive situation while others regard it as non-competition. The side-glance may be competitive for one and not for the other. In our analysis, we will devote more empirical attention to this question.

Third, by using the notion of 'side-glance', Geiger suggests that competition involves more than one glance. For competition to occur, competitors must also observe something more than each other—something for which they are both striving, which they both (or all) desire. Here, Geiger makes an important conceptual distinction between a struggle (*Zweikampf*) and a competition. In a struggle, the parties simply fight against each other, face each other. The objectives of the contestants are exhausted by the defeat of the opponent. In a competition, on the other hand, the contestants do not simply fight against each other but also for something else—what Geiger (1941: 12) calls 'the object'. In our analysis, we want to explore how this object can be defined in different ways in educational settings and how this is related to different forms of interplay between the glance towards the object and the side-glances between competitors.

For this purpose, however, we also need to go beyond Geiger's rather restricted conception of the object of competition. While Geiger mentions many different examples of competitive objects, he seems to understand them predominantly as things: prizes or possessions won through competitive success.

In this connection, we want to enlist Georg Simmel's theory of competition in order to gain a more nuanced approach to the object of competition. According to Simmel, competition, or, at least, 'higher competition' (see Chapter 1, this volume), is not simply a struggle for something but also a struggle for someone. If Simmel views competition as a social form (rather than pure anti-social destruction), this is not just because it links competitors to each other but also because it links them to a third party for whose favour they are vying (Simmel 1903/2008: 961).

The favour of the third party may take many different forms: it may be public opinion in politics, consumers on the market, the jury in a courtroom, or a loved one in courtship. In all these cases, Simmel claims, the key to competitive success is the ability to figure out what the third party wants—or, put differently, what the third party desires (1903/2008: 962). In this sense, desire is not simply what motivates the parties to compete but also the object for which they compete. The competitors strive to become (as in courtship) or at least to provide (as in market competition) what the third party desires.

In this respect, Simmel is close to French psychoanalyst Jacques Lacan's theory of desire, on which we will also draw in our analysis (and on which we have already implicitly drawn in the previous section). According to Lacan's famous formula, desire is 'the desire of the other' (2006; 2019). This means, on the one hand, that desire is socially constituted: our desire is not purely individual but is shaped by our side-glances towards others—our observations of other people's desires. On the other hand, desire can be understood as a desire to obtain the recognition, approval, or simply attention of the other. This (the Lacanian equivalent of the third party) is what Lacan calls 'the big Other'—the (imagined) figure to whom we want to appear in a certain desirable light.

In our analysis of competition in a contemporary educational setting, we want to use the insights of Geiger, Simmel, and Lacan to explore three sets of questions. The first set concerns the objects of desire offered to students in contemporary education. Which objects do contemporary educational authorities (from teachers to educational games and testing systems) invite students to desire and to which extent do they lead students towards competition or away from competition? The second set of questions concerns the volatility and unpredictability that may follow when you conceptualize competition as a mode of observation that also involves the agency of side-glances between students themselves. How do teachers and students respond to the potential for competition, which dynamics are produced, and what can we learn about the manageability of (non)competition in educational settings? The third set of questions focuses more specifically on ambivalences towards competition in contemporary education. Can the ambivalences relating to competition which run throughout educational history still be identified in contemporary education? And if so, how are they shaped differently in the context of today's dominant conceptions of education?

Organized (non)competition in the school class

Beyond scarcity: individual trajectories, prizes for all

If it seems timely to return to the question of competition in education, this is also because, in recent years, competition has resurfaced in education as an explicit motivational technology—most directly under the name of 'gamification'.

Basically, gamification means the introduction of game elements (new levels, prizes, leaderboards, etc.) into activities that are not in themselves game activities, so as to make such activities more exciting and thereby increase motivation. The term covers a number of very different activities, ranging from loyalty programmes to learning apps like Duolingo or Mathletics.

In the context of schools, the widespread use of Kahoot games is probably the best-known example of gamification. Here, however, we focus on a different example of gamification. CampMat is a digital maths game for primary school students, developed by the Danish learning company Alinea. We adopt two different perspectives on this game. First, we analyse two short videos that were produced by Alinea for marketing purposes. Second, we discuss how the game is actually played by second graders in a Danish school class.[1] We seek to identify the ways in which competition is organized both into existence and out of existence in the context of CampMat. We draw on our conceptualization of competition as a form of observation, and we look for invitations of competitive side-glances implying that *someone can only obtain the object of desire at the cost of someone else*. In other words, the competitive side-glance involves scarcity, a relation (without reciprocity), and a source of recognition (a third party).

We suggest that CampMat is a learning game that claims to provide the intensity of competition without the dark sides like failure and superficial motivation or demotivation. And it is apparent that the teacher works hard to organize (non)competition, giving the students responsibility for handling the perennial ambivalence regarding competition.

CampMat is clearly a game, and it makes abundant references to the best-known (or at least most-popular) arena of social competition: sport. The outcome of the game is not (for the most part) referred to as 'learning' but as 'training'. This reference is also quite clear in the very name of the game. The 'camp' to which the name refers is a 'training camp'—a space dedicated to optimizing your fitness and technical skills.

Nevertheless, Alinea's presentation material carefully eschews, or at least downplays, the competitive aspect of game-playing. In one of the videos, a student voice says about the game: 'Even though some of us have advanced further than others, we have all been rewarded with a radio' (an in-game prize). So what matters is not that some of the participants are ahead of others. What matters is that there are prizes for everyone. Recognition is an abundant resource, not a scarce one, and in this way competition is sidelined in the gaming context.

It is therefore no coincidence that the side-glance is virtually absent in the videos. Students are sitting in rows, each turned towards their own iPads. A boy who has just been awarded a star clenches his fist, exclaiming 'Yes!' However, such gestures of triumph do not appear to be manifestations of competition. The students are playing for stars, trophies, and prizes. In other words, they are playing for the recognition of the big Other—but they are not competing for this recognition. The algorithmic big Other differs from the classroom teacher to the extent that students do not have to compete for its attention. The game is based on an adaptive algorithm, which gets to know students while they are playing it. Thus, CampMat revolves around the intimate relationship between the algorithm and the individual student. This algorithm is a benevolent and generous big Other that works according to a logic of abundance rather than scarcity: each student has its undivided attention, and it offers recognition (stars and trophies) in abundance.

In using elements associated with competitive activities (stars, trophies, prizes, etc.), CampMat is not only related to modern computer games. It can also be viewed

---

[1] We have previously analysed this case in a Danish book on motivation (Christensen and Knudsen 2019).

as dovetailing with the tradition of emulation in education. It functions as a motivational technology that incites students to perform for the Other—to strive for the recognition of the algorithm. It instils a desire for learning in students by exploiting the reflective dimension of desire—by embedding desire for learning within the desire for the desire of the Other (stars, trophies, prizes, etc.).

As already suggested, however, CampMat is also profoundly different from other competitive activities because it seeks to eradicate the specifically competitive element in emulation. All the students can obtain the undivided attention and recognition of the algorithm. If competition is eradicated from the game, this is basically because the other students are irrelevant to each student's relationship with the algorithm.

In this sense, CampMat can be viewed as yet another manifestation of the discomfort with competition that has permeated education throughout history. However, this is a different kind of discomfort. In the 1970s, especially, educators criticized competition in the name of the social: competition was rejected as a threat to the school class as a collaborating social community. This is not the case in CampMat since the school class as a social community is virtually absent from the game. Competition appears not as an expression of individualism, which threatens communitarian relations, but rather as a social dynamic, which may distort the learning relationship between the algorithm and each individual student.

In this sense, the sidelining of competition involves less a concern for social relationships and more a concern for individual learning. Competition appears as a distraction that may divert students from their own individual learning paths (or, in other words, their own exclusive and intimate relationship with the big Other of the game). In this way, CampMat may exemplify how the educational critique of competition is re-articulated under the aegis of a new educational paradigm focusing on personalized or individualized learning (Thompson and Cook 2017). It also raises the question of how the social relations traditionally associated with the class are themselves re-articulated through this learning paradigm. In the next section, we address this question by examining the game in a different way—as a social practice in a Danish second grade.

Bringing the class back in

In the second grade in which we observed the use of CampMat, the game was played in a way that differed significantly from Alinea's promotion material. Most importantly, both the maths teacher and the students worked hard to supply the game with a social dimension—that is, to turn it into a class activity and not simply an activity for individual students.

They did this primarily in two ways. First, the class adopted its own rules for playing the game. CampMat consists of three different universes that are very close to the levels of conventional computer games. However, they differ from levels because in order to ensure individual learning trajectories CampMat allows players to move back and forth between the levels. However, the class had decided to ban this possibility, condemning it as a form of cheating that made it impossible to assess how far each student had advanced in the game. In this sense, the rules of the class prioritized standards that privileged social comparison of learning progress over individualized learning trajectories.

Second, CampMat's reward system was externalized—transformed from being an intimate relationship between the algorithm and the individual student into a public system of rewards that were visible to everybody in the classroom. In order to turn the game into a class activity instead of being an individual activity, the maths teacher had decided to duplicate the star system in the classroom. Whenever students had obtained a certain number of stars in the game, they were allowed to manufacture a yellow cardboard star, which they would then fix onto a cupboard at the back of the class.

For Helle, the maths teacher, this system served to incorporate the individualized learning trajectories of CampMat into the class as an overarching learning community. There were two main aspects to this reconstitution of the class. First, it sought to displace the function of the big Other from the algorithm to the class itself. On several occasions, Helle said that she had duplicated the star system because she thought that students' successes in learning should be recognized not only by the algorithm but also by fellow students. This is precisely what happened when students walked through the classroom in order to fix their stars to the cupboard. The function of the big Other was transferred from the algorithm to the class community (including the teacher herself). In other words, Helle's star system turned the individualized recognition of the algorithm into a way of obtaining the collective recognition of the class by placing your star on the cupboard under the gaze of the entire class. However, even as the source of recognition shifted, the form of recognition remained basically the same. Just like the algorithm, the class appeared as a benevolent and generous big Other that had recognition in abundance. Each student and learning achievement was recognized in precisely the same way—by walking down the 'catwalk' of the classroom displaying your star to the class.

Secondly, Helle's star system sought to re-embed the playing of CampMat within the class as a community of learning. As suggested earlier, CampMat describes itself as a 'training camp'—using an expression usually associated with sport. In an educational context, however, the notion of training is dangerously close to drilling—the repetitive inculcation of purely technical skills. For Helle, her duplication of the star system was one way of remedying this. She stated explicitly that the star system was her way of elevating CampMat from a training activity to a learning activity. According to her, the public display of stars created a space for students to relate to each other's experiences with the game. It created a communicative space where students could discuss and reflect on the game—and seek help on questions that had been successfully answered by other students. For Helle, it was this inter-subjective and reflective dimension of her reward system that elevated CampMat from the level of training to the level of learning.

Comparison and competition

By inventing her own classroom star system, Helle deliberately changed CampMat from an individualized activity (involving the algorithm and the individual student) into a social activity (involving the class and the individual student). However, in doing this Helle also re-introduced the dimension of sociality that the game itself had carefully eliminated—that is, the side-glance.

Helle's star system re-introduced the side-glance in the sense that it re-constituted the class as a space for comparison between students. Naturally, comparison is nothing new in classroom life. It is inherent to the class as a social institution. However, as mentioned earlier, since World War II in particular, comparison has been disavowed by an educational ideology calling for students 'not to compare' (in order not to open the gates of competition)—even though the education system systematically does so itself. While comparison is active in this kind of classroom context, it is implicit and disavowed. In Helle's classroom, on the other hand, it was explicit and public. It constituted a public grid of visibility that no student could ignore and to which they were all accountable.

As a medium of comparison, Helle's star system worked in an ambivalent way. On the one hand, it was a system of universal recognition in which all the students could have their learning successes recognized by the class. On the other hand, it worked in terms of more and less and ahead and behind. It did this because it made visible the different achievements of the students (the number of stars), as well as their overall degree of progression (levels completed).

If students could not ignore this grid of comparison, they could (and did) relate to it in different ways. The fact that the star system made students accountable for their learning in a highly public and visible way was revealed not least by the fact that most students openly discussed their relative positions in the game. To the extent that Helle's star system succeeded in inspiring reflection and communication between students, this was very much an ongoing and open-ended discussion of the meanings of comparative positions.

Even though the star system made comparative positions visible to all, this did not result in a general state of competition between students. The reason for this was the absence of a big Other—whether this is interpreted as the teacher or the class—inciting students to observe the grid of comparison as providing a ranking where only one could be number one (Esposito 2017). Indeed, it was highly unclear how the big Other wanted students to observe and make sense of their comparative positions. To the extent that the star system organized students' learning achievements on a scale of more and less, ahead and behind, it introduced a dimension of scarcity (one student's learning successes made other students less successful, and vice versa) that might be seen as inciting competition between students.

Still, it was left entirely unclear whether this was the correct way to observe comparative positions. In the class, one boy was acknowledged by everybody (including Helle) as being far ahead of the others in CampMat (and maths generally).

However, it remained unclear whether this boy was a model of excellence to be emulated by other students. In an interview with a Danish newspaper, Helle seemed to support this interpretation when she defended her star system by claiming that children are naturally motivated by competition (Nilsson 2019).

In our conversations with her, however, she argued differently, explaining that this boy was a very competitive student with a highly achievement-oriented family background. Competition here appeared as one particular mode of game-playing with no inherent superiority over others. In this sense, the boy did not stand out as the unambiguous winner of the learning game created around CampMat. Indeed, in the class one girl rivalled his position as a model learner—not by competing with him but by adopting the opposite approach to the grid of comparison created by Helle's star system. 'If you see that others are ahead', she told us, 'you may get an urge to overtake them. But then you realize that it's not about coming first, it's about being good.' This girl had realized that the overall objective was to focus on your own learning. So for her the learning ideal was not the student who came first but the one who was mature enough in her learning strategies to resist the temptation of competition and focus instead on her own individual learning trajectory. She expresses precisely the ambivalent attitude to competition in the current educational paradigm, with the distinction between intrinsic and extrinsic motivation dominating and interest focusing on the factors that promote learning most efficiently. The risk of utilizing an external reward system is that it leads to extrinsic motivation (Greer 2017).

In this sense, Helle's star system paradoxically reverted to the individualized approach of the game itself. No specific mode of observing comparative positions was imposed on the students. Instead, they were left to work out their own way of coping with universal comparison in the manner that best suited their individual modes of motivation. Here competition appeared as just one way among others of observing the classroom grid of comparison—a strategy that was neither superior nor inferior in itself, but one that students could adopt if this mode of observation was most efficient for their learning motivation. This individualized approach is reminiscent of many gamified learning apps (Duolingo, for instance), which are not directly organized in competitive terms but in which competition (leaderboards, etc.) is a function that can be switched on or off at will, depending on the motivational structures or current mood of individual learners.

Conclusion: competition as disavowed sociality in current education

Earlier pedagogical discussions on competition saw competition as a threat to community and cooperation, potentially undermining collaboration and socialization for democracy and equality. The current ambivalence towards competition is based less on moral and social concerns and more on a concern for individual learning. According to the currently dominating educational paradigm, students should maximize their own learning. This re-actualizes competition as a tempting solution to the problem of upholding the maximum intensity of investment in learning. The dilemmas regarding competition in the current educational paradigm therefore relate to the risk of alienating individual students from their own learning paths by being seduced to follow superficial goals or to compare themselves to others.

The current prevalence of gamified learning technologies in education can be viewed as an attempt to find a solution to these dilemmas. Such technologies are frequently based on adaptive algorithms that customize learning to suit the individual even though they rely on elements (like prizes) associated with competition. The intensity and motivation a student can experience by winning is desirable. At the same time, gamified learning technologies avoid the downsides of competition as a form of sociality: prizes for everyone should make sure that no-one is envious or disappointed.

In our analysis of CampMat we have explored how these current ambivalences with regard to competition play out—and mutate into new forms—in a classroom setting. We have seen how the teacher externalizes the reward system. She thereby simultaneously provides a system of universal recognition—a rating with stars for everyone—and a ranking of students that could incite students to observe the situation as competitive.

However, according to our analysis, this does not unambiguously mean that the teacher is inviting competition. Instead, we have argued that the classroom setting is characterized by a form of open organization that leaves undecided the question of competition or non-competition. To a large extent, each student is left to work out how to observe herself and her classmates. In this sense, the perennial ambivalence between competition and non-competition is displaced, becoming something for which each individual student must assume responsibility. Students must prove that they are reflective learners by deciding whether coming first or being good will be the most effective way of sustaining their investment in learning. The student should be aware whether learning is promoted more with the side-glance turned to her/himself or to the classmates. Simply forgetting yourself in the attempt to win is too easy, and competition becomes a temptation for the student and the disavowed form of sociality in current education.

The current ambivalence with regard to competition stems from a care for the individual's maximized learning. This means that even when the issue is forms of sociality, the starting point is the individual. Education has never been simply a matter of learning how to read and count; it has always been a question of socializing future generations. The current focus on learning makes basic questions like what kind of citizens do we want to educate, which virtues should they possess, and how do we want them to relate to each other difficult to debate among educational professionals. Sometimes the question of what kind of children we will get out of all this occurs in debates among educational professionals, but often in indirect ways, as 'a cold shiver down the spine' (Pors 2016). Focus on individual learning has impoverished our language for the social dimensions of education. By focusing on competition, we have sought in this chapter to direct focus back on sociality in education.

References

Allen, A. 2015. *Benign Violence. Education in and beyond the Age of Reason*. New York: Palgrave Macmillan.

Bjerregaard, R. 1977. 'Nedbrydning af barrierer, opbygning af fællesskab' (Breaking down barriers, building up community). *Uddannelse* 10 (8): 637–52.

Christensen, S. 2015. 'Healthy competition and unsound comparison: reforming educational competition in Singapore'. *Globalisation, Societies and Education* 13 (4): 553–73.

Christensen, S. and Knudsen, H. 2019. 'Komme først eller være god? konkurrence som prekær motivation for læring' (Winning or being good? Competition as precarious motivation for learning). In *At skulle ville: om motivationsarbejde og motivationens tilblivelse og effekter*, edited by K. Kousholt, J. B. Krejsler, and M. Nissen. Frederiksberg: Samfundslitteratur: 149–72.

Durkheim, E. 1938. *L'évolution pédagogique en France*. Paris: Puf.

Esposito, E. 2017. 'Organizing without understanding'. *Zeitschrift für Literaturwissenschaft und Linguistik* 47 (3): 351–9.

Fülöp, M. 2004. 'Competition as a culturally constructed concept'. In *Travelling Facts: The Social Construction, Distribution, and Accumulation of Knowledge*, edited by C. Baillie, E. Dunn, and Y. Zheng. Frankfurt/New York: Campus Verlag: 124–48.

Geiger, T. 1941. *Konkurrence: En Sociologisk Analyse* (Competition: a sociological analysis). Aarhus: København.

Greer, D. 2017. 'Motivation and attention as foundations for student learning'. In *From the Laboratory to the Classroom*, edited by J. C. Horvath, J.M. Lodge, and J. Hattie. London: Routledge/Taylor & Francis Group: 45–60.

Hattie, J. 2012. *Visible Learning for Teachers. Maximizing Impact on Learning*. London/New York: Routledge.

Husén, T. 1966 [1957]. *Pædagogisk Psykologi* (Psychology of Education). København: Nyt Nordisk Forlag Arnold Busck.

Knudsen, H. 2017. 'John Hattie: I'm a statistician, I'm not a theoretician'. *Nordic Journal of Studies in Educational Policy* 3 (3): 253–61.

Kousholt, K. 2016. 'Testing as social practice: analysing testing in classes of young children from the children's perspective'. *Theory & Psychology* 26 (3): 377–92.

Lacan, J. 2019. *Desire and Its Interpretation: The Seminar of Jacques Lacan Book VI*. Cambridge, UK/Medford, MA: Polity Press.

Lacan, J. 2006. 'The subversion of the subject and the dialectic of desire in the Freudian unconscious'. In *Ecrits: A Selection*. London and New York: W. W. Norton, 223–49 (translated by Bruce Fink).

Luhmann, N. 1995. *Social Systems*. Stanford: Stanford University Press.

Nilsson, K. 2019. De kalder det synlig læring: Alle børnene i 3. d ved, hvem der kun har fået én stjerne [They call it visible learning: All the children i 3.d. knows who only got one star]. *Politiken*, 5th of February 2019.

Pors, J. G. 2016. ' "It sends a cold shiver down my spine": ghostly interruptions to strategy implementation'. *Organization Studies* 37 (11): 1641–59.

Quintilian 1980. *Institutio Oratoria*: *Books I–III*. Cambridge, MA: Harvard University Press.

Simmel, G. 1903/2008. 'Sociology of competition'. *Canadian Journal of Sociology/Cahiers Canadiens de Sociologie* 33 (4): 957–78.

Staunæs, D. 2018. '"Green with envy": affects and gut feelings as an affirmative, immanent, and trans-corporeal critique of new motivational data visualisations'. *International Journal of Qualitative Studies in Education* 31 (5): 409–21.

Thompson, G. and Cook, I. 2017. 'The logic of data-sense: thinking through learning personalisation'. *Discourse: Studies in the Cultural Politics of Education* 38 (5): 740–54.

Undervisningsministeriet 2018. *Vejledning om de Nationale Test—Til Lærere i alle Fag* (*Guidance for National Tests—For Teachers*). Styrelsen for Undervisning og Kvalitet, København. Available at: https://www.uvm.dk/folkeskolen/elevplaner-nationale-test-trivselsmaaling-og-sprogproever/nationale-test/vejledninger.

11

Cooperating while competing in multinational corporations

Katarina Lagerström, Emilene Leite, Cecilia Pahlberg, and Roger Schweizer

In this chapter, we investigate the organization of competition within a formal and complex organization, the multinational corporation (MNC).* Competition among the subunits in an MNC has earlier been spoken about in terms of 'internal markets' (Andersson et al. 2015; Birkinshaw et al. 2005; Birkinshaw and Fry 1998; Birkinshaw and Lingblad 2005; Cerrato 2006; Fong et al. 2007; Gammelgaard 2009). As with other economic literature, such a focus on 'markets' narrows unnecessarily the perspective on competition. As will be shown in this chapter, much of the competition among the subsidiary units arises for things that are not traded in a market, such as attention and status. Compared to the organization of competition outside formal organizations, such as among schools in a municipality or in waste management, the organization of competition among the subsidiary units of an MNC is characterized by special conditions that renders this to be a particularly interesting setting in which to study the organization of competition.

The MNC is a complex formal organization where the subsidiary units are their own organizations but are owned by the 'parent company' that also manages the subsidiaries via its headquarters (Ambos and Mahnke 2010; Mudambi 2011). As a fourth party that organizes competition, headquarters can avail of a different set of organizing tools than many other fourth parties, including the possibility to introduce and manage transfer pricing among the subsidiaries, incentive models for distribution of resources and roles, encouragement and support for co-production, and co-marketing and creation of common processes for supply, distribution, and support (Fong et al. 2007; Luo et al. 2006; Paz-Vega 2009). Furthermore, the headquarters is in many cases not only the fourth party but also serves as the 'third party' in that it adjudicates between subsidiaries that vie for its attention or investments but it normally does not play the role of purchasing from the subsidiary.

* This work was supported by the Handelsbanken's research foundation—Jan Wallander and Tom Hedelius Foundation and Tore Browaldh Foundation [grant number P18:1078].

Katarina Lagerström, Emilene Leite, Cecilia Pahlberg, & Roger Schweizer, *Cooperating while competing in multinational corporations* In: *Competition: What It Is and Why It Happens*. Edited by: Stefan Arora-Jonsson, Nils Brunsson, Raimund Hasse, and Katarina Lagerström, Oxford University Press. © Katarina Lagerström, Emilene Leite, Cecilia Pahlberg, and Roger Schweizer 2021. DOI: 10.1093/oso/9780192898012.003.0011

Given this, competition should be easier to organize among the subsidiaries of an MNC than between organizations that are not part of a formal organization as there are tools to manage this process and a legitimate and capable buyer already exists. A further difference to many instances of organization of competition outside a formal organization is that the MNC is dependent on the overall outcome of all the actors active in the internal market; if the individual units fare badly in competition the overall performance of the MNC is negatively affected. This also means that there is, to an extent, goal congruence convergence across subsidiary units that also have goals of their own (Ciabuschi et al. 2012; Nohria and Ghoshal 1994). The headquarters can also alter the structure of the market by selling or acquiring units as it can thus define what constitutes the 'inside' versus the 'outside' of the market.

The above reasoning suggests that competition might be easier to organize in an MNC than in any other setting, but the goal-interdependence introduces concerns for the overall outcome of competition that are often not considered by other organizers of competition. In line with Becker-Ritterspach and Dörrenbächer (2011), we argue that competition among subsidiaries is likely to develop around the allocation of resources, system position and attention of headquarters to individual units, and the allocation of subsidiary mandates within the MNC. A central managerial question for headquarters when organizing internal competition is whether and when a competitive relationship hinders, or promotes, cooperative behaviour among the subsidiary units. We explore how headquarters manages to encourage competition and when and why competition is handled by subsidiary units that cooperate. In relation to each of the sources of competition, we draw upon empirical illustrations of intra-firm cooperative and non-cooperative behaviours among subsidiary units in six large MNCs.

Competition in an MNC setting

Competition within an MNC derives from a shared dependence across subsidiary units on the same scarce resources—either within or outside the MNC; they may desire the same R&D budget, allocation of manufacturing or marketing resources, or access to a market outside the MNC. The units that are likely to compete are thus the ones whose activities or objectives overlap. Birkinshaw and Lingblad (2005: 676), for example, define intra-firm competition in terms of 'the extent of overlap between charters of two or more business units in a single organization'.

Intra-firm competition is shaped by the subsidiary units' resources, performance, degree of autonomy, and relationships to headquarters (Cerrato 2006; Gammelgaard 2009) and also by the governance structures of the MNC as the allocation of resources, system positions, and mandates impact the bargaining power, status, and influence in the MNC (Birkinshaw et al. 2005; Luo 2005). The subsidiary units are heterogeneous when it comes to possession and access to resources. One of the main objectives for headquarters is to combine resources from different units in the most efficient way, and one way of achieving this is believed to be the orchestration of competition among the subsidiary units. Intra-MNC competition can also arise whether headquarters likes it or not.

Competition gives rise to a variety of behavioural outcomes. Often, it is assumed that those who compete do not cooperate with each other, but as argued by Ingram and Yue (2008) this is an assumption with doubtful empirical support. In the context of an MNC, the question of how competition influences the readiness for cooperation among the subsidiaries is of key managerial importance. *Cooperation* entails collaborating over access to existing resources for mutual gains (cf. Luo 2004). Hamel (1991) argues that cooperating with other units may be a way to either get access to or utilize each other's resources in the form of knowledge, skills, and technologies, or acquiring their resources. There is thus likely to be situations over time in given relationships where competition is dealt with by engaging in cooperative behaviour (Raza-Ullah et al. 2014).

Cooperation in response to competition

In this section we draw upon empirical illustrations from six case studies on cooperative and non-cooperative behaviour among subsidiary units in MNCs. Here the subsidiaries competed for three desirable things: resources, system positions, and mandates. MNC headquarters introduced and made use of various tools for governing and organizing competition for these three goods.

Resource allocation

Resources, that is personnel, money, and other assets that can be utilized for some purpose, are often both desirable and scarce within an MNC, and the allocation of these is a common source of competition. In order to avoid conflict around the resource allocation decision, a common method used by headquarters to allocate resources is to make it dependent on the subsidiary units' performance relative other units. This method organizes a comparative setting that can reinforce a sense of competition among the units (see Chapter 4, this volume), and the perception of a situation being competitive can stimulate the subsidiaries to cooperate or not (Cerrato 2006).

One example of how managers viewed competition is provided by a subsidiary manager in the telecom industry: 'cooperation and competition are both common ways of organizing within the multinational and employees are quite used to it.' He continues and highlights the following: 'We cooperate but also compete. We are all the time under evaluation and comparison with other subsidiaries.' Competition can thus be introduced through comparison, and it need not stop cooperation among subsidiary units. One way of attracting the attention of headquarters was to be creative and perform better than other units by, for example, transforming business concepts into commercially viable products. In order to do so, pooling resources from several units might become necessary. Consequently, subsidiaries sometimes engaged in cooperative activities to bring together not only financial resources but also human capabilities and knowledge.

Several subsidiary managers working for an MNC in the pharmaceutical industry stressed the importance of performance to gain access to resources: 'Getting resources is strongly related to performance. Deliver better and well. Create status, reputation, attention, and increase visibility. We compete for that.' When these subsidiary managers talk about resources, they emphasize the importance of financial resources as those provide the bottom-line prerequisite for being able to drive, for example, R&D activities, but they also emphasize the importance of human capabilities. The managers affirm that they are competing and try to get the best human resources assigned to their own projects. Nevertheless, they also explain that such behaviour does not work for some human capabilities where the scarcity is extreme. In those cases, they must rather find other means to be able to share these exceptionally scarce resources; that is they have to cooperate to find a solution for common exploitation of the resource in question.

Reward systems as organizational means for allocating resources were also mentioned by subsidiary managers working for a high-tech global engineering MNC. For example, R&D teams in the subsidiaries competed by showing good results stemming from innovation projects. The reward system was seen by headquarters as particularly important for achieving good results, and rewards were handed out in the form of medals and bonus checks. The system, intended to lead to competition among units, was implemented with the goal of motivating the teams to develop products and processes that could be used worldwide in the MNC. A subsidiary manager explains: 'My unit has never gotten a medal, but recently we were in the spotlight. We developed a type of technology that was recognized by headquarters as innovative, and as a result of that we were made responsible for competence development and training for other units.'

The subsidiary manager emphasized that during the development process the unit competed with other units to show its expertise and later on be rewarded for it. But once that goal was reached, it started to cooperate with other units to share the knowledge that had been created. While this subsidiary manager stressed the importance of reward systems to establish a sense of competition, a subsidiary manager in the telecom industry explained that he rather views reward systems as emphasizing the importance for cooperative activities. At the same time, he disclosed that there has to be a gain in cooperating for his unit, otherwise it is not worth it. 'I will share information and knowledge when there are particular gains from teaming up. My strategy is to cooperate with other subsidiaries in product development, but only if the process brings benefits to my unit.' The possible benefits are discussed in terms of 'projects that create interdependence and make the other subsidiary look to us as the choice to buy from or for developing things together'.

A reasonable conclusion is that strategies for allocating scarce resources, such as the implementation of reward systems, can lead subsidiaries to engage in cooperative activities. Most important, however, is that it indicates that it is difficult for headquarters to determine the outcome of the implemented organizational means. This is in line with previous research (Birkinshaw et al. 1998; Birkinshaw et al. 2005; Luo 2004) that shows that an MNC indeed can be seen as an internal competitive arena, where both cooperative and less cooperative behaviours exist in a dynamic interplay among the subsidiaries.

System position

The second thing that subsidiaries may compete for is for the position within the MNC's production system. The position has two important dimensions. The first concerns the subsidiary units' position in the value chain of the MNC—that is the position in the steps of production that the MNC is engaged in—and how this compares to the other subsidiary units. Some units are involved in only a single step, for instance manufacturing or R&D, while other units are positioned to span several steps. The second dimension relates to the attention that headquarters affords the unit, which in turn depends on the access of the subsidiary to resources and information and its ability to influence headquarters' decision-making (Gorgijevski et al. 2019; Luo 2005). Position is closely related to status, and there are feedback effects: a high-status subsidiary is more likely to get a greater share of headquarters' attention; it is also more likely that other subsidiaries are willing and prepared to cooperate with this unit.

The position of a subsidiary can change for several reasons. Organizational restructuring at the level of the MNC, change in top management, redistribution of resources and mergers and acquisitions are but a few examples that can impact the position and status of a subsidiary. One interesting example among the studied MNCs is where the position of a subsidiary changed several times due to changes in the composition of headquarters' top management team and the MNC's strategy. Initially, the position in the subsidiary's value chain was only to follow global processes and standards, but a strong and convincing head of innovation at the subsidiary managed to get headquarters' attention for what the subsidiary saw as special circumstances and requirements in the local market. The subsidiary was given additional resources for R&D to be used to develop products outside of the global processes and standards to meet the demands of the local market. However, a couple of years later, the MNC got a new top management team that withdrew the exceptions given to the subsidiary, forcing it back to its old position. A subsidiary manager commented: 'It is politics and strategy. It was not a sound business case that we should develop and produce a product outside the global processes and standards. But it was politics to move it [R&D] here. Now we have the people and knowledge, so now we are supposed to collaborate and do some here and some there.'

System positions can also change because of actions by the subsidiary, and the incentive to undertake such actions may come from comparisons with other subsidiaries. For example, a subsidiary in a promising emerging market expressed itself as aspiring to become 'at least as good as' other similar but well-established subsidiaries. The objective for this subsidiary was to become the preferred choice for other subsidiaries to turn to for R&D work; the subsidiary managers saw the subsidiary in a competitive situation with a single winner, which was also in line with the headquarters' intent. The headquarters had the idea 'may the best subsidiary win' and used a system of transfer prices and 'bidding' systems to allocate R&D resources and tasks across the subsidiary units. But in this case it realized that the subsidiary could not reach the position of 'being best' in a foreseeable future due to its lack of resources—financial, human, and knowledge—and also because of its modest reputation and status. The headquarters decided to sidestep its established system for allocation of resources and distribution of tasks in favour of the subsidiary in question. It transferred resources to the subsidiary outside of the system and also required other subsidiaries to allot a certain amount of work to the subsidiary outside of the 'bidding' system. In this way, the subsidiary unit, via the initial support from headquarters, was able to develop knowledge and human capabilities that eventually enabled it to reach a strong position and gain a reputation and status within the MNC on its own merits. This change increased other subsidiaries' interest to cooperate with it.

This example shows how headquarters' attention and support can alter the position of a unit. Furthermore, it is an example of headquarters as an organizer of the MNC that uses different means to obtain an intended strategic outcome. A manager in a pharmaceutical MNC described the process of having to compete for a position in a slightly different manner:

> We are a centre of excellence in the MNC, and the tasks we perform are not related to our market, but we do development work for other markets. We compete a lot with other subsidiaries for being assigned the tasks. In the structure we have, our position in relation to others is on display in terms of our performance, and it is being updated day-by-day. If a person does not like this competitive mindset, he or she will not fit in the organization.

Furthermore, the manager emphasized: 'competition is in the MNC's DNA; therefore, it is healthy and drives us towards better results.' In this case there is a view that to initially attain a position associated with high status as a centre of excellence—in competition with other units—is important and 'right'. Being constantly evaluated and compared to other units and continuing to compete to maintain the position may also be good, but it may also limit the readiness for cooperation. In this particular case, the subsidiary managers did not engage in cooperative behaviour as they were keen to reach or maintain the subsidiary's position in relation to the other subsidiaries.

The thought of being in competition with other subsidiary units for a position is present in all six MNCs. As shown in the examples, it is important to be able to get the attention from headquarters in order to get access to resources to build that position. The process of building a position is perceived to be done in competition with other subsidiaries, as both resources and attention are scarce, and the decisions on how this process is organized is ultimately made by the headquarters. A manager at the headquarters in one of the MNCs expressed:

> They [the subsidiaries] cannot live in a bubble, it is never good. For us to be able to compete in a global market, they have to be up to real, true competition internally....And of course, they want to compete with being bigger, having better results. So that is sort of healthy competition, but the decision regarding where to source is made centrally.

This example suggests that the headquarters' managers did not expect competition to stimulate cooperation. Yet, a few subsidiaries did collaborate to reach better positions in comparison to other more 'distant' units. For example, two subsidiaries in two different divisions located in the same emerging market decided to collaborate over the access to skilled human resources in a few specialist areas. The collaboration was especially important for one of the subsidiaries as it was established more recently than the other and needed to quickly build a strong position both internally and externally. It also had a somewhat problematic position in relation to the other units in the same division, and the collaboration was a way to improve that position. Managers at the two divisional headquarters as well as at the MNC headquarters were aware of this scenario and had no objections to it; rather, they saw it as a way to improve the utilization of company resources.

Several subsidiaries explained that once they had attained a strong position and acquired status in their designated area, they would be recognized by other subsidiaries as knowledgeable, which, in turn, often led to knowledge sharing and collaborations. For example, a head of innovation in a subsidiary in the manufacturing industry explained that his unit had become more focused on cooperation as it was now more engaged in knowledge sharing. However, he claimed: 'If another subsidiary is delivering better than us, I try to contact them and see what they are doing different from us. I am responsible for certain markets and I put my teams in contact with them to learn how to do the same task with the same efficiency in my unit.' Just as other managers at subsidiary units have expressed, competition seems to direct the attention of managers towards those that they compete with, which may also open avenues for collaboration.

In conclusion, the position of a subsidiary can be scarce and desirable and therefore a likely object for competition. From the headquarters' perspective, this competition is useful as it incentivizes subsidiaries to perform well in relation to other units, but it also increases the risk of units not wanting to cooperate to the extent that is the best for the entire MNC.

Mandates

Subsidiary mandates are closely connected to system position. A 'mandate' is formalized responsibility for a particular function within the MNC—for instance the responsibility to develop a particular product or to market something (Birkinshaw et al. 1998). Subsidiaries that are assigned a mandate often receive more resources, which, in turn, if used in a wise way, can lead to further capability development and then status in the MNC. Mandates are therefore desirable from the perspective of a subsidiary unit. The desire for a mandate may give rise to competition among subsidiary units, and headquarters often organize a competitive situation to distribute mandates (Birkinshaw et al. 1998). For instance, headquarters can sometimes give several subsidiaries the same mandate, as exemplified by a subsidiary manager in a Swedish MNC in the pharmaceutical industry: 'HQ provides us sometimes with the same tasks that many other subsidiaries are already doing. It happens in parallel.' This type of decision can only be explained by a belief that competition contributes to further improvements and innovations and that the extra costs due to duplications are compensated by the benefits of reducing innovation time and increased performance (cf. Maurer 2011).

Among the studied MNCs, subsidiaries received mandates depending on either their overall performance or headquarters' interest in investing in the development of capabilities in a specific unit in a specific market. For example, for one of the subsidiaries, the headquarters' decision to assign the mandate was motivated not only by the subsidiary's present performance but also by the belief in an important and growing future market in the country in question as well as by a conviction that it would be possible to develop the needed capabilities in that market. The subsidiary had already been engaged in some development activities although these were limited to product development for the local market. A manager at the headquarters explained why the subsidiary was given a mandate for R&D: 'We had some small technical activities in this location associated directly with factories doing relatively straightforward factory support and some level of product development for the market. The unit has changed from being an importer of knowledge to being a developer of knowledge. We work together with customers, developing products with them, specifically for that market.' The mandate was allotted to the unit with the goal of developing both knowledge and capabilities needed to meet local market demands, but also in order to enable support to units in other markets with R&D tasks. The process of managing the given mandate was not without obstacles, however, as the unit met strong resistance from other subsidiaries, resulting in some other subsidiaries refraining from cooperating with the unit in question, even though the mandate demanded them to do so. The situation was resolved when the headquarters put pressure on them through different governance means such as cooperation around specific tasks and common projects. Measures were also taken to build an environment for cooperation through the implementation of communication channels on several levels. Interestingly, managers at the headquarters and the subsidiary in question did not believe that the other units were afraid that the subsidiary would not be able to deliver. It was rather the opposite, that the subsidiary actually would be able to deliver tasks on time and with the right quality.

Mandates are temporary and may change over time. A subsidiary manager in the technology industry emphasized: 'Mandates are something that should be conquered; it also changes over time. Therefore, one of my intentions when visiting the headquarters is to highlight what we do and at what costs.' According to him, there was a need to communicate with the headquarters about issues concerning the existing mandate and the capabilities of the subsidiary but also to try to make sure that the subsidiary would get mandates in the future by pointing to future potentials and opportunities. But he also emphasized the importance of being known by other subsidiaries. He highlighted the need to travel a lot in order to accomplish that: 'I have a budget for traveling and therefore, I make sure to visit the headquarters and other subsidiaries to show best practices and our portfolio of solutions.'

A manager at the headquarters in an MNC described the process behind the assignment of a mandate to a subsidiary, with the aim of developing R&D capabilities in the MNC. In this case, four locations were possible—Holland, Germany, France, and Sweden—and competition for this mandate primarily among the last three options was intense as they were considered as being equally capable. The decision, however, was made to choose Holland, and the manager describes that it was based on two main reasons.

> The neutrality aspect became one of the main factors in this case. We don't have anything in Holland. Germans wanted it to be given to Germany, French wanted it in France, and Swedes wanted it in Sweden. Then, we said OK guys, let's stop fighting and put the centre in Holland. In addition, the Dutch Government has always given us good subsidies for R&D.

In this case, it was evident that all subsidiary units were competing over who should get the mandate for some designated R&D activities, but the headquarters saw that in order for the four units to be able to cooperate in the future, it had to make the decision not to select any of the three with the best and comparable capabilities but instead choose the fourth and—from many perspectives—the least likely option. This decision was accepted by the other three units, and consequently, a collaborative environment was saved. In this particular case, the ability to collaborate was extremely important in order to be able to keep up with the competition from other firms in the same industry.

These examples support the view expressed by subsidiary managers that the headquarters can influence the willingness of competing subsidiaries to cooperate or not. But subsidiaries may also actively choose to behave in a manner directly opposite to what is intended by headquarters if they interpret the situation differently.

Headquarters does not only give out mandates, but it also retracts mandates from subsidiaries. A subsidiary manager working in a robotic development centre explained that the subsidiary lost its status when the headquarters decided to change the internal structure resulting in that mandates for all different R&D tasks should only be distributed to three specific subsidiaries while the rest of the subsidiaries' responsibilities were limited to them being application centres. One way that the subsidiary manager circumvented this move was to cooperate more with the subsidiaries that now had been given the mandates: 'Our unit is recognized for being the most collaborative. We tend to be very ahead of sharing, developing together, and willing to help.... It creates visibility to the team; it is good for us also to develop here and present to the world.'

Once again, the example shows that the headquarters' strategy and governance with respect to mandates influence the subsidiaries' behaviour, but the outcome might not be completely in line with the expectations of the headquarters.

The complexities of managing competition

In this chapter, we have taken a step towards a more nuanced understanding of intra-firm competition while focusing on the three sources of competition, namely allocation of resources, system position, and mandates (Becker-Ritterspach and Dörrenbächer 2011). We focus particularly on how the perception of competition among subsidiary units relates to their willingness to cooperate with each other. In the MNC, the headquarters assumes the role as the fourth party by using different means to organize for competition (see Chapter 4, this volume), but it is evident from the cases that it is a challenging and ambiguous role.

In comparison to other instances where a fourth party seeks to organize competition, the MNC setting is a complex organization. The headquarters, to some extent, can rely on a formal hierarchical structure, with specified organizational boundaries of the MNC as well as of the subsidiary units it comprises, and an extent of goal convergence across all these units. This affords the use of management tools, such as bonus systems, mandate, and resource allocation as well as promotion and movement of personnel, in order to introduce and manage the outcomes of competition. This was evident in all six cases. Headquarters have the authority to, for example, implement systems for allocation of resources, direct their attention to certain subsidiaries, and distribute roles and mandates. It is thus not only a fourth but also a third party as it adjudicates many of the competitive situations that it organizes among its subsidiaries.

As with any attempt at management, the responses from the subsidiaries are not given. The subsidiaries are not only affected by the internal MNC structure but also by their local market context that is external to the MNC. Sometimes that context makes the subsidiaries behave in a different manner than anticipated by headquarters as the subsidiaries are more dependent on their 'outside' than their 'inside' relationships. Another explanation is that the subsidiaries, among themselves, can realize that cooperating with a chosen few within the MNC gives them a better position in relation to headquarters. They can thus circumscribe the means of governance implemented by headquarters. An example of this behaviour is that even if some subsidiaries competed for both mandates and system positions with each other, they realized that the gain for them all was greater when collaborating over scarce resources. It is also possible to conclude from the cases that cooperation does not take place in a random fashion. On the contrary, subsidiaries seek out other subsidiaries to collaborate with where they themselves can benefit. They search for subsidiaries with, for example, a resource advantage, a better or stronger position, and human capabilities, while they do not cooperate with other subsidiaries. Interestingly, these two behaviours are the outcome of the same measure taken by headquarters to organize for competition, which indicates that the role as the 'fourth party' is associated with challenges also in an MNC setting.

Another finding is that even if we could see several examples of competition leading to less cooperation, it could also lead to more. One possible explanation is the fact that having good internal relationships with peers is important, due to the external pressures from competing firms in the wider market context. The case studies thus indicate that the subsidiaries were less willing to cooperate when it came to their system position and mandate. A likely explanation is that the system position is important for their relationship not only vis-a-vis other subsidiaries but also vis-a-vis headquarters. The systems position is furthermore important for the status of the subsidiary in the MNC and can thus in turn influence the other objects for competition—the allocation of scarce resources and assignment of mandates. Consequently, it is possible to argue that organizing intra-firm competition is a socially constructed process that is impacted by different circumstances in the relationship not just between headquarters and the subsidiaries but also among the subsidiaries directly.

References

Ambos, B. and Mahnke, V. 2010. 'How do MNC headquarters add value?' *Management International Review* 50 (4): 403–12.

Andersson, U., Forsgren, M., and Holm, U. 2015. 'Balancing subsidiary influence in the federative MNC: a business network view'. In *Knowledge, Networks and Power*, edited by M. Forsgren, U. Holm, and J. Johanson. London: Palgrave Macmillan: 393–420.

Becker-Ritterspach, F. and Dörrenbächer, C. 2011. 'An organizational politics perspective on intra-firm competition in multinational corporations'. *Management International Review* 51 (4): 533–59.

Birkinshaw, J., Hood, N., and Jonsson, S. 1998. 'Building firm-specific advantages in multinational corporations: the role of subsidiary initiative'. *Strategic Management Journal* 19 (3): 221–41.

Birkinshaw, J., Hood, N., and Young, S. 2005. 'Subsidiary entrepreneurship, internal and external competitive forces, and subsidiary performance'. *International Business Review* 14 (2): 227–48.

Birkinshaw, J. and Fry, N. 1998. 'Subsidiary initiatives to develop new markets'. *Sloan Management Review* 39 (3): 51–61.

Birkinshaw, J. and Lingblad, M. 2005. 'Intrafirm competition and charter evolution in the multibusiness firm'. *Organization Science* 16 (6): 674–86.

Cerrato, D. 2006. 'The multinational enterprise as an internal market system'. *International Business Review* 15 (3): 253–77.

Ciabuschi, F., Dellestrand, H., and Holm, U. 2012. 'The role of headquarters in the contemporary MNC'. *Journal of International Management* 18 (3): 213–23.

Fong, C. M., Ho, H. L., Weng, L. C., and Yang, K. P. 2007. 'The intersubsidiary competition in an MNE: evidence from the Greater China region'. *Canadian Journal of Administrative Sciences/Revue Canadienne des Sciences de l'Administration* 24 (1): 45–57.

Gammelgaard, J. 2009. 'Issue selling and bargaining power in intrafirm competition: the differentiating impact of the subsidiary management composition'. *Competition & Change* 13 (3): 214–28.

Gorgijevski, A., Holmström Lind, C., and Lagerström, K. 2019. 'Does proactivity matter? The importance of initiative selling tactics for headquarters acceptance of subsidiary initiatives'. *Journal of International Management* 25 (4): 100673.

Hamel, G. 1991. 'Competition for competence and interpartner learning within international strategic alliances'. *Strategic Management Journal* 12 (S1): 83–103.

Ingram, P. and Qingyuan Yue, L. 2008. '6 structure, affect and identity as bases of organizational competition and cooperation'. *The Academy of Management Annals* 2 (1): 275–303.

Luo, Y. 2004. 'A coopetition perspective of MNC–host government relations'. *Journal of International Management* 10 (4): 431–51.

Luo, Y. 2005. 'Toward coopetition within a multinational enterprise: a perspective from foreign subsidiaries'. *Journal of World Business* 40 (1): 71–90.

Luo, X., Slotegraaf, R. J., and Pan, X. 2006. 'Cross-functional "coopetition": the simultaneous role of cooperation and competition within firms'. *Journal of Marketing* 70 (2): 67–80.

Maurer, J. 2011. *Relationships between Foreign Subsidiaries: Competition and Cooperation in Multinational Plant Engineering Companies.* Wiesbaden: Gabler Verlag, Springer Fachmedien.

Mudambi, R. 2011. 'Hierarchy, coordination, and innovation in the multinational enterprise'. *Global Strategy Journal* 1 (3–4): 317–23.

Nohria, N. and Ghoshal, S. 1994. 'Differentiated fit and shared values: alternatives for managing headquarters-subsidiary relations'. *Strategic Management Journal* 15 (6): 491–502.

Paz-Vega, R. 2009. 'International transfer pricing and subsidiary performance: the role of organizational justice'. *Thunderbird International Business Review* 51 (3): 219–38.

Raza-Ullah, T., Bengtsson, M., and Kock, S. 2014. 'The coopetition paradox and tension in coopetition at multiple levels'. *Industrial Marketing Management* 43 (2): 189–98.

12
Reversing competition: the case of corporate governance

Fabien Foureault

A key assertion in Chapter 1 is that competition is often organized by an actor who wishes to see competition—a fourth party. Competition can thus be a political tool of corporate governance, used by managers to effect changes in organizational settings. Several of the other chapters investigate how competition is introduced and organized. In this chapter, I nuance these questions by asking how a fourth party can tame competition in order to achieve cooperation. And, if so, what are the conditions under which it can?

To address this question, I study a case where competition already exists, and while the organizers do not want to suppress it, they want to develop parallel cooperating relationships in order to 'tame' it—that is reduce the overall level of competition within the organization. I will treat competition and cooperation as outcomes of an interaction process between (1) the acts of an organizer and (2) the interpretation of these acts and the responses of the organized, in a given context. By 'organizer', I mean a group of actors who try to impose a 'decided order' on some others, who will be the 'organized'. The organizer, or fourth party, is in this case a private equity firm (PE firm) associated with the headquarters' top managers of a company acquired through a leveraged buy-out (LBO) operation. The organized are the top and middle managers of the subunits of this multinational corporation. To identify some of the conditions under which competition can be reversed in this setting, I will ask an additional question: why did the organizers fail to induce cooperation and tame competition?

My case is a multinational corporation acquired through LBO during the 2000s. The PE firm tried to implement a strategy of value creation through a 'build-up' strategy, where the target company is merged with the competitors in a fragmented sector so that a new, more profitable and attractive 'industry leader' emerges. It is a case where the subunits are already competing, but the organizer wants to increase cooperation in order to achieve 'synergies' among these operating units. Despite their attempts, it will be evident that widespread cooperation did not emerge. Furthermore, at the end of my observation period, the target company was rife with internal competition that limited cooperation. This requires an explanation as many

Fabien Foureault, *Reversing competition: the case of corporate governance* In: *Competition: What It Is and Why It Happens.*
Edited by: Stefan Arora-Jonsson, Nils Brunsson, Raimund Hasse, and Katarina Lagerström, Oxford University Press
© Fabien Foureault 2021. DOI: 10.1093/oso/9780192898012.003.0012

of the prima facie conditions for cooperation seemed to be realized. The headquarters showed a strong will and had dedicated resources to implement synergies, for example when they set up working groups in the technical area and a customer management system in the commercial area. This policy was accepted by the subordinates who were willing to cooperate with colleagues from different units and countries. The barriers to such relationships were already low due to the development of technologies in transportation and communication during the 2000s. Finally, the CEO saw the economic crisis of 2009 as an occasion that would force operating units to develop new products and find new customers together.

In the rest of the chapter, I argue that the resulting 'untamed' competition can be explained by the discrepancy between the conception of control of PE firms and the moral economy of managers, especially engineers. A conception of control is the perspective shared by members of an organizational field on the legitimate competitive strategies and internal structures that should promote growth and survival of firms (Fligstein 2001: 35). The conception of control of private equity is to 'create shareholder value' by disciplining managers and reorganizing corporations through divestitures and mergers. A moral economy is the 'set of norms that specifically concern the economy—i.e. conceptions of what is morally appropriate economic behaviour' (Granovetter 2017: 27). The moral economy of engineering managers supposes that firms are collective entities designed to increase production capacity and create innovative products. My explanation for the observed non-cooperation is that private equity strategies are not legitimate among many managers and do not promote trust, which is badly needed when real uncertainty makes the cost of cooperation prohibitively high.

The methodology used will be comprehensive and analytical, as I want to explain a collective phenomenon, untamed competition, by reconstructing the individuals' reasons (Hedström and Swedberg 1998). In order to do so, I have conducted forty-three interviews in this corporation during the 'great recession' in 2009, with a focus on salespeople, engineers, and top managers. In the first section, I deal with the social context of cooperation: the governance model of private equity and the strategy used in this particular company. In the second section, I examine the numerous obstacles to cooperation and the persistence of competition. In the third section, I try to explain these facts by analysing the perceptions of the PE firm by managers, who thought that this or another shareholder could reshuffle or break up the company in the near future.

The push for cooperation

The corporation AdvancedTechnology was bought by a PE firm called Capital Investments. Private equity is a new model of ownership and control of firms to be distinguished from public equity (Baker and Smith 1998). Private equity's most common operation is called the LBO, where a small organization of financiers acquires the majority shares of a target company by using money committed by institutional investors and borrowed money from banks. After five years, the PE firm sells the stock of the restructured company and makes a return on investment, multiplied by the proportion of debt in the deal. The specificity of LBOs thus lies in its strategic use of debt to increase buying power, discipline managers, and magnify returns. This exposes the target firm to a higher bankruptcy risk. According to neo-classical economists, private equity is a new and superior form of financial capitalism because it is a response to the agency problems of managerial capitalism (Jensen 1989). In this model, property is not dispersed among a multitude of passive shareholders but concentrated in the hands of the PE firm. Top managers of the target firm do not control the acquired company but own a significant amount of its capital. Thus, there is an 'alignment of interests' between shareholders and managers. Moreover, the debt burden of the acquisition is repaid by using the free cash flow from the acquired company, its immediately available assets, which pressures the managers of target firms to implement operating efficiencies, as they otherwise cannot repay their debt.

According to my sociological interpretation, the LBO is an 'organizational weapon' used by a new segment of finance capital to reconfigure power relationships within firms by focalizing the attention of company managers on performance criteria such as return on equity. PE firms are thus new actors that can use LBOs as a practice animated by the 'shareholder value' conception of control (Fligstein 2001: 7). Directed primarily at top managers of target firms, this 'weapon' works on a simple behavioural heuristic: high debt induces the threat of bankruptcy and losing job and equity holding is a promise of a return with a possibility to become rich. The political theory behind this weapon is Hobbesian (Freeland 2005). Individuals are regarded as self-interested and as acting opportunistically, and 'good governance' means the design of the right incentives—negative sanctions (debt) and positive sanctions (equity). This political philosophy infused most aspects of the governance of AdvancedTechnology. Top management received an annual bonus, indexed on the financial performance of the firm as a whole, while middle managers received a bonus indexed on the performance of their operating unit. In addition, when the headquarters wanted to make salespeople share clients with their colleagues from different operating units, they made client-sharing a source of the bonus.

A PE firm owns AdvancedTechnology, which is a business group composed of operating units that are separate legal entities coordinated by three divisions (Figure 12.1). AdvancedTechnology is an Original Equipment Manufacturer in the optronics or electro-optics industry (Sturgeon 2002). It designs, manufactures, and commercializes optical systems to be incorporated in products in the defence or civil domains. It employs around 2,500 people in eleven operating units, which are located in the UK, Germany, the USA, Hungary, Singapore, and China. The headquarters, headed by a French CEO, is based in Paris.

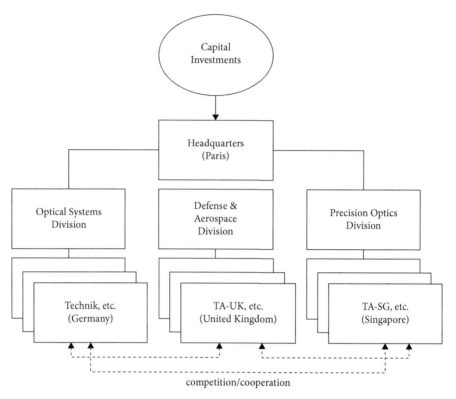

Figure 12.1 The organization of Advanced Technology in 2009.

The strategy that the PE firm and AdvancedTechnology' stop management agreed upon was not one of de-conglomeration and 'asset stripping', widely used in the 1980s (Davis et al. 1994), but one of organization building or 'build-up'. This was popular in the 2000s and helped spread LBOs because it was a way for top managers to buy their competitors. This movement most resembles the first merger wave at the turn of the twentieth century (Fligstein 1990). AdvancedTechnology, the target company, was first 'carved out' from a large French industrial group, which sold its share in its subsidiary in 2005 to Capital Investments, the PE firm. Then, the newly carved-out organization was structured by creating finance and marketing functions, by adopting a multidivisional form, and by implementing standard export procedures. However, from 2008, AdvancedTechnology was hit by the financial crisis, which turned into the 'great recession' in 2009. The crisis had two consequences: first, it spread insecurity within the company as it increased the risk of bankruptcy, and second, it led to a change in strategy in which internal, organic growth became a priority. One searched for synergies (i.e. cost reduction) and tried to develop cooperative relationships across operating units in order to design new products to sell to new customers. The PE firm, organizing this change, acknowledged a degree of internal competition among the subunits, but it wanted to 'tame it' by encouraging parallel cooperative relationships among the operating units.

Untamed competition

The success of AdvancedTechnology largely depended on its capacity to mobilize the skills of its employees, notably making middle managers—that is engineers and salespeople who represented 15 per cent of the workforce—cooperate not only within but also across these operating units. The engineers had different roles: on top of a hierarchical differentiation, they had a clear horizontal division of labour according to their specialization in different stages of product development. They could be optical designers, mechanical engineers, or even test engineers. The engineers could also be specialized, in particular optical designers, in narrow technical areas. Contrary to stereotypes, the environment in which they operated was quite turbulent. They described their work in terms of urgency as they tried to meet tight deadlines under uncertainty as new technical problems constantly emerged from the work process. The engineers were also connected to the organizational environment through professional networks, universities, and research centres.

In general terms, engineering work consisted of two main activities. First, engineers were to design and build a prototype that met the customer's technical requirements (specifications). Thanks to a form or drawing given by the salesperson, which described the technical characteristics of the product or demand, optical designers as well as mechanical and electronic engineers tried to realize those specifications. Second, they needed to resolve technical problems that arose in the course of product development or when the customer returned a defective product. Both of these tasks required close collaboration with sales and customers, and engineers were often organized into multidisciplinary teams.

It was in this context that engineers were encouraged to share their knowledge and skills with colleagues in other operating units. Top management, in particular the head of development and his subordinate, the head of research and development (R&D) at the headquarters, implemented a number of initiatives. They created a R&D seminar, but it was not considered to be very fruitful, in particular by top managers of AT-UK (UK) and Technik (Germany).

Q: What do you think of such seminars?

They're useful and necessary. But we don't get most value from them. The difficulty is making full use of Group capabilities as in some levels. For example, [AT-UK] is very busy so we are subcontracting to AT-SG and Hungary. But on technical matters, we don't do so much cooperation. I see two reasons: first, we are very careful about transmitting information. Because of [export compliance], which demands a process for transmitting data. Also, we are busy, so it's difficult to stop and think. It is true at the moment where AdvancedTechnology [he means: AT-UK] is very busy. (Interview with the technical director of AT-UK, 21 April 2009)

Top managers of these units (AT-UK, AT-SG, and Technik) wanted to negotiate the themes of the seminar, but as a result the discussions ended up being very general.

The headquarters also created working groups, one on surface analysis and one on stray light analysis. Each working group had conference calls and then were supposed to realize the tests. However, these tasks were not viewed as crucial by the management of the operating units. According to the head of R&D at the headquarters, the working group on stray light analysis was 'sleeping'. For him, the working group on surface analysis worked because it dealt with common problems that were not 'strategic' for operating units.

The idea was raised when Technik entered the Group. The idea is to cooperate, for example, on optical design. It's the way we benefit from different knowledge bases. There is one working group on metrology, one on surface analysis…the working group on optics has worked a little bit. There has been a common training session between AT-UK, Technik, and AT-SG, but they are sleeping. It's only the group on surface analysis that is working. […] In order for [this initiative] to work, it has to be win-win: not losing knowledge and acquiring knowledge. That's not necessarily supported inside operating units. (Interview with Group R&D director, 01 July 2009)

The common projects among the operating units were rare and more production-oriented than R&D oriented. They involved subcontracting between the central English and German units to peripheral units AT-SG (Singapore and China) and in Hungary. These projects were regularly interrupted—something that engineers could not explain, but they suspected it was for 'political reasons'. It seems that the absence of cooperation was in part intentional and due to each operating unit's strategic agenda. Engineers had a relatively positive view of collaborations because they wanted to learn new things and resolve their technical problems. However, their leadership was more reticent as they felt responsible for the know-how of their operating unit. This strategic and intentional aspect of non-cooperation was more visible in the sales and marketing (S&M) area.

Like engineers, salespeople had varied roles such as sales engineer, business developer, or sales director. These roles were differentiated, in terms of both level and content. Sales engineers dealt with setting prices for customer requests and with day-to-day relationship with clients, whereas business developers dealt with finding customers and getting orders. Sales directors, on the other hand, dealt with commercial strategy and supervising other salespersons. Their roles were more variable than those of engineers since their domains of expertise were much vaguer and because of their position at the boundary between the organization and its environment. Salespeople thought of their work according to two broad perspectives. One perspective was about finding needs and employed the vocabulary of help or support, whereas the other perspective was more aggressive and had to do with placing orders. The latter was thought of in terms of infiltration into potential clients and a struggle against competitors. Salespeople used different strategies to find an adjustment between what the customer wanted ('needs') and what the firm proposed ('capabilities'). These strategies involved getting information on technologies that actual or potential customers were developing, nurturing a personal network in technological milieus, being persuasive, and being on good terms with engineering colleagues.

The headquarters also wanted to foster cooperation among salespeople. In contrast to engineers, where non-cooperation was passive and took the form of a general apathy towards initiatives, in the case of salespeople it was more active and took many forms. These actions included hiding commercial information, forbidding or controlling access to a customer, selling the solutions of one's unit to the detriment of another, and offering parallel quotations. For instance, a salesperson, who was responsible for all of North America, explained that he could not coordinate with salespeople from different operating units:

Q: How do you coordinate with other companies?

[Laughing] not very well! There is not a Group direction to achieve that. [My position] is nothing more than key account management [explained later] with all the accounts but on a bigger scale. It gets very complicated. We have an individual mentality in sales. We don't think of the Group. To create that sales presence is very difficult. It's very complex and inefficient right now. We would need it, because they—the customers—can see the conflict.

Q: Do you have an example of this?

I just had a meeting last week in [a customer] with the senior manager. I invited [another unit, XXX] into the meeting. As we started going through the capabilities and how they worked, the person from XXX tried to interrupt the conversation. It was a constant battle. He tried to impose the XXX perspective, and have a direct conversation about 'what I can do for you'. That can become a conflict. Some conflicts are also within the other international organizations. AT-SG try to sell their capabilities. AT-UK is not as bad as this, we try to share the info over the Group. We present as different companies who compete against each other. The customers, they don't know who to talk to or what activity they should get involved in; it's bad for business. (Interview with regional sales director for North America, defence area, 21 May 2009)

These practices were of little visibility to top managers at the headquarters who thought that cooperation was more prevalent within sales than among engineers—in part because they had implemented a Key Account Management (KAM) system. In this system, sales directors wrote a list of important customers (key accounts), which were assigned to a salesperson (key account manager). This person was in charge of coordinating all actions concerning this client. Because one customer could buy capabilities of different units, the key account team comprised all the salespeople that visited the customer. A bonus system incentivized key account managers to share his/her client base with other salespeople. However, the bonus system did not eliminate competition among sales executives. In some instances, key account managers who were supposed to be 'neutral coordinators' for the Group were part of that competition and became 'partial intermediaries' for their own unit. Some of these managers were directly involved in conflicts over rules on how to interact with other salespeople.

Some informants suggested that the KAM system was used by some operating units to strengthen their control over particular markets, whereas the headquarters expected the KAM to balance power relationships within the Group. For instance, one salesperson, designated to the Singapore unit, was asked by colleagues to organize a meeting for a project with a French defence contractor. He immediately phoned the customer because of a tight deadline; however, he forgot to inform the key account manager who, when learning about the meeting, was furious and insisted on attending. The struggle over the control of markets can be seen in the conceptions that some key account managers had of their role. A salesman in the UK treated members of his team as subordinates who should report to him and gave them directions although this position did not give him hierarchical power over them. Another salesman in Germany, somewhat naively, said that KAM was helpful not only in generating business but also in keeping it at his operating unit. Another spoke of 'fighting Chinese suppliers' even though there was one in the Group. Their leadership, the directors of units and divisions, turned a blind eye or encouraged such attitudes and behaviours.

As with the engineers, these insights need to be interpreted in their larger context. Competition among salespeople was not only competition among individuals but also among different operating units, located in different countries, at different points in the value chain, and in different positions in the global division of labour. The three biggest units and divisions were in competition for access to and control of world markets. In particular, managers of Western units, AT-UK and Technik, both feared the upgrading of the Asian division, with its centre in Singapore (AT-SG) and its manufacturing unit in China. AT-SG had bought industrial capacity to realize more sophisticated solutions and wanted to use collaboration with other units to gain knowledge that it lacked. From the Western point of view, the Asian division represented a threat, which the headquarters aggravated by insisting on collaborations.

Indeed, it was the Singapore unit that benefited the most from the KAM system, which explained the defensive behaviour of some European key account managers. To show this, I have represented the flow of bonuses received and paid among operating units (Figure 12.2). When a salesperson sold a solution for another unit, the other unit had to pay a bonus that was proportional to the size of the contract. Such payments are represented by lines of different widths in the figure. For example, one salesman from the operating unit Optics shared some of his business with a salesman from the operating unit Technik. The latter unit had to pay the salesperson at Optics 1117 USD.

Three comments can be made about the figure. First, only six out of the eleven units participate in this exchange network. AT-SG is the only peripheral unit to be

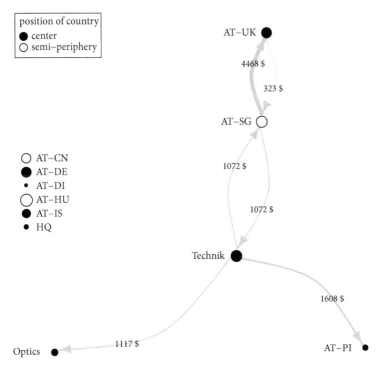

Figure 12.2 Flow of bonuses from the key account management system in 2008.

involved in the network. Second, there is a link between the unit heads of divisions AT-SG, Technik, and AT-UK. Despite being less dominant, AT-SG was in a strategic position as an intermediary between the two dominant units (AT-UK and Technik). Third, in terms of the resource flows, AT-SG is the unit that has given the most net bonuses for what it received (5540 USD), which implies that it was given the most contracts. The Western units (TA-UK and Technik) are not allied, as indicated by the lack of a tie between them. These units see themselves as being in competition as they are positioned at the same stage in the value chain and can sell similar capabilities for either defence or civil applications. Overall, the figure shows that cooperative relationships in the commercial area were very sparse but that AT-SG benefited the most from them. This explains why Technik and AT-UK were reluctant to cooperate with AT-SG. I now turn to the social mechanism that I think explains how competition limited cooperation.

Perceptions of the fourth party

The lack of cooperation in R&D and sales and marketing areas is intriguing because some middle managers were in favour of such collaborations, and most of them valued cooperation in itself. One classical explanation for this could be found in game theory. Thus, managers belonging to different units would not cooperate because the cost of cooperation would be too high or the expected benefits too low. For example, chief engineers would fear that risks of being overtaken by other operating units would be too great compared to the knowledge added from joint projects, or key account managers would consider that group bonuses were too low compared to what they could earn by meeting their own unit's objectives.

I find this explanation elegant but unconvincing for many reasons, notably because of empirical observations that indicate that managers (even salespeople) did not behave according to a pure 'logic of interest' (Granovetter 2017). My explanation involves putting emphasis on the 'non-strategic elements of strategic action' (Burawoy and Wright 1994)—on positive and normative beliefs, according to which actors evaluate the consequences of cooperation (moral economy). The conditions of cooperation at AdvancedTechnology were embedded in a social context with two levels. First, cooperation among colleagues in different units was influenced by their membership to their unit and the fact that they were under the authority of a top manager and ultimately the CEO of this operating unit. Second, cooperation among these top managers was influenced by the conception of control of the firm.

It is this second hierarchical level that is most crucial for the explanation because the top management of the operating units were the real power holders. They were in a position to decide about cooperation; specifically, by guiding their subordinates, they would be able to encourage or discourage cooperation. The mindset of these managers was influenced by beliefs about the intentions and future actions of the PE firm. Managers of AdvancedTechnology ascribed the PE firm managers a 'nexus of contracts' view of corporations, in contrast to their own view, which included a wish to build a 'real Group' that focused on internal growth and not on acquisitions and restructurings. As one top manager in Germany expressed, 'the perspective of the average employee is long-term', whereas this is not the perspective of the shareholders. Thus, the PE firm was not trusted and sometimes considered an illegitimate decision-maker that was both technically and managerially incompetent.

Hm, they [shareholders] are not skilled in management, these guys. One example is that they like to contact everyone…, which is not pleasant for management, the CEO especially. That is, if shareholders contact his colleagues, they can eventually give orders. We don't know who is the boss at one point. […] I remember clearly a reunion in Singapore. The two representatives of the shareholders wanted to see me. The CEO entered the room saying "can I be part of the reunion?" and they said "no we don't need you right now, we'll call you". [He laughs a bit] So, it's not in this domain that…that doesn't help create trust, on his part. (Interview with Group development director, 01 July 2009).

In this anecdote, the PE firm is declared incompetent concerning the 'human' aspect of management. In the moral economy of managers and engineers, financiers are perceived, not as 'captains of industry' in which the businessman becomes an institutional leader (Selznick 1957) but as raiders and liquidators, who flip companies for a 'quick buck'. Making money by financial restructuring is not considered legitimate, as opposed to seeking profit by making better quality and sophisticated products. An important reason not to cooperate was derived from such 'illegitimate' practices: the PE firm could sell the different divisions to different acquirers or the next shareholder could buy the whole package and get rid of the underperforming units. This top manager from the UK explained it most clearly:

There is also a concern about giving away too much technical information even if it stays within the Group. For example, ourselves AdvancedTechnology [meaning AT-UK], and Technik, were previous competitors in some areas. There is some reluctance to share information. No one is sure that in a few years' time we would be competing again. […] People who have been involved in optics have seen many changes: several owners, many reorganizations. We are aware that we have an owner this year, that the Group could be broken up and we could have different owners next year.

Q: This could happen?

Capital Investments' business model is to buy companies and keep it for three to five years and sell them. When that happens, there is no guarantee that the Group will stay as it is now. I have experienced this many times in my career. […] There is a concern. We're clearly divided into separate divisions. It's attractive to sell off different divisions to different owners. (R&D director of AT-UK, 23 April 2009)

In the context of 'permanent restructuring', induced by financialization and acceleration in the 2000s (Folkman et al. 2007), cooperating with a different operating unit meant sharing knowledge and clients with a possible future competitor and thus giving that competitor an advantage. This is why the responsible top managers were so reluctant to follow the headquarters' policy and to push for collaborations. It is important to note that this was a belief of 'moral economy' and not a certain or even the most probable outcome. It was considered a possibility by the headquarters, but top managers of operating units had no proof that it was going to be the case. They made this inference by ascribing the shareholder an intention, based on the idea that financial shareholders, and PE firms in particular, employ the least legitimate practices of doing business.

In 2014, Capital Investments sold the stock of AdvancedTechnology to one of its competitors, a US corporation also held by a PE firm. Faced with considerable difficulties after the financial crisis of 2009, Capital Investments was liquidated in 2018. Even though AdvancedTechnology lost 600 jobs after this fieldwork, there is no available evidence that the company was dissolved in 2014. In any case, it is clear that top managers of operating units adopted strategic, non-cooperative, behaviour not because they could foresee the future but because the owner could possibly behave in a way that the managers did not like, as they had a different ideology. Due to their beliefs, managers did not trust the PE firm whose strategies were not legitimate for them. The result was that they did not want to cooperate with operating units who may become official competitors if the PE firm dismembered AdvancedTechnology.

Problems of taming competition

AdvancedTechnology was a corporation that sought to design and build complex optical and electronic systems in the context of 'permanent restructuring' induced by global, financial capitalism. This context was made evident when the PE firm wanted to acquire it to create shareholder value by reorganizing the strategy and structure of AdvancedTechnology. Cooperation among its subunits was a major issue for AdvancedTechnology, which became paramount after the crisis of 2008. The intention to foster collaboration among its units failed, despite the interest of many middle managers. I have argued that the main reason was that top managers of these operating units thought that the PE firm was not a legitimate owner as it could break up the corporation, a belief inscribed in the 'moral economy' of managerialism. The existence of overlaps in capabilities among operating units was a necessary, but not sufficient, condition to explain the persistence of competition. The zones of competition were still active because top managers, who directed engineers and sales teams, did not trust the PE firm.

One can wonder if the social processes that we highlight are indicative of a vicious circle, where attempts at cooperation actually lead to increases in competition. This paradoxical reasoning is seductive, but we cannot answer the question because we actually do not know about the degree of competition and cooperation before the LBO. Answering this question would require at least two observation time points. However, there was a clear contradiction at work in AdvancedTechnology: the pressure on financial performance tended to force the operating units to concentrate on themselves, whereas developing cooperation could have increased financial performance in the long term.

This brings me to the initial question about the conditions of reversal of competition. The conception of control of private equity is problematic when seeking to tame competition and generating cooperation. The debt pressure focuses managerial attention on short-term goals such as return on equity and on a finite time horizon, which makes firm boundaries and membership status uncertain. Corporate governance based on sanctions and incentives does not build trust when it is most needed—as in times of crisis. Nonetheless, the most fundamental reason may be that private equity is not legitimate among many managers, for whom the firm is or should be a stable collective entity focused on long-term technical efficiency and not a nexus of contracts among individuals who work only to improve 'financial figures'.

In conclusion, there is a deep tension between the conception of control of private equity and the corporate strategy of build-up. The first tends to increase competition among individuals and de-stabilizes firm boundaries, whereas the second requires cooperation and integration of subunits into a greater whole. These contradictions would explain the negative perceptions of PE firms, and more generally of finance, in the moral economy of managers. We can thus conclude that competition is probably easier to tame in firms with different property and control structures, for example public firms with a 'manufacturing conception of control', family firms, or worker cooperatives. Competition may be more easily reversed in sectors where profit-seeking is prohibited and self-interested behaviour is less institutionalized, as in hospitals, schools, and the military. More generally, it seems that competition is difficult to tame if the fourth party, who organizes cooperation, is not legitimate among the organized.

References

Baker, G. and Smith, G. 1998. *The New Financial Capitalists: Kohlberg Kravis Roberts and the Creation of Corporate Value*. Cambridge: Cambridge University Press.

Burawoy, M. and Olin Wright, E. 1994. 'Coercion and consent in contested exchange'. In *Interrogating Inequality*, edited by E. Olin Wright. London: Verso: 72–87.

Davis, G. F., Diekmann, K. A., and Tinsley, C. H. 1994. 'The decline and fall of the conglomerate firm in the 1980s: the deinstitutionalization of an organizational form'. *American Sociological Review* 59 (4): 547–70.

Fligstein, N. 1990. *The Transformation of Corporate Control*. Cambridge, MA: Harvard University Press.

Fligstein, N. 2001. *The Architecture of Markets: An Economic Sociology of Twenty-First-Century Capitalist Societies*. Princeton: Princeton University Press.

Folkman, P., Froud, J., Johal, S., and Williams, K. 2007. 'Working for themselves? Capital market intermediaries and present day capitalism'. *Business History* 49 (4): 552–72.

Freeland, R. F. 2005. *The Struggle for Control of the Modern Corporation: Organizational Change at General Motors, 1924–1970*. Cambridge: Cambridge University Press.

Granovetter, M. S. 2017. *Society and Economy: Framework and Principles*. Cambridge, MA: Harvard University Press.

Hedström, P. and Swedberg, R. 1998. 'Social mechanisms: an introductory essay'. In *Social Mechanisms: An Analytical Approach to Social Theory*, edited by P. Hedström and R. Swedberg. Cambridge: Cambridge University Press: 1–31.

Jensen, M. C. 1989. 'Eclipse of the public corporation'. *Harvard Business Review* 67 (5): 61–74.

Selznick, P. 1957. *Leadership in Administration: A Sociological Interpretation*. Berkeley, LA: University of California Press.

Sturgeon, T. J. 2002. 'Modular production networks: a new American model of industrial organization'. *Industrial and Corporate Change* 11 (3): 451–96.

13
Debunking the holy trinity: competition, individualism, and meritocracy

Sebastian Kohl and Abraham Sapién

It is usually taken for granted that the most apt form of social organization for a world of independent individuals or 'market societies' is (economic) competition. Competition is thus not only taken as the natural extension of individualist positions in social ontology, the view that the social world is made up of separate, independent individuals (cf. Reisman 1968: 9). It is also taken as the best realization of individualist theories of responsibility or what is also called 'competitive individualism', the view that responsibility in competition can be attributed to individuals separately and that competition is the best meritocratic system for crediting deserving winners and blaming undeserving losers according to purely individual merit, a widespread view in sports and economic life. Competition, ontological individualism, and normative meritocracy thus appear to be an indivisible *holy trinity* that pervades market-liberal thought and policies.

This individualist take on competition, while not shared by sociologists (including in this volume), has deep roots in the history of economic thought (Dennis 1977). On the one hand, there is the Common Law notion defended by classical liberals that sees competition as protecting people from arbitrary domination because it *isolates* individuals from each other. This is reflected in the idea of 'perfect competition', in which individuals appear to be isolated price-takers. On the other hand, the liberal von Hayek (1948) conceives of competition as the perfect means to organize *decentralized* decision-makers as a source of innovative experimentation. The belief in individual merit, in turn, is paradoxically more widespread than ever, despite increasing levels of inequality everywhere (Mijs 2019). Michael Sandel (2020) even speaks of the 'tyranny of meritocracy' we have come to live under. Michael Young's (1958) social science fiction *The Rise of Meritocracy* might have partly become reality.

This chapter makes a non-trinitarian case: first, we argue that competition is based on collective relational intentionality, which defies ontological individualism. Second, we argue that individual winners and 'stars' do not deserve all the credit in

Sebastian Kohl and Abraham Sapién, *Debunking the holy trinity: competition, individualism, and meritocracy* In: *Competition: What It Is and Why It Happens.* Edited by: Stefan Arora-Jonsson, Nils Brunsson, Raimund Hasse, and Katarina Lagerström, Oxford University Press. © Sebastian Kohl and Abraham Sapién 2021. DOI: 10.1093/oso/9780192898012.003.0013 competition but that non-winning competitors, other team members, and the team itself can be more praiseworthy than the individual feted by meritocratic thought. By implication, the individualist trinity might not be that 'holy' after all: when competition regulators presuppose a strictly individualistic ontology of competition and act accordingly, they could in fact be endangering what Etzioni (1985) once called socially 'encapsulated competition', competition embedded in social rules. If competition is deeply collective and relational, then cultures that are too radically individualist in competition run the danger of destroying the social foundations on which competition rests. The collective collapse of competition can result in an outright struggle. Its relational collapse can prevent competition from functioning as a motor of mutual stimulation. When, in turn, competition regulators see competition in too individualistically meritocratic terms and act accordingly, they might not see or may even reinforce the growing dissatisfaction of (blamed) losers in winner-takes-all markets (Frank 2016). Competition obviously creates losers, but they seem to be more important than a purely individualistic meritocracy might assume. If conceived too individualistically then, competition does not only create material losers and winners but also widens the inequality of recognition between them. Moreover, 'among the winners, it generates hubris; among the losers, humiliation and resentment' (Sandel 2020). A less individualistic and meritocratic conception of competition would help to strengthen the social fabric overall and make competition a more gentle social game.

Our two main claims structure the following two main sections. Drawing on resources from the debate on collective intentionality (Schweikard and Schmid 2013), the *first*—ontological—section challenges the individualist view that competition is reducible to separate competing individuals. Drawing on resources from debates on collective responsibility (French 1984), the *second*—normative—section questions the link between competition and purely individualistic ascription of responsibility between competitors and within competing teams, which underlies a meritocratic ethic. We conclude by pointing to some implications for understanding and regulating competition, once the trinity view of competition, individualism, and meritocracy is abandoned.

Ontology of competition: a non-individualist understanding

It takes (at least) two to compete

Can you compete alone? 'Compete', as an intransitive verb, does not grammatically require an object. Semantically, by contrast, it does require an object, as do the common collective verbs that indicate cooperation. It takes two to compete, where the social grammar of competition is in principle open to any number of additional competing participants. An individualist of competition therefore also uses a basic relational verb to describe how atomized individuals interact in competitive market societies, but would probably claim that it is socially a much less demanding relationship than collective ones such as cooperation or solidarity.

Given that it is relational, however, does competing necessarily require two *different* persons? Can't I compete with myself on a lonely island? Again, there is nothing grammatically wrong in saying that I am competing with my former or future performances and these over-time comparisons are indeed frequently made when describing individual learning or training processes. But as with many other lonely-island scenarios, this way of speaking is rather derived from the two-person competitive situation. As competition is a rule-based artefact, one could ask—with Wittgenstein—how rule-following is even possible for an isolated individual. What is also missing in the scenario is the very directed intention to win against someone else, as well as the strong motivational push that mutual awareness produces in situations of rivalry. Also, the basic condition of scarcity is not present and needs to be fictitiously produced. These elements, which are not present when one 'competes with oneself', seem to be essential for a scenario of true competition.

When I am trying to improve my personal best for the 400 metres dash, no goal or resource is limited. We can improve, but that does not mean that we are winning. The one-person and the two-person situations are close enough to work with the help of these fictions, but the competition remains in 'as-if' mode. Only thanks to the conceptual resources developed in competitive situations can we even start thinking about our performance over time in these terms. One crucial element that allows us to build this analogical bridge is *comparison*. The across-participant comparison of performance concerning a specific goal is replaced by an over-time comparison for just one individual. But as important as comparison is in enabling competition, comparison alone is not competition and does not necessarily produce competitive situations. We can compare many things we cannot even reasonably compete for because we have no power over changing them.

Some authors even see a third person as constitutive for the competitive situation, namely the crowd in sports (Werron 2013) or the customers vied for in business (Simmel 1903/2008). Particularly when it comes to economic competition—in which what one is competing *for* is essential to the meaning of competitive actions—this is probably a reasonable argument, although one could also compete for things other than simply customers. Yet others (Chapters 1 and 4, this volume) even see a fourth type of actor—the competition organizers—as (not necessarily) constitutive for competition. For our current purposes, we can naturally side with any position that wants to populate the ontology of competition even more to make the case against this radically individualistic view of inter-person competitions.

Against the objectivist individualist notion of competition
We thus should reject a radical individualist who sees competition even in a one-person world. Individualists, such as Reisman (1968), could live with this rejection of radical individualism and simply retreat to the position that, given that there *are* at

least two individuals, they are still separate, isolated, and independent. However, the mere co-presence of two or more individuals acting in order to obtain something does not suffice to make a situation competitive. Two actors A and B are then said to compete by 'Y-ing' over Z in context C, if there is scarcity, an objective chance for both A and B to obtain Z, and no randomness, as in a lottery (Geiger 2012: 36). While being true to the individualist core, the main feature of this extended definition is *objectivism*—that is, an external observer could know that A and B are competing based on their observable individual actions alone.

For economic competition, this objectivist account entails identifying an object of scarcity and to count the number of competitors from a market observer's perspective, as practised in economic textbooks, but also in the network tradition of economic sociology. The advantage of such an account of competition is that it makes modest demands on our social ontology—that is competitors do not have to be equipped with any particular 'social organ', nor does any 'social game' have to be going on. It is particularly apt for grasping the kind of competition associated with the (social) Darwinian concept of evolution and thus provides a big tent for both human competition and situations in the animal realm, although perhaps *too* big a tent: where it is too demanding for the animal kingdom (Hirshleifer 1978), it seems too underdetermined for the human realm, so as to make the notion of competition inflationary. After all, if the presence of relative scarcity and individuals desiring something was enough to speak of competition, almost any situation could be described as one in which (relative) scarcity could be observed or simply externally attributed. Even cases of absolute abundance could be re-described as ones of relative scarcity, but without participants being conscious of themselves as competitors at all, which is not sufficient for the social game of competition. Hence, even economists or game theorists started to abandon the objectivist definition and to include subjective elements in their definitions of competition (Stigler 1957). Another way of seeing this is to start from the typical scenario used to describe collective intentionality in collaborative contexts (Gilbert 1989), such as walking together, which we competitively adapt as 'running together'.

Imagine two people running, side by side, in a park. From an external observer's point of view, two different situations may look the same and yet be different. In a first scenario A and B run alongside one another, a pure coincidence. This is not a collective action, but simply two individual actions added together. Now consider a scenario in which A and B are really going for a run *together*. The situation might phenotypically match perfectly with the previous one. One way of explaining the difference between them is that only in the second do A and B have a common intention: they have the plan of running together.

This shared intentionality makes all the difference. This extra element not only involves the fact that both actors have the intention of running in the park at a certain moment in time. It also implies that A and B hold important mental states about each other. A has the belief that B is willing to develop the activity with A, and vice versa. There is mutual motivation. Not only does A want to be running, but A also desires to perform the activity with *B*, and vice versa. What is more, *A* and *B* have certain obligations as part of their collective actions; one would be blameworthy if they started running at a pace that the other one clearly could not keep up with.

Now imagine the same scenario, but with the difference that our joggers not only go for a run together but also compete to see who is the most enduring. With both still running next to each other, there is again little phenotypical evidence that would help our external observer. The two individuals could moreover be involved in numerous other social activities. The objectivist notion of competition, besides inflating competitive situations into all domains of life, including the animal realm, is not fine-grained enough to distinguish merely coincidental parallel action from competitive ones. It needs to be enriched by the participant view. But understanding this situation to be constituted of purely collective intentions, as in the previous scenario, would not be sufficient. While it is still true that *A* and *B* are engaging in a type of collective activity when agreeing to go for a run together—which is clearly more socially organized compared with the coincidental parallel action of two individuals—their activity is produced by a different set of beliefs and desires from the standard cooperative case. It is this *collective competitive intentionality* that makes competitive action hard to grasp for both individualists and the standard tools of the intentionalist analysis of cooperative collective actions.

Collective competitive intentionality

The challenge is hence, first, to make clear in what sense competing is characterized by the *cooperative* intentionality that underpins such typical collective actions as going for a walk together, but also, second, to demarcate it as an *antagonistic* type of action: competitors acting against each other in order to win. Competition, despite its antagonistic features, is composed of collective actions, underpinned by collective modes of intentionality. It comes in various degrees of organization, stretching from the informal one of child's play to the highly structured one in publicly organized markets or auctions. It ranges continuously between the concrete forms of very local rivalry and distant relationships without detailed mutual knowledge.

Let us return to the example of the two park runners who just happen to be running side by side. Without mutual awareness, not even an external spectator could make this coincidence into a competition. But with mutual awareness, we can imagine how they might start to try to keep up with each other. They might even come up with a joint goal for which to compete, such as reaching the park gates. The situation is not too different from economic competition, when two shop owners start to offer similar products. Competition hinges on a joint intention of *A* and *B* to act on common grounds and rules. These are not only regulative rules—in Searle's (1995) sense—of how competition needs to be coordinated or what means are appropriate to achieve certain ends. They are also constitutive rules through which the institutional fact of the competitive game comes into being in the first place (Searle 1995).

We consider that a mutual awareness of another competitor is crucial for competition to take place. If you truly believe that there is no other agent striving for a limited resource, it is very hard to take the view that you are competing. Of course, the awareness of other competitors does not have to be by direct acquaintance. Another way to understand this is that one has to be aware of one's competitors *de dicto*, but not *de re*. This means that it is not necessary that one knows exactly which token, which precise person or group, is our competitor; it is enough that we know that someone fits the description, even if we do not directly know who that is. Yet another way of understanding this distinction is that we do not have to know indexically who the competitor is, by direct reference. We just need an awareness that there are rivals.

Hence, a collective intention of the implicit form 'we intend to set up this competition' is at the origin of any competition as an institutional fact, that is a social entity of the kind Searle (1995) opposes to brute facts, such as stones. In Searle's view, this collective intention is itself a primitive, not further reducible 'we-intentionality', but there are also less demanding relational understandings of how collective intentionality can be made explicit, prominent among which is Michael Bratman's (1999). Based on this view, we propose a *subjectivist*, intentionality-based approach to competition.

We intend to *J* (compete, in this case) if and only if

1. (a) I *intend* that we *J* and (b) you intend that we *J*.
2. I intend that we *J* in accordance with and because of 1a, 1b, and meshing subplans of 1a and 1b; you intend that we *J* in accordance with and because of 1a, 1b, and meshing subplans of 1a and 1b.
3. 1 and 2 are common knowledge between us. (adapted from Bratman 1999: 121)

This collective intentionality contributing to the constitution of competitive games is easily forgotten by individualists, and without it, competition might really look much more like what the individualist takes it to be. It is often forgotten because these rules of the game are not renegotiated each time competition takes place but have become part of a general 'background' that enables complex competitions to take place smoothly. Against this shared but only implicit background, it is easy to see individuals as only following individual intentions, where competitors appear only as restricting conditions. Individual competitors easily forget about the collective organization of the game they are part of.

We have just seen—against the individualist position—that competition, like other institutional facts, is very much founded on collective intentionality, but it is obviously different from the usual cooperative cases in that the collective background sets up an antagonistic game, where the goal towards which (sub)plans are directed is not a collective one. These features gain a number of relational elements that are hard for the individualist to grasp, but also render it distinct from cooperative actions.

Upon entering competitions, *A* and *B* obviously do not have the primary intention of competing for its own sake but do so as part of a general plan—to achieve market power, wealth, or simply success. This implies that the participants in competition can have very different general plans and that competition as a system is fairly flexible in accommodating very different individual plans. This flexibility makes competition such an adaptable and integrative coordination device. In contrast to cooperative actions in which the cooperation serves as a joint general plan, the only joint project serving as a common denominator in competition is the social game of competition itself. The individual actions making up the plan (to lower prices, invest money, or decrease costs) are also not intended so as to compete but rather constitute a competition indirectly, as when 'by doing X, A competes with B' (Goldman 1970). These sub-intentions for sub-actions that constitute competition also explain the indirect nature ascribed to the competitive interaction between A and B: they do not (necessarily) have the outright intention to outcompete, damage, or even ruin each other directly but mainly focus on mediating actions that do not have the competitor as the primary target.

This feature led scholars such as Georg Simmel to emphasize again competition's distinction from outright struggles. Both features—the competitor does not figure directly in the other's intentions and each competitor follows its own general plans and motives—also help us to understand why individualists are led to think of competition in individualistic terms. What should be collective about an arrangement in which A and B do not jointly form intentions to engage in cooperative projects, and do not even figure as primary objects in each other's action orientations and follow their respective individual plans otherwise? Contrary to condition (1–3) mentioned earlier, competitor A does not have to form the intention 'I intend that *we* do something'—their subplans can also be independent of B's and no mutual knowledge about individual intentions is required.

One reply against these individualist intuitions against the relational account is that the arrangement is basically founded on collective actions. But even once founded, the social game of competition entails more relational aspects than the individualist counter-intuition is willing to concede. For one thing, there is mutual awareness, without which competition cannot even get under way. We noted earlier that co-presence needs to be supplemented with mutual awareness and common knowledge of the rules of the game. But even beyond this initial awareness, the continuing mutual observation and interaction—what has been called the 'side-glance' of someone physically present or just imagined (Geiger 2012: 13)—is equally important for the unfolding of competition. Searle (1995) distinguishes the intention prior to action from the intention-in-action that continuously and self-referentially accompanies the execution of an action towards its success. The competitive side-glance then becomes an important non-individualist element in the competitors' intentions-in-action; whatever my opponent intends and does enters into my reconsideration of whether my course of action is still complying with my prior intention. Competition is not depicted as two stones rolling down a hill kicked off by the initial intent to win the game but rather as continuous steering, re-adjustment, and mutual challenging. The control over one's own actions and their execution, so central to our understanding of individual autonomy, is thus much more shared in competition than the individualist would admit.

Competitors thus also become a crucial motivational component in each others' intention to act. Competition's function of stimulating competitors to act in ways they would not otherwise have done without competition is a feature much cited by normative proponents of competition (Hayek 1948). This means that A's perceiving that B is working towards getting better at X motivates them to work harder towards being better at X themselves; B's action then becomes a causal contribution of A's further competing and perhaps even winning (plus symmetry on B's side). Hence, A's prior intention to compete might be an individualistic I-intention, but in the competitive process this becomes relationally diluted: A's intention-in-action to compete is caused by B's competitive action in a potentially long causal chain.

In summary, then, this two-tiered non-individualist view proposes that competition is first of all an institutional fact, explicitly or just implicitly founded by collective actions backed by collective intentionality, which can be interpreted in Bratman's relational terms. Against this we-intentional background, competitors indeed stage an I-intentional game that nonetheless contains irreducible relational elements, as the intentions-in-action make actors lose manipulative control over their actions and make one competitor an important contributory cause of the other's actions. While we used the example of a competition with local rivalry and acquaintance, our definition easily travels to constellations without it. Competitors can be distributed quite discontinuously across space and mutual awareness can be distributed quite unequally among a group of many competitors, with some having a perfect market survey and others having a hazy and perhaps even erroneous idea of the world of competition out there. Many features of competition can become different depending on how intensive local rivalry and awareness is, but without any, competition collapses into an observer-relative guess.

Collective responsibility in competition

Normative and ontological debates in social philosophy need to be distinguished, even if they are not completely independent. If the ontology of competition works relationally as proposed so far, it would nonetheless be surprising to assume that attribution of responsibility in competition works in neat separation of individuals as presumed in 'competitive individualism' or the holy-trinity view. In this latter view underlying a meritocratic ethic, competitions are races organized to produce unequal outcomes that are justified by crediting the winners' success to their own doings and by blaming the losers' failures on their own shortcomings. In this section, we question such neat distributions of merit and blame in two competitive contexts. First, we consider the distribution of responsibility *between* competitors in a simple two-person setting. Second, we consider the distribution of responsibility *within* competing teams.

Responsibility distribution in individual competitions

We have seen that competitions are complex social games in which the intentions, beliefs, and motivations of competitors *A* and *B* are closely intertwined. Given this strong ontological relationship between the constituents of competition, it should be *prima facie* surprising if pure notions of individual responsibilization were in place. And, indeed, there are important cases in which 'commonsense' blaming and crediting of competitors diverges from purely individualistic attribution of responsibility.

Individualistic ascription of responsibility as presupposed in a meritocratic ethic works best in success stories, in which winners in a competition can credit themselves with having causally brought about success. Another domain in which individualistic ascription occurs is in the case of the 'undeserving poor', people who, supposedly because of their 'moral deficiencies', brought about the plight they find themselves in, through fault of their own. A case for individualistic ascription is progress 'from-rags-to-riches', in which someone made it to the top thanks to their own efforts. In short, meritocratic legitimacy or delegitimacy is largely dependent on attributing responsibility to isolated individuals.

Another important factor in responsibility-attribution is that we have the strong intuition that people are praiseworthy and blameworthy *only* for actions that are under their control. Gauriot and Page's (2019) argument exemplifies this. Soccer players are *unfairly* judged about aspects of their performance that depend on luck. According to this control principle, we can establish that 'we are morally assessable only to the extent that what we are assessed for depends on factors under our control' (Nelkin 2019). From this, we propose the following principle of responsibility in competition:

> *Individualistic responsibility in competition*
> The respective responsibility (that is the praiseworthiness or blameworthiness) of competitors *A* and *B* is *fully* based on *their own* actions, intentions, desires, beliefs, and other relevant attitudes involved in their victory or loss over which they are in control.

One first doubt on this purely individualistic ascription of responsibility lies in the basic credit/blame asymmetry of responsibility-ascription in competitive situations: failures are much more frequently attributed to external circumstances than are successes. Huge profits, great returns, or salaries are bragged about, but losses, negative returns, or uncompetitive wages are attributed to the uncontrollable nature of fierce competition, market forces, or competitive pressures. These statements are probably not even excuses—for excuses would presuppose that it happens only exceptionally

(Austin 1956)—but their frequency rather indicates that they are justifications: we tend to accept the regular nature of uncontrollable forces intervening and justify them by pointing out why they are not surmountable. In many competitive situations, particularly when expected winners lose, it is common practice to attribute responsibility or blame to other individuals or even to external forces. If winners were to act symmetrically when claiming credit, reponsibility would be much less focused on few individuals.

A related case is the lucky winner. When winners win, they concede that at least part of their win was not due to their extraordinary effort or ability but to mere luck. Frank (2016) points out how the share attributed to luck is much lower, particularly among winners in a competition, than what luck is taken to explain, particularly in luck-intensive situations, such as winner-takes-all markets. The more complex the competitive situation—take prices on a stock exchange as an example—the more winners, but also losers, can refer to good or bad luck as what is (partially) responsible for the outcome. The implications of moral luck are important to enable us to make fair moral assessments (Nelkin 2019). Michaelson (2008), for example, argues that we must take into consideration the role of moral luck in business ethics, and 'if we cannot explain moral luck away, we should give consideration to moral risk in our moral judgments and the associated assignment of economic rewards regarding episodes in which moral luck plays a role'. We should be more careful when ascribing merit or blame with regard to how we build a meritocratic policy given that luck plays such an important role in competition outcomes.

Another case that goes against the individualistic ascriptivist derives from the relational element we identified earlier in our ontological definition of competition. A's intention-in-action to compete is motivated or caused by B's prior competitive actions, and vice versa. Motivation is bidirectional. Proponents of competition openly admit this interdependence in what is perhaps the strongest argument for introducing competition into a previously uncompetitive setting: its function of encouraging better performance, increasing productivity, and innovation. What this pro-competition argument implies, however, is that if better performance is not achieved by individuals alone, without competitive pressures, then they necessarily lose part of their credit, as well as blame in relation to the competitors or the competitive system. There can be no world record without good competitors.

This connects with another important feature of competition regarding merit or blame. How good or bad our adversary is plays a crucial role in the merit, or blame, that we obtain when winning, or losing. This is an element that is not present in other forms of collaborative action and, again, it is dependent on the parties' likelihood of victory, an important aspect that is needed to classify collective action as a competition. There is more merit in being the champion at world level than at a local one. These contextual features affect how we evaluate people's performance in competition, but they are not under their control. It is a matter of luck how well prepared my rival is. This might be affected by my own performance, of course, because we might even train together. But my rival's skills are a very important factor in my credit or blame, which are largely out of my control, and vice versa. Their capacity directly affects my merit when winning or losing against them. Losing against very skilled rivals incurs less blame than doing so against poorly skilled adversaries. Winning against much less skilled competitors entails less merit than shining among the stars. The underdog winner is special.

Furthermore, our motivation to compete and win is also influenced by the skills of our rivals and how we represent them regarding our own capacities. It is more motivating to win against strong competitors than weak ones. This can account for why competition can be used as a stimulus for better performance in diverse scenarios. That said, this does not imply that incorporating competition is ideal in all cases where we desire to increase productivity. Sometimes the competition occurs between groups, in which the members of each whole work cooperatively against another group. In these cases, internal competition can be detrimental to the main purpose of the whole: group victory.

Finally, winners depend on the collective in two different ways. *Causally*, winners in competition, even if mostly unacknowledged, have often relied on many collective institutions and external help to reach their goals successfully. As President Obama, pointing to American collective infrastructure as a precondition for the profits of individual entrepreneurs, put it in a 2012 speech, 'If you've been successful, you didn't get there on your own'. *Constitutively*, winners are simply winners because without collectively agreed rules, even if implicit, winning would not exist. These rules come into existence only through collective intentionality; only if others recognize these rules can a winner be a winner.

As we saw earlier, some scholars consider recognition from non-competing others—the general public or audience—as the most important thing in the production of winners and losers. For our purposes, it is enough to point out that collective recognition in general is an important precondition for attributing responsibility to individual participants. Take away the recognition from the audience, the money from customers, or the regulatory capacity of the competition organizer and the antagonistic game of competition—including all notions of winners and losers—will cease. This, again, is not under the competitors' control.

Taken together, these cases show that individualistic ascription of responsibility does not fully align with some of our ascription practices commonly used in economic contexts. First, competing individuals do seem to share the responsibility for competition outcomes much more than individualists think. Granted, the carriers of responsibility might still be individual competitors, but in the distribution of responsibility across individuals, the individualistic ascriptivist needs to concede certain shifts, even more so when collective institution and recognition is part of making people win. This is where an individualist meritocracy has its limits.

Secondly, in some cases, it is actually non-individualistic 'forces', moments of luck or structural 'pressures', that are invoked to justify one's losses in competition. This might be a mere *façon de parler*. Nonetheless, it reveals that individualistic ascription—no matter at what exchange rate—might err in complex competitive situations. The notion of individualistic responsibility in competition is not, of course, entirely mistaken, but it is not the whole story. This becomes even clearer when moving from the two-person competition to more complex forms.

Responsibility distribution in team competitions

Many competitions occur between very large groups of people. The individualist would expect that the responsibility of these groups could ultimately be explained with reference to the individuals within them. If the collective is the sum of its members, the responsibility of the whole should also result from the addition of the sum of its parts. This is not necessarily the case because, first, the responsible agent can be the group itself; second, there are examples where individuals are not responsible for the actions of their group; and third, there are cases in which people might be held responsible for a group action even when they played no significant causal role.

The group is responsible, not the individuals

There are many ways in which we might belong to a group. We belong to nations and, for the most part, this is out of our control. We may judge that a group has acted unfairly and we might be regarded as belonging to such a group even if our actions and intentions are not causally involved in such wrongdoings. We can cite a number of different principles concerning the type of responsibility-dependency between the whole and its parts that will be useful in attempting to explain the different forms of collective responsibility and, thus, of merit or blame:

> *Individualist collective responsibility*
> The responsibility (praiseworthiness or blameworthiness) of a group *(A, B, C*, and so on) is grounded in the sum of the responsibility of *all* of its members *(a, b, c*, and so on) *non-equally*.
>
> *Weak non-individualist collective responsibility*
> The responsibility of a group is grounded in the sum of the responsibility of *some* of its members, but not necessarily all of them.
>
> *Strong non-individualist collective responsibility*
> The responsibility of a group is *independent* of the responsibility of *all* of its members.

By *grounding* we mean a type of relationship between more and less fundamental elements. In this case the individuals ground the group, in the sense that they determine other less fundamental objects such as being a group. Individuals exist without groups, but not vice versa. Grounding is a relation of fundamentality that is distinct from an identity, causal or supervenience relations (cf. Bliss and Trogdon 2016).

Starting with the first principle, if we think of how collective action functions in very simple scenarios, it seems intuitive to think that individuals share responsibility equally. This is false. The moment we start considering more complex, albeit ordinary, situations, we can observe that responsibility is not equally distributed. Within a team, some individuals are more, some less responsible for the overall outcome. But even if not all members play the same prominent role and thus deserve different degrees of merit or blame, the fact that together they constitute a group or a team implies that all of them have a certain degree of responsibility; their shared collective responsibility makes them part of the same team.

This is controversial. There is an important literature on collective responsibility according to which collectives can be regarded as agents with a full portion of morality, that is the strong non-individualist view of collective responsibility (French 1984). 'A collective *behavior* is a doing or behavior that is the result of a collective, though not the result of its intentions. A *collective action* is caused by the beliefs and desires (wants) of the collective itself, whether or not such beliefs and desires can be accounted for or explained in individualistic terms' (Corlett 2001: 575). Not only can we not explain collective action by referring to individuals' actions, but it is the collective that acts.

This understanding of agency goes against an important individualist tradition of responsibility, such as that of Rawls, in which it is not clear how a metaphysical person can be constituted by a collective. 'There is, perhaps, a certain logical priority to the case of human individuals: it may be possible to analyse the actions of so-called artificial persons as logical constructions of the actions of human persons' (Rawls 1971: 244–5). It is hard to make sense of a collective being praiseworthy or blameworthy in itself. However, one reason to think so is that, otherwise, we should blame individuals whose intentions do not seem to be connected to the group action. Even more, such individuals' intentions might be the opposite of the collective's. 'It would be unfair, whether we are considering a result produced by more than one person's action or by a single person, to blame a person for a result that he or she did not intend to produce' (Sverdlik 1987: 86).

We can think that *only some* people are responsible for these actions. We could take a weak non-individualist approach. This seems naturally intuitive for many scenarios. But there is also a possibility that only the collective being responsible exists. 'For a corporation to be treated as a moral person, it must be the case that some events are describable in a way that makes certain sentences true: sentences that say that some of the things a corporation does were intended by the corporation itself' (French 1984: 39). When a firm takes a decision, such as joining a cartel, the truth of such an intention can be independent of the truth of a specific individual's action. When an oil corporation decides to join a cartel, this means that 'in these circumstances the executives voting is...the corporation deciding to do something' (French 1984: 45). The truth of the sentence 'the oil corporation decides to join a cartel' is independent of the intentions of the members that constitute it, and this shows—French and many others think—that the responsibility of the group can be independent of its members.

There might be scenarios in which responsibility for collective action cannot be explained in terms of particular responsibility. When it comes to competition, something similar may happen. A firm can be out of the market for external reasons or uncontrollable factors, which excuse the members of a group from responsibility. Imagine a soccer final in which all the members of a team were poisoned and lost. The team lost as a collective. However, all the players would be excused from blameworthiness because the bad result would have been beyond their control. The same could happen to a firm losing an important case or an enterprise going bankrupt. Because the merit or blame of a collective's action is attributed to that collective agent, this reshapes our notion of meritocracy: a group can have merit or blame without any of its members being held responsible for it. Even if a CEO seals a great deal, they might have no merit in that connection at all.

Only some individuals are responsible

Even if there seem to be examples in which group members are not responsible for the collective's actions, there are many cases in which we can ascribe responsibility to individuals. Friedman (1970), for example, notices that it is ultimately individuals who are responsible for actions in corporations—although that is not necessarily the case, as we saw in the previous section. 'Presumably, the individuals who are to be responsible are businessmen, which means individual proprietors or corporate executives.'

That said, the distribution of group responsibility is often uneven. We think that such inequality can be understood in two main ways: (a) there are levels of responsibility to the extent that some members are not even responsible—in other words, they are not blameworthy or praiseworthy; and (b) some members of the group may be judged to be responsible in a form of moral luck, in the sense that they may be morally responsible to a certain extent for things that they have no control over.

The notion of cheating is useful for understanding unequal distribution of responsibility, as when companies flout cartel agreements by undercutting prices. The distribution of responsibility among members of a group is distributed depending on the impact that a person's actions have on the evaluated outcome. Blame is also distributed unequally. Executives are more blameworthy for corporate cheating than others because their actions play a much bigger role in the final outcome. This can be explained counterfactually: if Steve Jobs hadn't been the leader of Apple, it would have been much less likely that the enterprise would achieve such success. The leader of a team has a crucial role in winning competitions.

The extent to which the rest of the team members are blameworthy depends on how much their agency is involved in the result. If a team member has no intention of cheating but knows about it, they would be more responsible than one who is not even aware of it. Furthermore, a team member might have tried to act against the cheating, and the other team members might have deceived them about it. In this case, that person would not be responsible. Ontologically, all its members constitute the team. However, the responsibility for the team's outcomes is not distributed equally among its members and some of these may not even be responsible at all for some of the team's actions. Again, this shows how our merit or blame is nuanced by the collective, by other agents, who we do not control.

Something similar can occur in economic competitions, such as different enterprises trying to dominate the market. The final outcome may depend almost entirely on the actions and decisions of a few. The responsibility and consequences of these competitions can be dramatically different among its members, and also unfair. In some cases, the team may win something without one of its members really contributing to the victory. Similarly, a member of a firm may suffer terrible consequences as a result of the CEO's actions. Why is it that a member of a group receives punishment, such as losing their job, if they are not responsible for the outcome, over which they have no control? There are various ways of explaining this.

The simplest solution is that sometimes—maybe too often—legal consequences do not reflect morality. We may lose our job or enter a big economic crisis without doing anything wrong. However, this is not the type of scenario that we are concerned with here. We consider that in some cases people who belong to a collective have no moral responsibility at all. This is because they have an excuse exempting them from responsibility. If, for example, a team member was poisoned and, due to that, was incapable of playing in a game, they are not blameworthy for the team losing the match. This becomes clearer the larger the group is, because agency becomes more unequal among the constituents of a whole.

When different nations compete to achieve high economic growth, winning cannot be fully understood by appealing to the intentions and actions of each of the individuals that constitute the nation, even if the responsibility can be explained in terms of the agency and decisions of some of its individuals, such as the president or other relevant politicians. However, there are cases in which the responsibility of a collective seems to be independent of its individuals. This applies to collectives in general, but it is accentuated in competition contexts in which the credit or blame, when winning, losing, or cheating, cannot be understood based on a purely individualist approach to collective responsibility.

Different forms of responsibility

However, there are cases that are not so easy to explain in such a fashion. People might be morally responsible, even if their actions and intentions are not causally linked to the outcome. This can be explained in terms of moral luck—that is, based on the fact that we might judge people to be good or bad, better or worse, independently of their intentions, actions, and things that are not under their control.

We normally think that we cannot be morally assessed in relation to a state of affairs over which we have no control. Or to put it another way, two situations in which people have the same intentions and actions should be judged equally. This, although intuitive, is not the way we tend to judge certain moral cases: sometimes we are morally judged about things that are not in our control. Imagine two people who plan an identical murder. They take the same precautions and actions, but, by accident, one fails. It seems as if an attempted murder is not as bad as an accomplished one, even if the intentions and actions are the same.

Many situations in our lives depend on factors outside our control. Among the many things we cannot control, but that we benefit or suffer from, is the competence of the groups that we belong to, both in competitive and in non-competitive scenarios. Can we be morally judged about the outcome of collective actions if we are not in control of the results? Are we, as individuals, praiseworthy or blameworthy if victory or defeat did not depend on our individual control?

Competition in groups maintains the intricacies of individual competition, but it adds an extra layer of complexity. Consider responsibility: being simply a spectator at a lynching makes us part of the lynch mob, but we may be there by accident; we did not cause it and have no real power of stopping it. However, we are still part of the lynch mob. Similarly, some individuals belonging to competing groups are constituents of the group without playing a major role in the groups' agency, and yet they are part of the relevant crowd and play different roles, even if their actions and intentions are not ultimately decisive in the merit of winning or the blame of losing.

We propose that a good way of making sense of the disproportionate responsibility in group competition is to put it in terms of moral luck. There are two possible strategies. First, to deny the existence of moral luck in order to keep the notion that one can only be morally judged about things that one has control of. That is to say, all members of a group have a certain degree of responsibility—if you have no responsibility whatsoever in relation to the group's agency, then you simply could not be a member of that group. This, we think, leads to too inflexible a way of judging collectivity. We prefer a more nuanced approach, because it captures not only the degrees of responsibility but also the different forms of belonging to a group.

We interpret certain cases of group activity as examples of moral luck, together with a non-individualist understanding of collective responsibility. First, regarding the non-individualist aspect of it, we think that an individual may be ontologically a member of a group, or a competing team, but have zero responsibility *in a certain sense*. There are different types or roles of moral luck (Nelkin 2019): resultant, circumstantial, constitutive, and causal. These different types of luck track uncontrolled aspects in virtue of which we morally judge someone, depending on the uncontrolled results, circumstances, and so on. Consider again the example of the two murderers. They are equally guilty in a causal sense; they did the same things to cause a homicide. However, the resultant luck is not the same; by mere chance one only attempted murder and the other succeeded. One might also be judged based on the circumstances counterfactually.

We think that competitive scenarios can be judged similarly to cases of *circumstantial luck*, that is, by considering who we are and the situation we find ourselves in. We sometimes are part of a group or a team, without being able to fully control to which team we belong to and, in particular, without controlling who are the other members of our team and their actions. These uncontrolled factors will determine how we will be judged, how much credit or blame we will receive as members of these groups, and the likelihood of our victory or our loss. We might be judged in terms of circumstantial luck, but not on the grounds of our actions and intentions playing a *causal* role in the merit or blame of the whole. We are responsible insofar as we belong to a group, but not in all possible senses. The winner of a world cup who sat on the bench the whole tournament has very little merit *causally* with the team winning even if they might have some individual merit *circumstantially*.

After examining collective competition, collective responsibility in competitive settings is more complex than we might think at a first glance. There are cases in which, although rare, a collective could win or lose without its members being blameworthy or praiseworthy for it. In other circumstances—much more common—members of a collective are not responsible for the outcome of its performance. Moreover, even when the responsibility is distributed among the members of a collective, even if not all of them, there are nuances. The degree of the impact of our actions and intentions affects our responsibility. However, even in cases in which we are not causally responsible for the collective's actions in competition, we can still be held responsible in other senses, which can be understood as forms of moral luck, such as circumstantial ones. All in all, we are not always responsible for our team's victory or loss, at least not in all possible ways. To the extent that large parts of our life, in competitive or non-competitive contexts, take place in or are organized through groups, easy individualistic attributions of responsibility as required in a meritocratic ethic thus become problematic as a feasible gold standard.

Conclusion

This chapter set out to question the stability and coherence of the trinity of competition, individualism, and meritocracy. If we are right, the three not only do not go together naturally, but competition actually weakens an individualist ontology and is not as clearly meritocratic as previously thought. In liberal thought and market radicalism, competition serves at least two important functions. First, it is the least demanding form of social organization for the separate and independent individuals that alone are supposed to figure in the ontology of individualists. Second, it is meant as the central meritocratic mechanism that justifies the inequality of winners winning and losers losing, particularly in competitive capitalist systems. This chapter was meant to show that the implicit concept of competition presupposed in these two functions might not work because supposedly individualistic competition is much more collectively enmeshed than is usually thought. This has two broader implications.

First, if competition is deeply collective and relational, then too radically individualist cultures in competition run the danger of destroying the social foundation on which competition rests. The collective collapse of competition can result in an outright struggle. Its relational collapse—as perhaps practised in the French *loi Chapelier* outlawing all cooperation between employers or employees or the US Supreme

Court jurisprudence on employer associations—can deprive competition of functioning as a motor of mutual stimulation. Second, competition obviously creates losers, but the distribution of responsibility between winners and losers is more complex than simple individualistic ascription. Team competitions are also more complex than notions such as the merit of superstar players or CEOs and the blame of the lower ranks allow us to understand. Denying the latter recognition and concentrating it at the top can be a dangerous source of societal discontent. Reassessing less individual-centric forms of competition would help to strengthen the overall social fabric and make predatory competition a gentler social game.

References

Austin, J. L. 1956. 'A plea for excuses: the presidential address'. *Proceedings of the Aristotelian Society* 57: 1–30.

Bliss, R. and Trogdon, K. 2016. 'Metaphysical grounding'. *Stanford Encyclopedia of Philosophy*. Available at: https://plato.stanford.edu/archives/win2016/entries/grounding (accessed 20 June 2020).

Bratman, M. E. 1999. *Faces of Intention: Selected Essays on Intention and Agency*. Cambridge: Cambridge University Press.

Corlett, J. A. 2001. 'Collective moral responsibility'. *Journal of Social Philosophy* 32 (4): 573–84.

Dennis, K. G. 1977. *Competition in the History of Economic Thought*. New York: Arno Press.

Etzioni, A. 1985. 'Encapsulated competition'. *Journal of Post Keynesian Economics* 7 (3): 287–302.

Frank, R. H. 2016. *Success and Luck: Good Fortune and the Myth of Meritocracy*. Princeton: Princeton University Press.

French, P. 1984. *Collective and Corporate Responsibility*. New York: Columbia University Press.

Friedman, M. 1970. 'The social responsibility of business is to increase its profits'. *New York Times Magazine* 13 (33): 122–6.

Gauriot, R. and Page, L. 2019. 'Fooled by performance randomness: overrewarding luck', *Review of Economics and Statistics* 101 (4): 658–66.

Geiger, T. 2012. *Gesamtausgabe. Wirtschafts- und Betriebssoziologie. Konkurrenz*, Frankfurt a. M.: Peter Lang.

Gilbert, M. 1989. *On Social Facts*. London: Routledge.

Goldman, A. I. 1970. *A Theory of Human Action*. Princeton: Princeton University Press.

Hayek, F. A. von. 1948. *Individualism and Economic Order*. Chicago: University of Chicago Press.

Hirshleifer, J. 1978. 'Competition, cooperation, and conflict in economics and biology'. *American Economic Review* 68 (2): 238–43.

Michaelson, C. 2008. 'Moral luck and business ethics'. *Journal of Business Ethics* 83 (4): 773–87.

Mijs, J. J. B. 2019. 'The paradox of inequality: income inequality and belief in meritocracy go hand in hand'. *Socio-Economic Review*. Available at: https://doi.org/10.1093/ser/mwy051.

Nelkin, D. K. 2019. 'Moral luck'. *Stanford Encyclopedia of Philosophy*. Available at: https://plato.stanford.edu/archives/sum2019/entries/moral-luck/.

Rawls, J. 1971. 'Justice as reciprocity'. In *John Stuart Mill, Utilitarianism*, edited by S. Gorovitz. Indianapolis: Bobbs-Merrill: 242–68.

Reisman, G. 1968. 'Platonic competition'. *The Objectivist* 7 (8–9): 504–22.

Sandel, M. 2020. *The Tyranny of Merit. What's Become of the Common Good?* London: Allen Lane.

Schweikard, D. P. and Schmid, H. B. 2013. 'Collective intentionality'. *Stanford Encyclopedia of Philosophy*. Available at: https://plato.stanford.edu/archives/sum2013/entries/collective-intentionality/ (accessed 20 June 2020).

Searle, J. R. 1995. *The Construction of Social Reality*. New York: Free Press.

Simmel, G. 1903/2008. 'Sociology of competition'. *Canadian Journal of Sociology/Cahiers Canadiens de Sociologie* 33 (4): 957–78.

Stigler, G. J. 1957. 'Perfect competition, historically contemplated'. *Journal of Political Economy* 65 (1): 1–17.

Sverdlik, S. 1987. 'Collective responsibility'. *Philosophical Studies: An International Journal for Philosophy in the Analytic Tradition* 51 (1): 61–76.

Werron, T. 2013. 'On public forms of competition'. *Cultural Studies ↔ Critical Methodologies* 14 (1): 62–76.

Young, M. 1958. *The Rise of the Meritocracy. 1870–2033*. New York: Penguin Books.

14

Competition unbundled: taking stock and looking forward

Stefan Arora-Jonsson, Nils Brunsson, Raimund Hasse, and Katarina Lagerström

The origin of this book was the observation that although competition has become an increasingly important aspect of everyday life, social science engagement with competition has been largely confined to the workings of competition within markets. Missing is a vibrant discussion about the origins of competition, its various expressions, and the meaning of competition in its many forms to society at large. The purpose of this book is to open competition to social science engagement. Towards this end, Chapter 1 proposed a definition of competition that allows scholars to ask new, more fundamental questions about competition. Central to our definition is the parsing of competition into its constituent elements of actors, their relationship, scarcity, and desire, and the insight that these elements can be constructed by three types of actors: those who compete, those who adjudicate the competition (third parties), and those who organize the competition (fourth parties). With this definition, we can study the institutional and organizational foundations of competition, and thereby gain a deeper and fuller understanding of its origins, workings, and consequences. In this final chapter, we discuss how the preceding chapters illuminate some fundamental questions about competition: how competition is constructed, how the behaviours resulting from competition are managed, what consequences competition may lead to, and how competition can be removed. In doing this, we hope to provide an outline of a social science research programme on competition that is long overdue.

How competition happens

Economists and other social scientists have devoted surprisingly little attention to the construction of competition. Students of competition tend to take as their point of departure a situation in which there already *is* competition, and few researchers have asked when and how a situation that was not characterized by competition *becomes* so. This could be one reason why competition seems so ubiquitous and

Stefan Arora-Jonsson, Nils Brunsson, Raimund Hasse, & Katarina Lagerström, *Competition unbundled: taking stock and looking forward* In: *Competition: What It Is and Why It Happens*. Edited by: Stefan Arora-Jonsson, Nils Brunsson, Raimund Hasse, and Katarina Lagerström, Oxford University Press. © Stefan Arora-Jonsson, Nils Brunsson, Raimund Hasse, and Katarina Lagerström 2021. DOI: 10.1093/oso/9780192898012.003.0014 almost invincible; the efforts and sometimes unsuccessful attempts at introducing competition have not been studied. Even when there are institutional foundations suitable for competition or when there have been attempts to organize for competition, competition does not necessarily arise.

A central message of the book is that competition seems ubiquitous but that it should not be naturalized as an inevitable aspect of human existence. Its emergence, maintenance, and change may be the result of institutions, or of intention and purposive efforts. How competition is organized, by whom, and for what purpose matters not only for the way resources are allocated and for the legitimacy of competition but also for its role in status ascription and social cohesion. Apart from the cases discussed in Chapter 3, in which competition was shown to emerge by mutual adjustment among house decorators and among actors in the fashion industry, the chapters in this book have covered two main ways in which a situation can become constructed as competition: through institutionalization of the elements of competition and through organization as an intended or unintended effect.

Competition often requires both institutional foundations and organizational effort. As argued in Chapter 4, some of the most significant institutions of modern society have laid foundations for the construction of competition. Modern society celebrates actorhood in many forms; individuals, organizations and states are expected to have desires and to see others as capable of creating scarcity. An aspect of actorhood is a sense of identity, which in turn lends itself to considerations of social positioning, a greater willingness to compare oneself to others, and a greater willingness to improve upon or, at least, maintain one's status. Actorhood thus lays the groundwork for constructing a situation as competition.

Even the idea of competing can be infused with value and be taken for granted, as was most clearly seen in the case of the subsidiary managers in Chapter 11 who extolled the virtues of competing and competition. These managers did not consider it necessary to explain what good competition would do; they merely believed it to be 'right'. The reformers of higher education described in Chapter 6 strongly believed in competition, although they were vague about what universities should be competing for. In these cases, competition is highly institutionalized, and no further efforts are required to maintain it. The good that one is competing for can also be taken for granted, as when auditors, clients, and even scholars who study auditing have found it natural that auditing firms compete for contracts with clients, rather than for the appreciation of the investors who are their main stakeholders (Chapter 8).

Competition as an intended or unintended construction

Often, competition is constructed as the intended result of organizational efforts, as when someone makes decisions in order to influence others, in hopes that those others will perceive the situation as competition. A good part of latter-day public-sector reforms can be understood in that way, when a state, local government, or department seeks to introduce competition among organizations that did not previously see themselves as competing (cf. Hasse 2003; Hood and Dixon 2015; Le Grand 2009). In some cases, it means changing who is constructed as the third party in an ongoing competition. This happens when users of public services become customers, and interdepartmental competition for budget allocations from top management is transformed into a different competition: a competition to be chosen by the users of the services. Chapters 5, 6, 10, and 11, in particular, treated in that way situations in which there was an interested fourth party—the politicians in a municipality, rankers, teachers, or the headquarter managers of multinational corporations (MNCs)—people who expended considerable effort on the construction of competition. Competition can also arise from decisions that are made without the intent of introducing competition; it can be an unintended outcome of organization. Some of the rankings, ratings, and meta-organizations discussed in Chapters 6 and 7 are cases in point.

Those who try to convince others that competition exists may not need to consider all the elements of competition. There may already be an institutionalized sense of desire, scarcity, relationships, or actorhood. In Chapter 5, for instance, the school principals already desired to have students, and they had established relationships with other schools prior to the introduction of competition. What required intervention was their legitimate ability to act in order to attract students (the actorhood of schools) and the sense that students were scarce and that the actorhood of other schools could influence this scarcity. Similarly, in Chapter 6, universities already had relationships with each other but needed to develop their actorhood and desire for status in order for the situation to be constructed as competition. For rankers of the waste-disposal organizations in Chapter 7, the main question was how to make the organizations connect their desire to the own ranking system. In Chapter 8, auditors were already in established relationships with each other, but to turn these relationships competitive required the construction of a third party—a buyer of their services. In constructing the audited firms as the third party, the auditing firms collectively organized their situation as competition.

Alternatively, the construction of an element of competition may be hindered by earlier organization or institutions. The professional role of auditors, a central aspect of their actorhood, initially discouraged auditing firms from advertising to promote their individual firm rather than promoting the accounting profession (Chapter 8). Competitive relationships among the auditing firms did not develop, but remained residual. Similarly, the professional norms of university researchers and teachers may limit their willingness to promote their own university if it is seen to be at the expense of their profession (Chapter 6). A possible corollary to these findings is that the competitive actorhood of organizations develops at the expense of the actorhood of professions that cut across organizations. Although competition among professions is a central theme within research on professions (Abbott 1988), we need to learn more about the relationship between organizational competition and professional autonomy.

Interrelated constructions

The institutional or organizational impact on elements of competition may be indirect. The ideal of education as equalizing rather than elitist, as seen in Chapter 10, gave rise to a striving for equality in student outcomes among teachers, which hampered the construction of a desire among pupils for prizes and other forms of segregating rewards. Chapters 6, 7, and 11 suggest that there could be a trade-off between competition for status, money, and attention (the desire for one could exclude the other), or conversely, one of these desired goods could serve as the means to achieve the other. An example of the latter case occurred when subsidiaries in an MNC that were successful in the competition for headquarters investments gained over the other subsidiaries in the status competition. But we can also see the reverse; success in the competition for money may have a negative impact on status among artists, fashion designers, or underground musicians.

More broadly, actors are often engaged in different competitions in several arenas simultaneously: athletes compete on the track, for sponsors, and for the status of their sports; and firms compete for customers, suppliers, investor money and governmental support. Actions and outcome in one competition can influence the result of another competition, as when a firm loses customers because it implements austerity measures required by its investors or when athletes whose individual successes on the track help attract sponsors that increase the status of their sport. Such relationships must also be considered if we are interested in the question of how various competitions affect each other. If we believe that there is more competition than ever, we need to know more about what may be labelled as an *ecology of competitions*.

Actors can play several roles in the construction of competition, and their role at a particular time can be ambiguous. In formal organizations, a management that wants to see competition among its subunits regularly takes the role of both organizer and adjudicator of the competition. In Chapters 5 and 11, the municipality and the headquarters were both organizers of competition, and were in many respects also its adjudicators. Earlier work on the introduction of competition (for instance Dobbin 1994) has investigated instances of a single role, as when a state seeks to introduce competition among its railway firms. Multiple roles have not been well investigated and this issue is of great interest, as it is likely to raise managerial issues and issues about the legitimacy of competition. Schools in the Swedish municipality that were becoming less attractive were provided with extra students, and subsidiaries of an MNC that were lacking financial resources were supplied outside of the previously decided allocation system. In the case of the MNC, subsidiary managers saw this situation negatively as one of 'politics and strategy'. The question of the role of fourth parties and how they maintain the legitimacy of competition has not been treated in earlier research.

Competition needs not be so difficult to create, however. Chapter 9 illustrates how one can slide into competition without really being aware of what is happening, while chasing a seemingly innocuous prize. Among fashion producers and fashion users, efforts at being the 'first with the latest' easily translates into a situation of competition, as illustrated in Chapter 3. Competition can be promoted in indirect ways, by alluding to what is thought to be competitive. The reformers described in Chapter 5 tried to instil competition by organizing a practice that seemed to be common 'competitive market practice'—a fair for the schools—although it is uncertain whether it had much effect on the extent to which principals or students constructed competition. Universities developed strategy documents for handling an imagined competition. On a similar note, one could speculate that auditors competed for clients partly because of the common but careless conflation of competition and market. The auditing clients in Chapter 8 were already in a market arrangement with the auditors, in which they exchanged money for audits, and that situation may have led them to assume that it was the market-exchange actor, rather than other stakeholders, that should be constructed as the third party for whose favour they should compete.

Sometimes, as seen in Chapter 12, it is difficult even to avoid a situation being constructed as competition; headquarters in that case tried to encourage R&D units to share information, but the various units did not comply because they thought of each other as possible future competitors. As we suggested in Chapter 1, and this case accentuates, although the past can be important to its construction, competition is about the future, and the enactment of that future has profound effects on the present. In our experience, it is common that those using competition as an argument for change refer to the imagined threat of future competition rather any existing one (Forssell 1992). A corollary is also noteworthy: competition can cease in anticipation of the deconstruction of one of its elements—a pending merger that collapses several actors into one, for instance.

Competition for what?

Although most literature related to competition within economic markets deals with the case of competing for someone else's money, the chapters in this book expand the study of what can be competed for. Not only money but also skilled people, status, and in many cases attention are constructed as desirable and scarce. Earlier literature has in its limitation to money, missed a significant dimension of the complexity of competition: the nature of its object. Money is a unique and arguably unproblematic good to be competed for, as it is constructed as a neutral medium of exchange. This is not the case with many other things for which competition can develop. When schools compete for students, as seen in Chapter 5, their resulting distribution matters profoundly to the education the students receive; the quality of a student's peer group has consequences for learning and for the formation of networks. Students are not a neutral and value-free good, and their distribution across schools matters to the students themselves, to the schools that compete for them, and to a society that expects an even quality of students throughout the country. Furthermore, attention is not something neutral to be competed for; as seen in Chapter 10, attention from the teacher can be more valuable to pupils than is the attention of other pupils. There are things like status that can be competed for, that may have value in themselves, whereas other goods, such as money, are valued not for themselves but are seen as resources, valued only for the other goods to which they can provide access. (See Chapter 6.)

The nature of competition may differ, depending on the goods involved. In Chapters 6 and 7, the authors discussed the particulars of status competition, whereas the authors of Chapters 9 and 10 demonstrated how competition for attention can be organized. Because attention is fleeting, it is its *acquisition* that is crucial whereas successfully attracting customers' money—which can be stored—manifests itself primarily in *retrospect*. Although attention is visible to others only in the moment it is lavished, money won from customers accrues to an asset that leaves traces in bookkeeping and in an organization's various reports and publications. Once acquired, money can be protected by the institution of ownership, whereas status and attention won in earlier competitions is more ephemeral. Furthermore, as described in Chapter 6, the behavioural responses to competition may vary according to the organization of the distribution of a good. Actions contemplated and undertaken in the competition for money in markets are likely to differ from actions contemplated in competition for money in a budget process, and the behaviour when status allocation is organized is likely to differ from behaviour exhibited in situations in which it is not organized.

Competition may not be the unitary concept that is often assumed. Previous literature has sometimes distinguished between episodic (in the awarding of contracts or in political elections, for instance) and continuous competition (for the money of consumers, for example), but there are other ways of systematically categorizing competitions. It may be necessary to distinguish among competition for different goods, such as status, attention, and money and more. Furthermore, these goods are often convertible, but there can also be a trade-off where gaining one means losing another. How they interact and reinforce each other differs in different situations of competition. There is a need for more research about different types of competition.

Moreover, as noted, the construction of different competitions and their behavioural outcomes may interfere with each other within what could be thought of as an ecology of competitions. This can happen when political parties deal with competition for voters in ways that undermine the status of the democratic system. It can also happen when competition *among schools* is translated into competition *within schools* and *among teachers*, as principals seek to promote their school by ranking the performance of individual teachers. The boundaries of and connections among competitions are key questions for further research.

Asymmetries of construction

Following from the conceptualization of competition as construction, competition is likely to be constructed differently across different actors and actor types. There can be many reasons for these asymmetries. As demonstrated in Chapters 2, 6, and 8, asymmetries can be based on different imaginations about other actors—when the construction of a third party is partly imaginary, for example. Chapter 2 demonstrated the variation in construction across restaurant managers and among scholars subscribing to different economic theories. This finding illustrates the limitation of standard practices of determining whether or not competition exists. It is limiting to consider only the number of actors and the characteristics of their offerings as defining competition, in that such approaches cannot determine why some of these actors see competition where others do not. Investigating, instead, whether organizers, competitors, or customers have constructed the four constituent elements of competition enables a nuanced understanding of when and why some situations are competitive to some people but not to others.

Competition can be constructed by three types of actors: those who think that they are competing, third parties who determine their success, and fourth parties who organize in a way that affects competition. Earlier work on competition has treated the perception of competition of a single type of actor at a point in time. These scholars seem to have accepted the implicit assumption that competition is taken for granted among all actor types, and they have not considered that the actors may differ in their constructions. But in many cases, the construction is asymmetric across actor types. Chapters 2, 5, 6, 8, 10, 11, and 12 all detailed examples of such asymmetries. As described in Chapter 5, the municipality perceived competition among its schools differently than did the principals of the schools—the actors who were supposed to compete.

There can also be heterogeneity in the construction of competition *within* each of the types of actors, as when one party sees another party as a competitor, but the opposite is not true. In Chapter 10, pupils differed in the extent to which they saw other pupils as competitors. As described in Chapter 8, both the firms to be audited and the investors who desired information about these firms are possible to construct as the third party for the auditors to consider. As the auditors constructed the audited firms as the only third party, the content and form of their offering developed in a manner that did not serve other stakeholders.

Asymmetries in the construction of competition are likely to fuel organizational efforts. In Chapter 5, the municipal officials who did not think that school principals constructed the situation as competition intensified their organizational efforts. Conversely, Chapter 12 detailed the way headquarters failed to see the competition among its subsidiaries that managers of the subsidiaries saw, and this asymmetry led to organizational efforts to increase cooperative activities as well as managerial resistance to cooperation across units.

Consequences of competition

The standard expectation is that competition leads to improvements and innovations in the activities of competing parties. As described in Chapters 10 to 12, these expected effects had motivated the organizers of competition in schools and large corporations, whether it concerned the learning of pupils or the activities of subsidiaries or other units in firms. But the chapters have also illustrated a number of other possible consequences of competition, including effects on attention, on autonomy, on interactions, on the status of winner or loser, and on conflicts.

Attention and goal drift

Competition can direct attention to the area where it occurs and can divert attention away from other areas where competition is not present. As argued in Chapter 9, competition is a form of social drama that easily attracts interest and involvement with an attractiveness that may be trumped only by conflict. Thus, those with an interest in social drama—journalists, for instance—will be interested in competition, an observation that is borne out by the great interest in reporting from TV show competitions and sports contests. If such a predilection exists, it would suggest that journalists prioritize social areas of competition over areas without competition as described in Chapter 9, and they may describe ambiguous situations as competitive rather than uncompetitive. In this way, competition may receive more public attention than warranted, and may therefore seem more ubiquitous than it is. As seen in Chapter 10, competition as a teaser for interest is used frequently by educators who are hoping to interest pupils in learning over other aspects of school life.

But the attractiveness of competition can be treacherous as well. As argued in Chapter 9, observers may fail to notice other, more significant, phenomena when they concentrate on competition. As demonstrated in Chapters 6, 8, and 9, competition may lead to a goal drift in organizations, in which the goal of winning a competition or achieving goals related to a competitive area become those attended to, while other, perhaps more fundamental, goals are neglected. (For a related discussion see Ethiraj and Levinthal 2009; Power 2021.) In auditing firms, the very rationale for financial auditing to provide information for investors has been increasingly neglected in favour of goals connected to the competition for money from audited customers. Disproportionate attention and money may be spent in attempts at reaching a high position in university rankings, and research and teaching activities may be adapted to the relatively simple measures used in those rankings, potentially at the expense of attempts to improve a university's quality according to professional norms. (See also Bromley and Powell 2012.)

Perhaps, as suggested in Chapter 9, contests are particularly prone to attracting interest, as the enormous interest in public sports contests would suggest. In fact, the central purpose of these contests is entertainment, which means that the contest itself constitutes a fundamental meaning of the competition (cf. Leifer 1995; Stark 2020). Other contests may be perceived in a similar way; participation is difficult to resist, whether one is likely to win or not and irrespective of the value or usefulness of the prizes or status involved. Such a situation makes goal drift even more likely. Pupils may concentrate excessively on winning the competition rather than improving their learning. People may bring ideas and values from sport contests into other contexts—as when the media describe political debates in preparation for general elections as contests in which there are winners and losers or when they speculate that voters admire and tend to elect upcoming underdogs that seem to receive increasing support.

Loss of autonomy

Competition affects the autonomy of individuals, organizations, and states. As argued in Chapters 3, 6, and 13, seeing oneself as competing with another party is to perceive oneself as dependent upon the activities of that party and on the desire and actions of a third party and the organizing activities of the fourth party. Although competition requires that there be actors with the capacity to make their own decisions and therefore possess some level of autonomy, competition limits that autonomy (Dennis 1975). It comes as no surprise, therefore, that competitors often seek to avoid competition by escaping into niches. As discussed in Chapter 3, the formation of markets provides ample evidence for such responses to competition.

As Simmel (1903/2008) suggested, the relationships and dependencies that connect people through competition may even make them more attentive to other people's desires. Rather than seeing competition as disruptive, he argued, it binds society together. And, as explained in Chapter 13, competitive actions are collective and relational.

The cohesive aspect of competition should not be confused, however, with the fact that competition may have disruptive rather than cohesive outcomes for society at large. When competition is used to allocate money and other goods, it serves to legitimize the outcome. As was argued by Simmel (1903/2008) and elaborated upon in Chapter 13, it can legitimize inequalities that may not be possible to legitimize without it. (See also Wolff 2006.) In a school setting, like the one seen in Chapter 5, a municipality lost some of its managerial ability to pursue its ideals of equality in educational opportunity when privately owned schools gained a larger share of students through competition. Furthermore, there are organizations, such as courts, auditors, and universities, the independence of which is a widely held ideal. Consequently, it is not unproblematic that in their competition for customers auditors become highly dependent on those they are supposed to audit (see also Carruthers 2016) or that universities competing for high rankings become dependent on the journalists who construct those rankings (Pallas and Wedlin 2013). Competition may thus combine the disadvantages of two worlds: less cohesion at the societal level and less autonomy for organizations that society has decreed should have greater autonomy.

Interactions

In most chapters, we saw examples of the type of behaviour celebrated by proponents of competition—attempts to adjust behaviour to the wishes of the third party, whether that third party consisted of corporate headquarters, teachers, or a computer game. Such behaviour does not require interactions with others—neither with third or fourth parties nor with one's competitors. But it does not preclude those interactions.

Managers of corporate subsidiaries may, as described in Chapter 11, try to stay in contact with managers at headquarters in order to gain their attention and convince them of the subsidiary's present or future potential. Rankers in the field of higher education often contact universities in order to obtain information, and this interaction could, at least in principle, be used to affect the rules applied by the rankers, although in most cases, this potential to influence is limited to high-status universities (Wedlin 2006). As privately owned schools began to attract a greater share of students in the municipality, the municipal schools described in Chapter 5 interacted with each other more closely than they had previously done, thus creating a new type of relationship and even the construction of a meta-organizational grouping, 'the municipal schools', in contrast to 'the private schools', and competition could then be partially lifted from the level of the individual schools to these two groups of schools. We saw similar processes among the waste-handling firms in Chapter 7.

Competition can also stimulate interaction among competitors. Trying to learn from and imitate winning competitors is called emulation in Chapter 10, and, as illustrated in Chapter 11, it can be done by contacting and interviewing the winners about how they did it. Competition can also lead to various forms of cooperation among competitors. In order to cooperate, competitors often form organizations with their peers—meta-organizations for organizations: international governmental organizations for states and business associations for firms; professional associations and unions for individuals. Chapter 6 illustrates this point with respect to sports and university associations. And within organizations, competition among subunits often leads to cooperation among those units. Such cooperation may be initiated by top managers, as described in Chapter 12 on corporate governance, but it may also happen without their support or even against their will, as illustrated in Chapter 11 on MNCs. Cooperation may be motivated by common interests among competitors, such as an interest in influencing the fourth parties or even acting as a fourth party themselves, as is the case of cooperation in many business or sports associations. Such cooperation among one type of organization can also be an attempt at winning the competition with another type of organization, or at least an attempt at not losing it, as evident with respect to the universities discussed in Chapter 6 and the waste-handling organizations in Chapters 7.

In the cases described in Chapter 11, cooperation among some organizational units was initiated as a way of improving the results of each unit, or even acquiring the knowledge of personnel that all of them needed but that only a few of them would obtain without cooperation; scarcity generated by competition motivated cooperation. As illustrated in Chapter 12, cooperation among units in an organization may be crucial for the success of the organization as a whole—a typical rationale behind the creation of a formal organization. It is noteworthy that competition among the units, regardless of whether top management wishes for it, does not necessarily hinder that cooperation. One critical issue for future research is the type and aspects of competition that hinder or promote various forms of interaction among competitors, in which one can expect that conditions differ as the social setting differs, as exemplified by the settings within or outside formal organizations.

Winning or losing competitions

One reaction to competition is avoidance, especially when one has lost a competition or expects to lose it (Murayama and Elliot 2012). This reaction can take at least four different forms: avoiding desire for a scarce good, fuelling desire for goods that are not scarce, playing down the perception of actorhood, and avoiding relationships in situations with the potential of producing competition. Limiting one's interest to a third party or to oneself, without side-glances to others is another strategy, often recommended to pupils. Some pupils described in Chapter 10 were thus able to avoid competition, even in a contest-like situation (dealing with a game) and even when comparisons with others were designed to be easy.

One can also try to restrict the sense of competition to areas in which one has a decent chance of winning or at least emerging from the situation well. There are often several goods one can compete for and several ongoing contests one can try to win; alternatively, one can construct other contests. Some pupils in a class can choose not to relate to their classmates in a competitive way in sports, for example, but continue to compete in mathematics. As described in Chapter 7, firms that did not fare well in environmental waste-handling rankings could concentrate on scoring high rankings for the most environmentally friendly gas production.

One could also question whether it is always advantageous to win a competition. Cases described in Chapter 11 provide a reminder that winning may be a mixed blessing. Winning in what is considered an unfair way may create problems in the future—in winning future competitions for status or appreciation, for instance. When one subunit won a 'mandate' through headquarters' ad hoc decision rather than by 'a sound business case', it was not received well by competing subunits who became reluctant to engage in future cooperation. In another case, when managers at headquarters realized that giving a mandate to one of three equally good subunits would create bad feelings, they gave it to a fourth, less advanced candidate. More generally, too much attention to a winning organization may hinder economic success in situations in which it is crucial to remain discrete. The cases can be seen as empirical illustrations of the ambiguity of competition when it comes to allocating responsibility for its results, as discussed in depth in Chapter 13, in its treatment of competition, individualism, and meritocracy.

Competition and conflict

As Simmel (1903/2008) suggested, competition is sometimes organized as a way of handling conflict—when conflict means diverging opinions about how to handle something of common interest. Arranging elections in democracies constitutes an example: conflict among political parties about what the state shall do is transformed into a competition for seats in the parliament. Thus, conflict in another meaning of the term is avoided: the use of violence for determining who shall decide. Simmel argued that competition is 'a civilizing force', a position that was shown by Hirschman (1997) to have been a strong argument for the early legitimization of market competition in economic and political theory.

The relationship between conflict and competition can also be reversed, as when competition gives rise to conflict. Many wars have occurred as a result of a competition for new territories. The managers described in Chapter 12 had strong but differing opinions of what constituted acceptable forms of interaction in a competition. In markets, the behaviour of competing firms is a relatively common source of conflict. In some such situations, there are laws to refer to what allows or forbids certain forms of behaviour, and there are courts or mediators that can decide which of the conflicting parties is right. Similarly, in some countries, conflicts about proper behaviour in elections can be the object of court decisions. In sports there is usually a referee present to settle such differences immediately. It is the competition among states, firms, parties, or sport teams that constitutes the origin of such conflicts and provides them with energy. Without competition, there would be fewer or weaker conflicts, but a key instrument for solving conflict would also be missing.

The conceptualization of competition that has been developed in this book profoundly affects the way we can look at conflict. Just like competition, conflict requires at least two parties equipped with actorhood; we can hardly be in conflict with animals, the climate, or abstract principles. Conflicts among actors also constitute a relationship. Not unlike competition, conflict and the handling of conflicts are often highly institutionalized, and there are various means of organizing their handling, such as court systems, mediation procedures, or even the organizing of open conflict, as exemplified in international rules of war (Jepperson et al. 1996).

The various relationships between competition and conflict offer an intriguing area for future research. A first and necessary step is careful specification of the meaning of not only the concept of competition but also the concept of conflict. Such specification will help to avoid conceptual vagueness and ambiguity, which otherwise threatens to confuse empirical research—both the questions that are posed and the answers that are given.

Removal of competition

Many, or perhaps most, competitors do not appreciate competition, whether it has resulted from institutions or organization. Efforts to introduce competition may be resisted or ignored, as did some of the school children described in Chapter 10. In other cases, such as those presented in Chapter 7 on food waste and in Chapter 8 on auditing, the area of competition can be shifted on purpose—or, as shown in Chapter 8, simply not attended to intensely.

When ignoring competition is not sufficient it may be necessary to seek its removal. As described previously, for the individual or a single organization that wants to remove competition, it is enough to revoke one of its four elements. One may turn several competitors into one actor, as when firms buy their competitors. Marriage is an attempt (although often unsuccessful) to finalize competition for affection by withdrawing legitimate actorhood. Restricting one's interest to niches can be seen as an attempt to cease the desire for scarce goods, as shown in Chapter 3.

Institutional changes may weaken or end competition. Public discourse, a problematizing and delegitimizing of any of the four elements of competition, may transform competition into something else in the long run. Competition can be ended by a deconstruction of what used to be viewed as actors or by the obsolescence of relationships to potential competitors. Similarly, institutional processes can alter scarcity evaluations and desires. What used to be status relevant, for example, may become irrelevant and no longer desired, which is most obvious in the case of fashion, discussed in Chapter 3.

Competition can also be reduced as a side effect of decisions that primarily concern things other than competition. Competition for jobs can be reduced by political decisions—boosting the number of jobs or reducing the desire for a job by providing more generous welfare allowances. Given the variety of its potential effects, third and fourth parties and the broader society may also seek less competition, or may even avoid it. Particularly when the actorhood of individuals and organizations is contested and when there are manifest moral concerns not to produce losers from competition, the legitimation of competition can erode. (See Chapter 10.) Fierce competition in children's sports has become problematized, for instance.

A relevant question, for which there are currently few answers, is whether and how third and fourth parties can revoke competition. A fourth party may have different organizational tools at its disposal. Third parties, on the other hand, are central to the construction of competition in so far as they control the desired goods. When they have full control over what is desired, they could revoke competition by refusing to choose—but in the usual case, in which they each control only a small part of what is desired, revoking competition may necessitate the use of social movement tactics (Lounsbury 2001; Schneiberg and Lounsbury 2017).

In principle, it seems easy to organize away competition. If something can be decided in one way, it should be possible to decide it in another way as well. Competing firms can be merged; competitive relationships among schools can be broken by decisions to reduce students' freedom of choice; rankings can be turned into ratings that abolish scarcity; and desire can be changed by deciding on new goals for organizations. As described in Chapter 10, there has been an attempt to remove competition among pupils by trying to avoid scarcity or by encouraging them to avoid competitive relationships with their peers.

Attempts at revoking competition, however, may be as unsuccessful as some attempts to introduce competition have been. Experimental research into the removal of competition at the individual level suggests that competition is 'sticky' (Buser and Dreber 2015; Johnson et al. 2006); it is easier to prime individuals to act as if there is competition than to undo that priming. As seen in Chapter 12, competition among the former firms may well continue in a merged company, although the outcome is decided in a different way within the firm than it was in the market. Illegal markets—such as a market for illicit drugs—are often combatted by decisions that express attempts to remove the actorhood of organizations and individuals or by attempts to alter scarcity or desires, but often with little success. Attempts at reducing competition in children's team sports involve abolishing the scarce good of winning matches and table positions. But the result is uncertain: sports constitutes one example of a decided competitive order that has become institutionalized over time and therefore more difficult to challenge and change.

As described previously, however, individuals and organizations may be able to resist the lure of competition, particularly in situations in which they can choose among several competitions. In a society in which competition is highly valued, it may be impossible to avoid all competition, and controlling which competition one is exposed to may be the only hope.

Competition is one of the master trends in society, and its origins, workings, and consequences are far more complex and subtle than is normally considered in the economics and other social science literatures that address it. We have attempted to establish what we are sure will be a fascinating field of study on competition—as something significant and urgent but also fragile and ultimately of our own making, and unmaking.

References

Abbott, A. 1988. *The System of Professions—An Essay on the Division of Expert Labor*. Chicago: University of Chicago Press.

Bromley, P. and Powell, W. W. 2012. 'From smoke and mirrors to walking the talk: decoupling in the contemporary world'. *Academy of Management Annals* 6 (1): 483–530.

Buser, T. and Dreber, A. 2015. 'The flipside of comparative payment schemes'. *Management Science* 62 (9): 2626–38.

Carruthers, B. G. 2016. 'Credit ratings and global economic governance: non-price valuation in financial markets'. *Contractual Knowledge: One Hundred Years of Legal Experimentation in Global Markets*, edited by G. Mallard. Cambridge: Cambridge University Press: 324–9.

Dennis, K. G. 1975. *Competition in the History of Economic Thought*. Oxford: University of Oxford.

Dobbin, F. 1994. *Forging Industrial Policy: The United States, Britain, and France in the Railway Age*. Cambridge/New York: Cambridge University Press.

Ethiraj, S. K. and Levinthal, D. 2009. 'Hoping for A to Z while rewarding only A: complex organizations and multiple goals'. *Organization Science* 20 (1): 4–21.

Forssell, A. 1992. *Moderna tider i Sparbanken om organisatorisk omvandling i ett institutionellt perspektiv*. Nerenius & Santérus.

Hasse, R. 2003. *Wohlfahrtspolitik und Globalisierung*. Wiesbaden: Springer.

Hirschman, A. O. 1997. *The Passions and the Interests—Political Arguments for Capitalism before Its Triumph*. Princeton: Princeton University Press.

Hood, C. and Dixon, R. 2015. *A Government that Worked Better and Cost Less? Evaluating Three Decades of Reform and Change in UK Central Government*. Oxford: Oxford University Press.

Jepperson, R. L., Wendt, A., and Katzenstein, P. J. 1996. 'Norms, identity, and culture in national security'. In *The Culture of National Security: Norms and Identity in World Politics*, edited by P. J. Katzenstein. New York: Columbia University Press: 33–75.

Johnson, M. D., Hollenbeck, J. R., Humphrey, S. E., Ilgen, D. R., Jundt, D., and Meyer, C. J. 2006. 'Cutthroat cooperation: asymmetrical adaptation to changes in team reward structures'. *Academy of Management Journal* 49 (1): 103–19.

Le Grand, J. 2009. *The Other Invisible Hand: Delivering Public Services through Choice and Competition*. Princeton: Princeton University Press.

Leifer, E. M. 1995. *Making the Majors: The Transformation of Team Sports in America*. Cambridge, MA: Harvard University Press.

Lounsbury, M. 2001. 'Institutional sources of practice variation: staffing college and university recycling programs'. *Administrative Science Quarterly* 46: 29–56.

Murayama, K. and Elliot, A. J. 2012. 'The competition–performance relation: a meta-analytic review and test of the opposing processes model of competition and performance'. *Psychological Bulletin* 138 (6): 1035.

Pallas, J. and Wedlin, L. 2013. 'Governance of science in mediatized society: media rankings and the translation of global governance'. In *Global Themes and Local Variations in Organization and Management: Perspectives on Glocalization*, edited by G. S. Drori, M. H. Llerer, and P. Walgenbach. New York: Routledge: 295–308.

Power, M. 2021. 'Modelling the micro-foundations of the audit society: organizations and the logic of the audit trail'. *Academy of Management Review* 46 (1): 6–32.

Schneiberg, M. and Lounsbury, M. 2017. 'Social movements and the dynamics of institutions and organizations'. In *The Sage Handbook of Organizational Institutionalism*, edited by R. Greenwood, T. Lawrence, R. Meyer, and C. Oliver. London: SAGE: 281–310.

Simmel, G. 1903/2008. 'Sociology of competition'. *Canadian Journal of Sociology/Cahiers Canadiens de Sociologie* 33 (4): 957–78.

Stark, D. 2020. *The Performance Complex: Competition and Competitions in Social Life*. Oxford: Oxford University Press.

Wedlin, L. 2006. *Ranking Business Schools: Forming Fields, Identities and Boundaries in International Management Education*. Cheltenham: Edward Elgar.

Wolff, J. 2006. 'Libertarianism, utility, and economic competition'. *Virginia Law Review* 92 (7): 1605–23.

Index

Note: Tables and figures are indicated by an italic "*t*", and "*f*", respectively.